Escaped Nuns

TRUE WOMANHOOD AND THE CAMPAIGN AGAINST
CONVENTS IN ANTEBELLUM AMERICA

Cassandra L. Yacovazzi

OXFORD
UNIVERSITY PRESS

OXFORD
UNIVERSITY PRESS

Oxford University Press is a department of the University of Oxford. It furthers
the University's objective of excellence in research, scholarship, and education
by publishing worldwide. Oxford is a registered trade mark of Oxford University
Press in the UK and certain other countries.

Published in the United States of America by Oxford University Press
198 Madison Avenue, New York, NY 10016, United States of America.

© Oxford University Press 2018

CIP data is on file at the Library of Congress
ISBN 978-0-19-088100-9

9 8 7 6 5 4 3 2 1
Printed by Sheridan Books, Inc., United States of America

Contents

Illustrations

Acknowledgments

I AM DEEPLY grateful to many people for helping me with this book, and it is my pleasure to thank them. Several of my colleagues read the entire manuscript and multiple chapter drafts, providing helpful comments, questions, suggestions, and encouragement. In this regard, I would especially like to thank John Wigger, my doctoral adviser, colleague, and friend. He has fostered an academic community, the collaboration and friendship from which have benefited this book and enriched my life. A special thanks to my colleagues and friends in this group, including Jonathan Root, Joshua Rice, Darin Tuck, Jennifer Wiard, Hunter Hampton, Brandon Flint, Luke Schleif, Meaghan Collier, Josh McMullen, T.J. Tomlin, Craig Forest, Benjamin Park, Armin Mattes, and Victor McFarland. Their voices come through this book every step of the way.

I am indebted to the Department of History at the University of Missouri for granting me a dissertation fellowship, without which I would not have been able to make timely progress on this project. The Department of History also generously awarded me a summer research grant, enabling me to visit archives and libraries in Massachusetts, New York, and Indiana. It is my pleasure to thank the faculty and staff with the Kinder Institute on Constitutional Democracy for awarding me a Kinder Dissertation Fellowship. The department staff, including Nancy Taube, Patty Eggleston, Melinda Lockwood, and Lynn Summers, provided various kinds of encouragement and support, answering my many logistical questions. I am also grateful to the Department of History for offering me a Postdoctoral Teaching Fellowship, a position that has allowed me to turn a dissertation into a book.

At the University of Missouri Libraries, I would like to thank Delores Fisher, senior library specialist, who tracked down numerous items through Interlibrary Loan. Marie Concannon, data archivist, helped me locate Massachusetts government documents. The University of Missouri Special Collections and Rare Books and the Missouri Historical Society staff offered a number of valuable resources for this project.

I would also like to thank Nancy Barthelemy, Boston provincial archivist for the Sisters of Notre Dame de Namur, for scanning and sending me archival material. William Kevin Cawley, senior archivist and curator of manuscripts at the Archives of the University of Notre Dame, helped me find a number of crucial sources for this project. At the American Antiquarian Society, Elizabeth Watts Pope and Paul Erickson guided me through the archives and made me aware of additional sources. The staff at the New York Public Library extended gracious hospitality and clued me in to the Order of the United Americans records. I am thankful to Mike Whalen for sending me a private online screener of his excellent documentary, *A Question of Habit*, which provided much inspiration for the epilogue. Sister Jane Frances Behlmann, archivist at the Sisters of St. Joseph of Carondelet, provided generous assistance during my visit. Denise P. Gallo, provincial archivist of the Daughters of Charity in Emmitsburg, Maryland, promptly answered email questions, helping me to piece together parts of this project. Michael Pera, archivist at the Society of the Sacred Heart Archives, acquainted me with rich sources on Sacred Heart convents in the US.

A number of colleagues in the Department of History at the University of Missouri and at other academic institutions have selflessly offered their time and expertise. Catherine Rymph, Steven Watts, Jeffery Pasley, John Evelev, John Frymire, and Kathleen Sprows Cummings carefully read my dissertation and extended useful feedback, helping to make the eventual book project much better. John Turner graciously offered his assistance on my chapter exploring anti-Mormonism. I am thankful to Sara Crosby for taking an interest in this project and helping me as I pursued publication. My undergraduate professors, Jay Case, Shawn Floyd, Greg Miller, and Jacci Stuckey, encouraged me to think in ways I had not before, imparting an appreciation for the life of the mind. I am grateful for their continued support and friendship.

It has been a pleasure to work with the staff at Oxford University Press. I am thrilled and honored to be publishing with them. A special thanks to Cynthia Read for giving my proposal a chance, to Drew Anderla and Richa Jobin for their friendly assistance, and to Danielle Michaely for her expert copy-editing.

Without the moral support of friends and family, this would have been a much more grueling and lonely process. I am thankful for my friends, especially Jonathan Root, Sarah Lirely McCune, Claire McGraw, Dan Murphy, Tim Gibbons, Jessie Bivens, Dave Dittmer, Jenna Rice, and Will and Tina Witham. My friend Dan Murphy graciously gave of his time, reading every chapter and offering comments, suggestions, encouragement, and good conversation. Thanks to Thomas and Carolyn Loew, my "Missouri parents," for all your love and support.

My sisters, Tiffany Bodis and Natalie Yacovazzi, and my near sister, Ann Marie Romans, offered reassurance and laughter even from a distance. I am deeply thankful for the encouragement provided by my mom and dad, Debie and Mark Yacovazzi. Just knowing you cared and were proud of me was a constant comfort.

Any institution which prevents a woman from fulfilling those duties as wives and mothers, which
God has appointed, should not be permitted to exist for one instant in any civilized land.

—WILLIAM C. BROWNLEE, "Nunneries Are Unconstitutional," 1836

Introduction

THE AMERICAN CAMPAIGN AGAINST CONVENTS

IN 1836, TWO popular anti-Catholic periodicals operating out of New York City
published ringing endorsements of a convent exposé by "escaped nun" Maria Monk.
The *Downfall of Babylon* offered an engraving of a "shocking sight" at the Hotel
Dieu Nunnery described by Monk:

> In one part . . . we see a Nun throwing a murdered infant into a deep pit in
> the cellar of the Nunnery. At a little distance from her, a Priest is seen rising
> up through a trap door, from the subterranean passage that leads from the
> Seminary . . . to the Nunnery. Against the wall are two solitary cells, in which
> are confined two Nuns. . . . The white substance which appears about the
> mouth of the pit is lime, which is thrown upon the bodies when they are cast
> into the pit, in order to consume them, and prevent noxious exhalations. Poor,
> helpless, inoffensive babes . . . born but to breathe a few short pangs, then to be
> strangled by fiends in human shape, called Nuns and Priests!

The Protestant Vindicator also reported on the "great sensation" Maria Monk's
book ignited throughout the country. "It is most fiercely assailed by the Catholic
periodicals," the article granted, but "the credibility of Miss Monk is powerfully sus-
tained by very vigorous and able writers in some of our most valuable periodicals."
Offering one (in a list of eight) reason "for confidence" in the book, the author

listed, "They are just what we should expect from a community of unmarried females placed entirely under the control of unmarried men."[1]

Before the Civil War, Maria Monk's *Awful Disclosures of the Hotel Dieu Nunnery* (Figure 0.1) became the second-best-selling book in the US, just after *Uncle Tom's Cabin*. Five weeks from its publication in January 1836, *Awful Disclosures* sold over twenty thousand copies, making Maria Monk a household name. Her shocking convent exposé, full of licentious priests, tortured nuns, illicit sex, murder, and infanticide, gripped the nation. By 1860, readers had purchased over three hundred thousand copies. Prominent citizens of the US and Canada took the book's

Maria Monk.

FIGURE 0.1. "Maria Monk."
Courtesy of HathiTrust.

allegations seriously, launching public investigations of the convent. The book occupied newspaper front pages as editors detailed the latest developments of the saga and debated the veracity of Monk's disclosures. Despite the eventual unveiling of Monk as an impostor who never lived in any convent and the revelation that in fact a group of men wrote the book, *Awful Disclosures* continued to sell well, inspiring a host of spinoffs. Maria Monk herself never profited from the book that bore her name, but she helped launch a campaign against convents that would envelop the country, from reformers, pastors, writers, and politicians to consumers of popular culture, for the next three decades. This book explores that campaign, seeking to uncover why so many Americans loved to hate nuns.[2]

Far from a curious aberration, Maria Monk's book was part of a much larger phenomenon of anticonvent culture. Two years before the book's publication, a group of men attacked Mount Benedict, a convent and female academy in Charlestown, Massachusetts, in one of the worst acts of nativist violence in American history. As women and children scrambled out of their beds, the rioters marched toward the three-story brick building. They torched the convent, raided the mausoleum, and destroyed the grounds, inflicting over $50,000 in damages that would never be repaid. The "haughty" Mother Superior of the convent and rumors of "imprisoned females" prompted the attack. Following the burning of Mount Benedict, *Six Months in a Convent*, by former novice there, Rebecca Reed, became an instant bestseller. When Maria Monk's book wildly surpassed the popularity of Reed's, offering a more horrifying and sensational picture of convent life, a new genre was born.[3]

Escaped nun and convent tales saturated the literary market, with titles such as *The Escaped Nun, Priests' Prisons for Women, The Captive Nun, The Haunted Convent*, and *The Convent's Doom*. In the 1840s, as reformers began establishing common or public schools, convent schools came under attack. How could women, who were not themselves wives and mothers, bring up the nation's female students—"the future ornaments of our most refined society, the future mothers of American citizens"? Books such as *Protestant Girl in a French Nunnery* warned of the perils of convent schools, which only served to "destroy" "feminine sensibilities."[4]

Rather than being eclipsed by the growing antislavery movement, the campaign against convents was bolstered by it. Abolitionists presented slavery as a threat to female purity, the marriage institution, and happy homes, citing the rape of female slaves and the harrowing experience of family separation through sale. While abolitionists relied on factual testimonies, crusaders against convents, relying on unsubstantiated evidence, also presented the nun's life as the antithesis to female virtue, marriage, and domesticity, striking a nerve with middle-class sensibilities. Indeed, many Americans saw no contradictions in their efforts to free African Americans from slavery and to "liberate" women from convents, or what some referred to as "white slavery." George Bourne, who championed immediate abolition before William Lloyd Garrison and inspired the great abolitionist, wrote the first convent narrative to be published in the US in 1832. His antislavery and anticonvent works sounded remarkably similar.[5]

The campaign against convents was also reinforced by a movement to combat corruption in new urban centers. In the face of rapid industrialization and urbanization, Americans at once marveled at the progress of civilization and faced a host of new challenges and temptations. Some reformers took up arms against "dens of vice" that caught the unsuspecting in lives of alcohol, gambling, and sex. No one received more attention as a symbol of city corruption than the prostitute, pictured as both a tempting villain to be scorned and a victim in need of rescue. In a new genre that highlighted the sins of the city, writers contrasted prostitutes with "the pure and gentle woman," the "wife and mother." Like convent narratives, these city mysteries promised to unveil a world of hidden debauchery and unfolded cautionary tales of women seduced into lives of misery and sexual deviance. Convent narratives themselves compared nuns to prostitutes, convents to brothels, priests to seducers, and abbesses to madams. As the movement to rescue "fallen women" and the campaign against convents merged, the nun-prostitute figure became iconic.[6]

Even anti-Mormonism, culminating in a war between the federal government and the Latter-day Saints on the eve of the Civil War, drew on, merged with, and bolstered the anticonvent movement. Mormon captivity narratives related stories of innocent women who found themselves trapped, tortured, and defiled in polygamous marriages. In this way, plural marriage and convents became interchangeable threats to American womanhood. One Mormon captivity narrative even blatantly echoed Maria Monk's story, being titled *Awful Disclosures of Mormonism*.

Tying together many of these strains of reform or reaction in antebellum America, a growing group of nativists who railed against "foreign influence," also advanced the American campaign against convents. For nativist fraternal organizations, such as the Order of United Americans and the Sons of the Sires, convents symbolized the pinnacle of Catholic dangers, an *imperium in imperio* from which American daughters needed protection. So entrenched was the anticonvent movement in America that by 1855, even as the country faced a sectional crisis that would tear the nation apart, state legislators formed a "Nunnery Committee" to investigate convents without incriminating evidence and with the full support of their constituents.[7]

There are a number of questions that drive this book. What made Maria Monk so popular? Why did *Awful Disclosures* cause such a sensation, and how has it remained continuously in print? What led otherwise regular citizens to torch convents full of women and children? What kept readers purchasing and turning pages of convent narratives throughout the antebellum era? And how did opposition to nuns and convent life reach such heights as state-sponsored nunnery investigations? In short, what made nuns so offensive to American sensibilities? In attempting to probe these questions, this book explores the American campaign against convents closely, analyzing convent narratives; tracing the story of Maria Monk, her supporters, and her detractors; placing antinun rhetoric in the wider context of antebellum reform, gender ideology, and print culture; and eventually considering this story alongside modern nun kitsch culture reflected in bobble-head nuns, sexy nun costumes, and iconic scary nuns on screen today.

Nun hating was not unique to nineteenth-century America. It dated back to the Protestant Reformation. When Martin Luther nailed his *Ninety-Five Theses* to the All Saints Church door in Wittenberg, he initiated a sweeping revolution in religion, politics, and gender roles. Luther's theology rejected chastity and the nun's life as the ideal role for women, believing celibacy to be nearly impossible for both men and women. In its place Luther upheld the household, rather than the monastery, as the cornerstone of society. This represented a dramatic shift from one of the central expressions of Christianity, especially for women. While the image of Mary had for centuries embodied a virginal model for Catholics, Luther's Protestantism and subsequent Reformation theology looked to Mary as the ideal wife and mother, a picture of domestic obedience. In Luther's mind, this exemplified both the true Christian vocation for women and liberation from a supposedly oppressive system. Yet this redirection removed the only vocational option other than marriage open to women at the time and often rendered the single woman suspect or deviant.[8]

When England formally embraced the Protestant Reformation between 1532 and 1534, under decree of King Henry VIII, one of the biggest transformations related to monastic life. The new supreme head of church and state wasted little time before plundering the over 650 religious houses that dotted the landscape throughout England and Wales. As a result, many women religious, sometimes as an entire house, moved to the continent. While the dissolution of the monasteries was likely more an effort to replenish the nearly bankrupt exchequer than one rooted in theoretical opposition, the nun subsequently became a distinctly foreign and anti-Christian symbol in England, especially as Catholic France and Spain emerged as hated enemies. These views migrated with British colonists to the New World, making their way deeply into British North America, only to be revived in full force in the rapidly changing society of the early nineteenth century.[9]

Some of the earliest novels in the English language reflected intense loathing of convents. *The Monk* (1796), published in London by Matthew Lewis, became an instant bestseller throughout England and Europe. A gothic novel set in Spain, *The Monk* told of two young men who lost their brides-to-be, Agnes and Antonia, to conniving clerics. During her confinement, Agnes had an erotic encounter with a priest before the jealous abbess murdered her. Unaware, Raymond broke into the convent to rescue her, lifting the veil of his beloved only to reveal the "Bleeding Nun," a decrepit woman dead and punished for her sexual sins. Meanwhile Antonia abandoned her beau after falling for a dissolute and ambitious priest, Ambrosio. Full of lust, violence, and even incest, the novel caught readers' attention. In true gothic form, it also delivered a gloomy medieval environment, complete with church cemeteries, subterranean passages, and vaulted monasteries. Gothic literature operated in the vacuum left by Catholic belief in England and often included distinctly Protestant views of anticlericalism. *The Monk*'s near-obsessive focus on Catholic abuses of power, sexual repression, and transgression easily fit this model and would become a mainstay of later convent narratives throughout the nineteenth century. Its message advanced a tradition of suspicion of monastic life, especially for women, in contrast to the domestic vocation of marriage and motherhood.[10]

Other anti-Catholic works published in the eighteenth century prominently featured convents, including *The Master-Key to Popery* (1724). The book went through a series of reprints in England before being translated into German, Dutch, and French. With a telling subtitle—*How Haunted Virgins Have Been Disposed, and Devils Were Cast Out to Let in Priests*—the book promised to unlock the "many errors" of Rome, female monasticism being one of the most grave. The book provided a litany of bitter fruits produced by celibate vocations, including illicit relationships among priests and nuns, illegitimate births, and dangerous attempts to escape by nuns who faced the prospect of the Spanish Inquisition. In explaining why a woman might choose life in a convent, the author concluded dismissively that women were tricked. *The Master-Key* was later republished in the US as *The Great Red Dragon*, enjoying wide popularity during the height of the American campaign against convents.[11]

Anti-Catholicism in America was older than the nation itself, dating back to the colonial era. But a steady influx of German and Irish immigrants to the country in the early nineteenth century and a rapidly changing society wrought by urbanization and industrialization, challenging the status quo, reawakened latent fears of Rome, prompting what Ray Allen Billington dubbed "the Protestant Crusade." From 1800 to 1860, anti-Catholic publications proliferated, with over two hundred books, twenty-five newspapers, forty-one histories, forty works of fiction, thirteen magazines, and a bevy of pamphlets, gift books, and almanacs. Newspapers unambiguously titled *Downfall of Babylon, The American Protestant Vindicator, Priestcraft Unmasked,* and *The Anti-Romanist* enjoyed steady subscriptions offering weekly tirades against Romanism. National organizations dedicated at once to spreading Protestant Christianity and combating popery sprang up across the country, including the American Protestant Association, the Home Missionary Society, the Protestant Reformation Society, and the American Tract Society. The New York Protestant Association declared its sole purpose to be the promotion of "the Reformation . . . which shall illustrate the character of Popery." Its first meeting addressed the topic: "Is Popery That Babylon the Great?" Many of these organizations would publish or promote escaped nun tales, advancing the American campaign against convents into the far reaches of the expanding US.[12]

In the 1830s, immigration to the US increased dramatically. Sixty thousand immigrants arrived in America in 1832, and about as many flowed in each year that decade. Between 1840 and 1844, preceding the Irish potato famine, the number reached almost a quarter of a million. In 1847, numbers spiked to 234,000, and reached 380,000 in 1851. Figures continued at this unprecedented rate until 1854. Most of the 2.75 million newcomers who reached American shores in this seven-year period were practicing Roman Catholics. Germans made up a large percentage and Irish even more, with a quarter-million Irish men and women arriving in 1851 alone. Beginning as a small minority, Catholics counted only 70,000 in America in 1807. By 1840, church membership swelled to 660,000. Numbers reached 3.1 million in 1860, making Catholicism the single largest religious group in the nation. In thus a short period of time, Anglo-Americans witnessed a dramatic change in their environment, both ethnic and religious, a change that would make the populace susceptible to conspiracy theories and fearmongering as to the fate of the nation.[13]

As the Catholic presence grew, nuns especially stood out. Their distinct dress or habit, their unmarried state, and their self-supporting, communal celibacy, independent from the traditional household modes of female production rendered them directly opposed to domestic civic relationships, middle-class companionate marriage, and Protestant feminine ideals. As Emily Clark put it in her study on the New Orleans' Ursulines, "the nun was an ideological outlaw." She stood in stark contrast to Protestant American constructions of femininity. While revolutionary rhetoric praised what historians now refer to as "republican motherhood" as the bedrock of virtue and civilization in the new nation, nuns appeared superfluous if not outright threatening. One anti-Catholic periodical from the 1830s contended that "nunneries of all places are the most unfit for the preservation of female virtue." That many orders of nuns springing up in nineteenth-century America came from Catholic Europe only contributed to the view of convents as foreign and un-American. Representing religious, gender, and ethnic fears, the nun became one of the greatest targets of anti-Catholic hostility.[14]

During the colonial era, British colonists prohibited religious communities from founding convents. Prior to the nineteenth century, the new nation housed only two religious houses, the Carmelites and the Poor Clares, both in Maryland, a former

Catholic stronghold. Soon after the Ursulines of New Orleans entered the nation through the Louisiana Purchase, the number of orders of women religious grew. Between 1803 and 1830, Catholic women founded ten female orders. Indigenous orders constituted five of these, including the American Sisters of Charity founded by Elizabeth Anne Seton in 1809. New orders assumed the French model of the Ursulines, taking up active apostolates such as teaching, nursing, and running orphanages and other charitable institutions. By 1845, Catholic women religious resided in the nation's North and South, in major cities, agricultural hubs, and the expanding frontier. Beginning in 1812, the Sisters of Loretto and the Sisters of Charity of Nazareth served in the remote frontier area of Bardstown, Kentucky. By the 1840s, the Mississippi Valley—already a haven of French Catholicism before becoming part of the territorial US—housed the Sisters of St. Joseph of Carondelet, the School Sisters of Notre Dame, and the Sisters of the Sacred Heart, along with a number of other orders. In northern urban areas, some orders included the Sisters of Charity, Sisters of Mercy, and Sisters of Notre Dame de Namur. The number of conventual houses rose to thirty-one by 1850 with 1,941 Sisters.[15]

As the number of convents in America increased, signs of what historian Barbara Welter described as the "cult of true womanhood" were everywhere. In novels, magazines, and prescriptive and religious literature, Americans learned that the ideal woman embodied "piety, purity, submissiveness and domesticity." Yet, as many historians have pointed out, gender roles and family structures were in flux. In the wake of the so-called market revolution, more women went to work in northern urban areas. Their labor as domestic servants, seamstresses, launderers, and factory workers led to debates about women's place in society. At the same time, women of more means, part of a new urban middle class, banded together, forming charitable societies to raise money for missionaries, help orphaned children, fight the abuses of alcohol, and end slavery. These women upheld and even based their activism on the ideology of true womanhood and domestic feminism, arguing their piety and purity made them better suited to weigh in on social issues that affected women, children, and the home. In effect, these activist women used the cult of true womanhood to expand their roles.[16]

While the middle class was diverse in a number of ways, historians have pointed to a shared "cultural belief system, including views about women, the family, and republicanism." Subscription to this belief system often served to delineate the respectable or the genteel from the rest. These beliefs, fears, and values played out on the pages of the printing revolution that swept across the North, making New York City the hub of a new publishing empire. Reform literature, novels, religious tracts, newspapers, and magazines spoke to the concerns of changing gender roles, desires to protect the family, and the impulse to define the character of the republic. At the same time, the proliferation of more affordable penny papers and paperbacks created a growing appetite for entertaining, easily digestible literature. Perhaps more than any other genre, the convent narrative at once reflected middle-class Protestant domesticity, forging acceptable and nonacceptable roles for women, while offering readers the sensational stories they were coming to crave.[17]

This work draws heavily from the contributions of Jenny Franchot, Marie Anne Pagliarini, and Tracy Fessenden on the subject of gender and anti-Catholicism in early America. Franchot highlighted the centrality of sexual deviance in anti-Catholic literature of the antebellum era, arguing that such literature at once bolstered Protestant identity while indirectly expressing Protestant fears of and fascinations with Catholicism. Expanding on this, Pagliarini more closely examined the stock figures of the "pure American woman" and the "wicked Catholic priest" in anti-Catholic print culture. When the ideal of the pure woman as wife and mother gained near-religious status, the image of "innocent young women defiled in the confessional or convent" served as a powerful indictment of Catholicism. In turn, the "sexually depraved" priest reflected and reinforced the belief that celibacy was unnatural and dangerous. In rejecting "marriage and family life," the priest morphed into a "social degenerate" fixed on ravaging innocent women. Together these characters rendered Catholicism "a threat to the sexual norms, gender definitions, and family values that comprised the antebellum 'cult of domesticity.'" Fessenden also identified anxiety over female gender roles as the nexus of the "nun-as-whore figure" in nineteenth-century literature. She pointed out similarities among literary depictions of nuns and prostitutes, two kinds of women decidedly outside of the "Protestant woman's sphere." Despite appearing "to stand at opposite extremes," Fessenden argued that imaginings of both nuns and prostitutes clashed with "constructions of legitimate femininity as domestic, maternal, pious, and separate from the working market." Depictions of convents as clandestine brothels only reinforced this association, helping to preserve the Protestant woman's sphere.[18]

Rather than arguing against this scholarship, my work builds on it. Unlike Pagliarini's analysis, which examines married Catholic women who visited confessionals and nuns, my project focuses entirely on nuns and convents. I ask what it was in particular about the nun herself throughout the antebellum era that invoked such fierce disapproval. In addition to examining the "wicked priest" as a risk to female virtue, I explore the nun herself as a threatening image to dominant gender norms and national identity. While Fessenden hones in on literary depictions of nuns and prostitutes, I expand beyond this to compare nuns to portrayals of enslaved women, Mormon plural wives, and the "Jesuit spy." And while Franchot extended a general depiction of American Protestant fears and fascinations projected through anti-Catholic literature, I concentrate on convents, asking what the emotions stirred by these institutions tell us about American culture, female gender ideals, and notions of nationhood.

While some women used their ascribed piety to justify moving into more public roles, the ideology of domestic feminism could still be used to outcast, typecast, and punish certain women. In the antebellum US, this was no truer than for nuns. At a time when talk of female virtue pervaded cultural, religious, and political rhetoric, nuns were a barometer of American attitudes toward women. The image of the veiled nun appeared as the inversion of the true woman needed to sustain the nation. She was a captive of a foreign power, a fallen woman, a "white slave," a "useless drone," and a "foolish virgin." In contrast to the woman who found happiness, usefulness, and security as wife and mother in sentimental literature, nuns appeared miserable, wasted, and in constant danger. It was not merely pursuing what could be described in contemporary terms as a career that placed nuns outside of the bounds of acceptable womanhood; it was her unmarried state. Only through marriage could women reach their full potential as selfless caregivers, taming the wild passions of men, raising children to be virtuous citizens, and contribute to the household economy. In blatant defiance of this role, the nun appeared to disrupt the cosmic order of things. As Americans wrestled with the nature of their experimental republic, many agreed that the nun had no place for even "one instant in any civilized land." The ensuing campaign against convents would play a crucial role in the battles to define proper womanhood, republican government, and American identity.

Abbreviations

AAS   American Antiquarian Society
NYPL   New York Public Library
RSCJ   Society of the Sacred Heart, US Province Archives
SSND   School Sisters of Notre Dame Archives
SSNDEN   School Sisters of Notre Dame de Namur Archives
UNDA   University of Notre Dame Archives

ESCAPED NUNS

How unexpected to them will be the disclosures I make! Shut up in a place from which there has been thought to be but one way of egress, and that the passage to the grave, they considered themselves safe in perpetuating crimes in our presence and in making us share in their criminality as often as they chose.
—*Awful Disclosures of the Hotel Dieu*, 1836

I used to look upon the nun as the happiest of women, and the convent as the most delightful place of abode.
—*Awful Disclosures of the Hotel Dieu*, 1836

1

An Escaped Nun

MARIA MONK AND HER AWFUL DISCLOSURES

ALONE IN HER home in Montreal, Canada, on the evening of November 9, 1834, Mrs. Robertson heard an insistent pounding at the door. Two men in working clothes and a disheveled but attractive young woman stood anxiously in the cool night air, asking to speak with Dr. William Robertson. Mrs. Robertson refused to move from her position in the entryway, forcing the lot to explain themselves in the cold. The men relayed how they had come across the woman by the canal, near the St. Joseph suburbs. They had interrupted her near attempt to drown herself, persuading her away from the rocky banks. As the men explained their story, expectantly waiting for a flash of recognition in the eyes of the figure in the doorway, the young woman peered up at Mrs. Robinson, her expression unreadable. "Are you not her mother?" the men finally inquired. "She told us Dr. William Robinson was her father." At this Mrs. Robertson shut the door in their faces, sending the suspicious lot back into the night as she waited for her husband's return.[1]

When William Robertson came home that night, his wife told him about the strange visitors, speculating that they took the poor girl to the watch-house. Although it was late, Robertson put on his coat, heading back outside. The watch-house held "the most profligate women of the town," taken off the streets for "inebriety and disorderly conduct." Despite being full to capacity that night, the wardens found the girl who a few hours earlier had stood outside the Robertsons' home. The doctor took a seat beside the young woman whose long, dark hair lay matted against her shoulders and back, in what was likely a noisy room with sleepless inmates. He spoke calmly to her as he might to one of his patients, prompting her to explain her story. The girl acknowledged that she was not his daughter. For the past four years, she told him, her parents kept her locked up in the cellar, chained like a dog because she suffered from bouts of "temporary insanity." She was desperate to escape. She could not return home. Robertson examined her wrists, noting no signs of "the wearing of manacles, or any other mode of restraint." But Maria told him her mother took care to "cover the irons with soft cloths." The doctor was suspicious, but he took pity on the unkempt, yet somewhat charming woman. Clearly something distressing must have led to her now sitting alone in a cell in the middle of the night. As a justice of the peace, he ordered her release from the watch-house. He also looked into her identity, learning that her real name was the somewhat poetic-sounding Maria Monk.[2]

In August the following year, at ten o'clock at night, the Robertsons once more received unexpected visitors. This time two distinguished men of the city stood outside the door. Invited in, the men exchanged casual remarks with the Robertsons before explaining that "some very serious charges" had been made against the priests of the city and the nuns of the general hospital. The Hotel Dieu ("Hostel of God") was a hospital run by nuns from the French order of Religoius Hospitallers of St. Joseph. Would Dr. Robertson, as a magistrate, make an inquiry regarding these charges? The accusations, explained one of the men, came from "a female who had been a Nun in that Institution for four years." She divulged "horrible secrets," another chimed in, including the "criminal intercourse between nuns and priests" and "their murdering their offspring of these criminal connexions." As Robertson questioned the men further, he soon discovered that this was the same woman who visited his house last November. Her story, he learned, would soon be published in New York under the title *Awful Disclosures of the Hotel Dieu Nunnery of Montreal*.[3]

"How unexpected to them will be the disclosures I make!" read the opening lines of Maria Monk's *Awful Disclosures*. Her exposé promised to reveal to the world what went on "within the walls of that prison house of death," the Montreal convent. "Shut up in a place from which there has been thought to be but one way of egress, and that the passage to the grave," it continued, "they considered themselves safe in perpetuating crimes." What amounted to an over three-hundred-page book traced Monk's reception into the convent back to her "want of religious instruction at home," particularly a lacking on her mother's part. Though a Protestant, Mrs. Monk was "not accustomed to pay attention to her children" and "rather inclined to think well of Catholics." Young Maria admired the nuns until the day she "took the veil," thus becoming initiated into the ways of a convent. Once a vowed member of the Hotel Dieu, she learned to her "utter astonishment and horror" that her chief duties as a nun included ignoring her conscience and living in "criminal intercourse" with the priests. As a first-hand witness, Monk led readers through every trap door and chamber within the convent; inside interior apartments; down into the dark cellar, "where two sisters were imprisoned"; and through hidden subterranean passages that connected the priests' seminary with the convent for "impure purposes." While other nuns took their horrific stories to the grave, Monk managed to escape and to expose to the public the truth of convent life.[4]

Sex and sadism defined daily life in the Hotel Dieu. "Every one of [the priests] was guilty of licentiousness," confirmed Monk. Their "holy retreat" merely allowed them to receive treatment "for the many diseases they contract[ed]" from a sinful lifestyle. Another product of their "abominable ways" was the birth of many babies in the convent. These infants "were always baptized and immediately strangled" before being tossed into a giant pit in the cellar floor, which was covered with a "quantity of lime." Monk attested to "at least eighteen or twenty" instances of infanticide while she resided at the Hotel Dieu. She also recounted the violent murder of one of the nuns, who was seized, gagged, and tied to a bed on which a second mattress was thrown. The nuns and priests joyfully "jumped upon the poor girl" until they "smothered and crushed [her] to death." When they realized Sister Francis was dead, "they began to laugh . . . rallying each other in the most unfeeling manner," one remarking mockingly, " 'She would have made a good martyr!' "[5]

An illustration featured the murder of Sister Francis. (Figure 1.1) Catholic symbols of the crucifix, portraits of saints, and the garb of nuns and priests appeared prominently alongside depictions of horrific violence, suggesting the union of the two. As *Awful Disclosures,* and soon after an engraving in the popular anti-Catholic newspaper *Downfall of Babylon,* revealed, the murder of Sister Francis was a group event, a sanctioned rite, flowing naturally from the very unnatural state in which nuns and priests lived. The murdering nuns in the image contrasted sharply with ideals of womanhood from the time. Rather than sentimental, maternal, and moral "true women," these ladies were cold-hearted, immoral, and masculine. Indeed, their trampling of Sister Francis for her opposition to infanticide symbolized the idea that convents stamped out maternal instincts among the female "inmates," inverting the ideals of moral motherhood.

Awful Disclosures related the terrible fate of nuns who resisted instruction. For the smallest insubordination a nun could be chained to the cellar floor or made to starve to death. One of the worst punishments Monk ever saw was "the cap." The Mother Superior fastened this device onto the heads of nuns who "washed their hands without permission." It would "throw [them] into convulsions . . . [that] no human being could endure for an hour." Other nuns had "their flesh burned off their bones with red hot irons." The Mother Superior, a "heavy, lame," and arrogant woman who

FIGURE 1.1. "The Smothering of St. Francis, a Nun at the Hotel Dieu of Montreal," printed in *Downfall of Babylon* (1836).
Courtesy of the American Antiquarian Society.

encouraged the other nuns to "foster a superstitious regard for her," often gagged nuns and tied their hands behind their backs "to teach submission." She made them drink the water in which she had washed her feet. The Mother Superior and priests called these "brutal obscenities . . . meritorious before God," justifying their actions among a host of brainwashed nuns who, forbidden from reading the Bible, believed "the priests could do no sin." The Hotel Dieu was thus a dangerous place where men without wives and women "superiors" with too much authority reigned over "homes," tyrannizing "poor female victims."[6]

Before her initiation into convent life, Maria Monk claimed that she looked on nuns as "the happiest of women, and a convent as the most peaceful, holy, and delightful place of abode." But she soon discovered the opposite to be true. The cloister robbed women of any happiness, health, or hope they might otherwise wish for in life. Monk related seeing multiple women chained up in various chambers throughout the Hotel Dieu for minor offenses or offenses of which she never learned. They languished away for years, often facing an early death. "Many a nice, young creature has been killed in this nunnery," she reported. One nun "spoke like a woman in feeble health, and of a broken spirit." Monk experienced a similar wasting away, noting, "My wearisome daily prayers and labors, my pain of body, and depression of mind, which were so much increased by the penances I suffered . . . the shame, remorse, and horror, which sometimes arose, brought me to a state which I cannot describe." No happily-ever-after scenario awaited these brides of Christ. Their beauty, health, youth, and ideals wilted before the gloomy walls of a convent, where they lived tortured, burdensome, lonely lives of despair, the apparent consequences for rejecting traditional marriage and motherhood. Rather than the "happiest of women," these were the most wretched.[7]

The one relief Monk enjoyed before her final escape was the company of Sister "Mad" Jane Ray, who constantly played tricks on the residents or "inmates" of the Hotel Dieu. Though deemed insane, Jane Ray was the smartest of all the nuns in the convent. She knew English, had a keen sense of justice, and could always outwit her fellow Sisters. Once "Mad Jane" sprinkled holy water all over the floor so that the nuns would trip and "break the silence." She moved the boards beneath the beds "so that at night nearly a dozen nuns fell down upon the floor in getting into bed." One night, Jane Ray dressed a broomstick in a white cloth, lifting it up before the Mother Superior's chamber windows. "Oh, Mon Dieu!" the woman screamed in fright, heaving her plump body into the lap of the Sister beside her. The other nuns, who "all believed in ghosts," were equally terrified. Monk's brief respite was cut short, however, when she found "Mad Jane" hanging dead from the ceiling, her hands tied behind her back and her mouth gagged, a scene very similar, Monk recalled, "to that of the Inquisition." Mad Jane Ray not only provided readers of this otherwise dark tale with some comic relief but also reinforced the alleged foolishness of the nuns' vocation. These were not pious, educated women to be taken seriously.[8]

The first edition of *Awful Disclosures* ended abruptly with Monk's "liberty" from the convent. After allegedly being impregnated by Father Phelan, a well-known priest of Montreal, she narrowly escaped to save the life of her unborn child. The first edition included no mention of Monk's visit to the Robertsons'. The second edition, released soon after a number of affidavits appeared in opposition to Monk's story, included a lengthy sequel. Here the author explained that she had slipped into a "fit of melancholy" after her escape and attempted to drown herself along the canal in St. Joseph, only to be saved by two workmen. She addressed an affidavit contributed by Robertson, claiming, "It appears . . . that Dr. Robertson felt a peculiar desire to represent my character in the most unfavorable light he could." Attributing her rescue to divine providence, Monk described her subsequent special mission to expose the horrors of popery.[9]

Alone and friendless, she traveled to New York, hoping to find "protection from [her] enemies, as it was in a Protestant country." Among American Yankees, instead of Canadian Catholics, she believed she would find a more receptive audience. Famished and exhausted by the time she arrived, Maria allegedly once more attempted to end her life before being rescued by a few men who took her to an almshouse. Relatively new, almshouses, like other correctional facilities, began popping up in America's urban centers in the decades that followed the 1820s. They represented an institutional approach to dealing with society's delinquents and dependents during the early days of industrialization. Feeling near death, she requested to tell her story to the house chaplain, reportedly none other than the famed evangelical reformer Arthur Tappan. The minister encouraged her to "search the scriptures" and publish her story. Monk took up Tappan's advice and soon after, with the help of certain "Protestant protectors," published *Awful Disclosures of the Hotel Dieu Nunnery of Montreal.*[10]

Awful Disclosures became an overnight sensation, enjoying unprecedented popularity in the US and abroad. In the first five weeks of its publication, the book sold over twenty thousand copies. By 1860, sales surpassed three hundred thousand, making it second in the nation only to Harriet Beecher Stowe's *Uncle Tom's Cabin.* The manuscript was initially presented to Harper Brothers by Monk's "Protestant protectors," the Reverends William Hoyte, J. J. Slocum, and Theodore Dwight and the famed abolitionist George Bourne. Harper turned down the manuscript, anxious to protect their reputation against such a graphic tale. But sensing the potential gain from such intriguing allegations, the brothers commissioned two of their employees to set up a dummy press for its publication. Under the names "Howe & Bates," the book appeared for the first time in January 1836. Harper secured a note signed by Maria Monk in which she swore to the truth of her disclosures before they manufactured the book, supplying the printing machinery and material. Harper Brothers' historian, Eugene Exman, later described *Awful Disclosures* as the "most disgraceful book the brothers ever had connection with."[11]

Two years before *Awful Disclosures* appeared, two staunchly anti-Catholic periodicals went into publication. Each avidly previewed Maria Monk's story as evidence of the corruption and danger of Catholicism. Samuel S. Smith, a self-styled "late popish priest" and regular speaker for the New York Protestant Association, established and ran *The Downfall of Babylon; or, The Triumph of Truth over Popery.* The paper first appeared in Philadelphia in 1834 before Smith moved it to New York in 1836. Smith promised to unveil dark secrets of the Catholic Church "that w[ould] shake the mighty Babylon to its center." Before the book's publication, Smith devoted ample space to bawdy stories of nuns and priests, referring to "Nunneries" as "mere brothels." After its publication, *Downfall of Babylon* ran excerpts from the book, included lengthy editorials confirming Maria Monk's allegations, and even commissioned engravings of the "dreadful scenes" in *Awful Disclosures.*[12]

The president of the Protestant Reformation Society and minister of the Dutch Reformed Church, William C. Brownlee, edited the biweekly newspaper *American Protestant Vindicator and Defender of Civil Religious Liberties*, running from 1834 to 1842. With the endorsement of twelve clergymen, Brownlee stated the paper's mission to be founded on "the conviction that Popery ought always to be loathed and extricated, not only by all Christians, but also by every patriot and philanthropist." Of *Awful Disclosures*, Brownlee confirmed "no candid person . . . can read this straightforward narrative of Maria Monk without deep conviction of its truth." Brownlee referred to the book to denounce convents as unconstitutional. In what became a heated controversy over the veracity of *Awful Disclosures*, both newspapers tirelessly devoted space to updates and "final proof" of Maria Monk's allegations. George Bourne, one of Maria Monk's Protestant protectors, regularly contributed pieces in Brownlee's *Protestant Vindicator*. In one article, he confirmed the "truth" that nuns lived as captives in convents and warned that such institutions would "exterminate the family."[13]

Monk's so-called Protestant protectors, all active reformers, lent an aura of credibility and respectability to her story. Arthur Tappan, who raised no objections to his name appearing in over three hundred thousand copies of the book as the chaplain she first encountered at the New York almshouse, was a respected New York reformer, minister, and businessman. Tappan gave generously from his business fortunes to support various evangelical causes. He helped establish and fund the American Tract Society, managed the American Bible Society, and actively supported the American Temperance and Home Missionary Societies. Arthur and his brother Rev. Lewis Tappan were among those who spearheaded radical abolitionism, sitting on the founding board of the American Anti-Slavery Society and working closely with William Lloyd Garrison. In 1830, Arthur bailed Garrison out of jail. The hefty sums of money he and his brother donated to various reform movements made them national figures, known by the public simply as "the Tappan brothers." The association of their name with Maria Monk carried great weight with the general public.[14]

William Hoyte, one the fiercest defenders of Monk and likely the father of her child (instead of Father Phelan of the Hotel Dieu), had been a Methodist minister and missionary in Canada. For undisclosed reasons he was dismissed from the ministry before he met Maria Monk. While Hoyte mostly lived in obscurity before his association with Monk, George Bourne was a household name by the 1830s. He also spent time in Canada as a missionary among the nation's Catholics, subsequently publishing a travel guide, *Picture of Quebec in Its Vicinity* (1830). After emigrating to the US from England, Bourne became a Presbyterian minister and active abolitionist. Bourne also established the first anti-Catholic periodical in the US, simply entitled *The Protestant*, which began in 1830 in New York. Three years later, he authored the first convent narrative in the country, dedicating it to Arthur Tappan. *Lorette: The History of Louise, Daughter of a Canadian Nun, Exhibiting the Interior of Female Convents* sounded strikingly like *Awful Disclosures*.[15]

J. J. Slocum and Theodore Dwight were likewise ministers and reformers. Slocum actively participated in the New York Protestant Association. Dwight, the great-grandson of the sage of New England Jonathan Edwards, worked as a lawyer and leading member of the New York State Prison Discipline Association. A few months after *Awful Disclosures* appeared, Dwight published *Open Convents; or, Nunneries and Popish Seminaries, Dangerous to the Morals and Degrading to the Character of a Republican Community*. In his book, Dwight promoted *Awful Disclosures* as a "plain, unvarnished account of the enormities practiced in a convent." "No person who has any regard for female virtue," Dwight stated, should hesitate, after reading Monk's book, to endorse the civil inspection of all Catholic convents. The eminent New York mayoral candidate, painter, and inventor Samuel F. B. Morse also pledged support to Maria Monk and even considered proposing marriage to her. The association of these prominent men with Monk suggests the vast popularity of *Awful Disclosures*. The book's message resonated with society, especially those associated in one way or another with the burgeoning antebellum reform movements of the so-called benevolent empire, of which "regard for female virtue," as Dwight put it, was the ultimate focus.[16]

Awful Disclosures enjoyed a broad readership and inspired a host of imitations. The editor of the *Quarterly Christian Spectator*, a respected New Haven journal of theology and literature, referred to the "almost universal credit" given to Monk's story. Polemicists along with "well-informed and intelligent men," explained the article, believed and supported Maria Monk without question. "Immense editions of the work were sold in rapid succession and gained to an astonishing degree, belief among all classes of readers," the article announced. The stories of other allegedly escaped nuns, which remarkably resembled Maria Monk's, appeared almost immediately after Monk's debut, contributing to an "anti-nunnery" obsession. *Rosamond Culbertson; or, The Narrative and Suffering of an American Female Under the Popish Priests in the Island of Cuba* (written by Samuel Smith) appeared just a few months after *Awful Disclosures*. Inviting readers to "read, blush, and weep," Smith detailed the dark practices of Catholic priests in Cuba, which included confinement of women in convents and "stealing young negroes for the purpose of cutting them up and making them into sausages." Among others, *The Nun of St. Ursula* (1845), *The Convent's Doom* (1854), and *The Escaped Nun* (1855) all went on to become bestsellers before the Civil War. *The Escaped Nun* described nuns as "so many foolish virgins" of which a nation had no use. *The Nun of St. Ursula*, written by a well-known romance and adventure novelist, Harry Hazel, included a happy ending in which a charming man rescued a nun from a convent and married her. The height of Maria Monk's infamy as the escaped nun from Montreal would only last a few years, but the legacy of her story—the belief that nuns were not the right kind of women and that happy endings included marital vows rather than religious ones—would have a much greater reach.[17]

The rising tide of anti-Catholicism in America during the 1830s created a receptive market for stories like that of Maria Monk's. A small minority in the colonial era, Roman Catholics grew in number from three hundred thousand at the beginning of the century to about six hundred thousand in 1830. The number of priests, nuns, seminaries, convents, and Catholic newspapers and benevolent institutions proliferated as well. Internal or American conversion to Catholicism constituted one aspect of this growth. As many as two thousand people from New England alone converted to Catholicism between 1820 and 1840. German and especially Irish immigration, however, ushered in the greatest number of Catholics to the US. The ethnicity of the newcomers reinforced growing nativist thought that foreigners— their character, religion, and culture—threatened the country. In 1836 an article entitled "Our Country," published in Brownlee's *American Protestant Vindicator*, argued: "The vast increase of the number of foreign emigrants, most of whom are Catholic—the strenuous efforts of Papists to establish schools, nunneries, and colleges in every part of our country—are objects which we have feared by their combined influences would soon prostrate our liberties and make our noble country a wreck."[18]

To combat the spread of Rome in America, Protestants sponsored anti-Catholic literature, public debates, and associations. Believing that Protestant Americans had strayed from their founding ideals and that the religious background of many immigrants further threatened the Protestant character of the nation, these groups sought a revival of the Protestant Reformation in the nineteenth century. The Home Missionary Society formed in 1826, followed by the New York Protestant Association in 1830, and the American Society to Promote the Principles of the Protestant Reformation in 1836. To broaden their sphere of influence, George Bourne and William Brownlee, among others, pushed forward a merger of the latter two groups, forming the Protestant Reformation Society, an organization that would grow rapidly, exerting significant influence in the following decades.[19]

Awful Disclosures reflected quintessential anti-Catholicism. Ray Allen Billington argued that the book was "far more influential than any single work of nativist propaganda preceding the Civil War." But more important, *Awful Disclosures* struck a nerve with ideas of womanhood, the home, and the family. The publication of *Awful Disclosures* coincided with the rising feminine model of what Barbra Welter termed "true womanhood." The nuns of *Awful Disclosures* appeared decidedly out-side the bounds of true womanhood, being superstitious rather than pious, "fallen" rather than pure, and single as opposed to domestic wives and mothers. The inver-sion of good womanhood, seen especially in the image of the nun-mother callously dropping her infant into a pit, represented a direct inversion of the iconic Victorian gentlewoman, easily moved to tears at the slightest sentiment.[20]

The book mocked not only single women but also women with authority. Of the two Mother Superiors in the Hotel Dieu, the first was "bold and masculine . . . cruel and coldblooded." The second "was so heavy and lame that she walked with diffi-culty." The convent too appeared as the direct opposite of home, not warm, loving, and inviting, but cold, lonely, and dangerous. The Hotel Dieu confirmed the dire implications of women who lived outside the realm of marriage and motherhood. Monk's nightmarish depiction of what befell such women reinforced the perceived dangers of single womanhood. While *Awful Disclosures* enjoyed a ready-made audi-ence prone to believe the worst about Catholics, it also played on deep fears, desires, and expectations regarding female gender roles.[21]

Nuns resisted easy categorization in antebellum America, neither working out of necessity entirely as women of the emerging working class, nor justifying their foray into the public sphere on the basis of their maternal sensibilities as middle-class Protestant reform-minded women often did. Women who joined convents not only led lives of prayer but also worked as nurses, teachers, and administrators. While female religious communities often suffered financial privation and had to supple-ment incomes through manual labor, and while there was often a hierarchy of labor, they traveled, made business deals, owned property, and saw themselves as integral parts of larger communities that stretched beyond the nuclear family. In some ways, they were the first career women.[22]

The nuns of the Hotel Dieu, or the Hospitaliéres de Saint-Joseph, were part of a French order whose existence in Montreal dated back to 1659. By the 1820s the Hotel Dieu was one of five hospitals in Lower Canada, each operated by Catholic nuns, who served in the field of health and welfare. In particular, they assisted those suffering from floods, fires, and disease epidemics along with the large numbers of poor Irish immigrants. *Awful Disclosures* mentioned none of this, combating the notion of nuns as independent, educated women. Instead, the nuns of the Hotel Dieu appeared without agency, as captives, slaves, and "inmates" of licentious, power-hungry priests who joined convents out of a naïve hope for a blissful ex-istence away from the strife of the world. Rather than intelligent women, nuns of the Hotel Dieu in *Awful Disclosures* randomly placed capital letters in the middle of words, knew nothing of geography or the Bible, and muttered senseless Latin prayers.[23]

The Canadian press was the first to respond to the accusations in *Awful Disclosures*. The *Montreal Courier* denounced the work as "abominably false." Feeling it their duty to "defend the defamed," the editors set out to "expose the falsehood" perpetuated in Monk's book. They confirmed the good character of the nuns and priests of the Hotel Dieu, writing of their "unimpeachable conduct" and "unwearied Christian charity," especially during the "two years of pestilence" (referring to a cholera epidemic in Lower Canada). This was not simply a defense of the city's Catholic institutions, the editors claimed. As themselves Protestants who "glory to be so," they nevertheless took personal offense at the accusations in *Awful Disclosures*. "We should regard ourselves to be degraded in the eyes of the world," explained the article, "did we live in a community where such abominations existed, and not dare to denounce the perpetrators."[24] Their condemnation of *Awful Disclosures* was thus a defense at once of the Hotel Dieu and of the people of Montreal.

In part, the editors were responding to anti-Canadian sentiment. Due to the country's association with French and later Irish Catholicism and its status as a British colony, anti-Canadian feeling prevailed in the US during the Jacksonian era. These prejudices were only heightened as working-class Canadians migrated south to find work in New England's textile factories. After his missionary ventures in Canada, George Bourne, one of Monk's Protestant protectors, described the country as "debased by the prevalence of Roman supremacy." *Awful Disclosures* expressed a similar sentiment. When describing her decision to travel to the US instead of staying in Montreal, Monk claimed, "I well knew of the ignorance and prejudice of the poor Canadians, and understood how such a person as myself must appear in their eyes." Aware of this unfavorable reputation, the Canadian press acted to defend their countrymen and -women in the face of what they considered to be a libelous work against Lower Canada.[25]

A few presses in the US were also quick to denounce the book. The *Vermont State Paper* rebuked it as a "miserable catchpenny" that would "disgrace a brothel." The *Boston Statesmen* blasted it as "miserable libel from beginning to end." Other papers criticized the book for pandering to anti-Catholic bigotry. The editor of the *New Hampshire Sentinel* lamented that "thousands will likely purchase, read, and believe" the book because nothing was "too bad for *Catholics*." The *Vermont State Paper* likewise relegated the readership to those who "find in the Catholic religion a theme of continued crimination." The New York *Sunday Morning News* contended that no "sane man" would believe that a "whole religious community . . . is a murderer and worse than a murderer." "We cannot deem it founded on truth—the statements are too shocking for belief," read the *New Yorker*, whose editor concluded that the book would only appeal to those of "the most depraved taste."[26]

Yet the readership of "depraved tastes" appeared to prevail. Numerous presses and associations, Protestant or otherwise, expressed full-fledged belief in *Awful Disclosures*. A month after its release, the *New York Journal of Commerce* admitted that "there is strong internal evidence of the truth of the stories." The *Baltimore Literary and Religious Magazine*, a fiercely anti-Catholic paper, never wavered in its support of Monk. "On the authority of Maria Monk," the paper condemned all convents as prisons of "misery and superstition." In another article, the editors supported Monk's alleged request to lead an examination of the Hotel Dieu. "How quietly she might take someone to the spot in which have long been deposited the murdered bodies of the nuns and their children!" exclaimed the author. *Zion's Herald*, published in Boston, professed continual support of Monk even after investigations suggested the falseness of her story, writing by September 1836, "we have always said that Maria Monk's book bears irrefragable, irrefutable evidence of truth." The paper also included nearly fifty articles on Monk during 1836 alone. The Protestant Association of New York likewise pledged unyielding support to Maria Monk, officially challenging the bishops of Montreal to open the Hotel Dieu to investigation. As these challenges mounted, new editions of *Awful Disclosures* featured a picture of Maria Monk, clad in a nun's habit with a baby on her lap and an inscription that read: "Bring me before a court."[27]

Maria Monk's soaring popularity in the US as the brave and lovely escaped nun took a hit when her mother formally testified against her. That same August of 1835, when the Robertsons heard of the allegations against the nuns and priests of Montreal, Isabella Monk, Maria's mother, also received a number of strange visitors to her home and had an unusual encounter with her daughter. The city of Montreal collected her testimony, along with Dr. Robertson's and those of other city residents, as formal affidavits against the veracity of *Awful Disclosures*. The *Montreal Courier* and the New York *Catholic Diary* published the affidavits shortly after their release. The *Protestant Vindicator* dismissed Mrs. Monk's testimony as "forged and fallacious," but its release marked the first substantial setback for Maria Monk's disclosures.[28]

Mrs. Monk testified to receiving a strange visitor in mid-August, a "decently dressed" man who introduced himself as Reverend Hoyte of New York. Sitting inside Mrs. Monk's modest parlor, the minister apologetically explained his situation. He and Maria had a five-week-old baby girl, he informed Mrs. Monk. He wanted to take care of them, but Maria ran away from him and the child where they were lodging at "Goodenough's Tavern" in town. He questioned Mrs. Monk about her daughter's whereabouts. When Mrs. Monk, apparently unmoved, shrugged and waved the man off, he became indignant. How could a mother not care where her daughter was or about the well-being of her own granddaughter? Mrs. Monk later claimed that Hoyte vehemently demanded she help him find Maria, firing a series of questions at her that she could not answer.[29]

The minister also spoke "very bitterly against the Catholics, the Priests, and the Nuns," Mrs. Monk recalled. Hoyte told her that Maria had been in a nunnery where she had been tortured, starved, and coarsely handled by priests. Mrs. Monk again appeared indifferent. She denied that Maria had ever been in a convent except when she attended a day school at age eight. Moreover, as a child she had broken a slate pencil in her skull and ever since was "deranged in the head." She would make up "the most ridiculous but plausible stories," explained Mrs. Monk. Perhaps to convince him that she was not unduly obstinate, Mrs. Monk told Hoyte that she was a Protestant and "did not like the Roman Catholic religion." Nevertheless, she respected the priests and nuns of Montreal as the most "charitable persons I ever knew," refusing to believe his story. At that, the reverend left in a huff.[30]

The next day, Hoyte reportedly returned to Mrs. Monk's home. He explained that he had found Maria and that their little family planned to depart for New York City the following day. Mrs. Monk expressed no wish to see her daughter or granddaughter before their departure. In the affidavit, she offered no explanation for the hostility between herself and Maria. Writing forty years later, Maria Monk's daughter described Mrs. Monk as a callous woman who had kicked Maria out of the house for "some indiscretion," forcing her to take refuge in an asylum for "fallen women" or prostitutes. Mrs. Monk did, however, include testimony of Hoyte offering her a bribe. If Mrs. Monk would only say that her daughter had been a nun, "it would be better than one hundred pounds." She would be "protected for life," and could move away from Montreal should any hostility with her neighbors arise. According to the affidavit, Mrs. Monk responded that "thousands of pounds would not induce me to perjure myself." At this, Hoyte got "saucy and abusive to the utmost." And then he went away, leaving Mrs. Monk's for the last time. She would not hear about her daughter again until Maria was an international sensation for her shocking exposé of the Hotel Dieu convent.[31]

Isabella Monk's formal testimony led some US newspapers to switch their positions. The *Barre Gazette* of Massachusetts renounced their endorsement of Maria Monk published "a week or two ago." "It turns out to be all a humbug," stated the article, since "the mother of Maria Monk has since sworn that her daughter was never in a convent." The *New Bedford Mercury* admitted to being convinced "by a number of affidavits from Canadian papers" that Maria Monk was not the true author of *Awful Disclosures* and that she was a "woman of bad character" and "mental derangements." Other affidavits mounted against the veracity of Monk's allegations. William Robinson testified to her mysterious appearance at his home the previous year. Based on his "knowledge of her character," Robertson stated that he "did not believe a word" of her story. Another resident of Montreal, Nancy McGan, attested to being closely associated with Maria and her mother. During the same year that Maria appeared at the Robertsons', McGan claimed Maria told her she had discovered "the father of her child." Maria explained she would not go with him, "for he wanted her to swear an oath that would lose her soul forever, but . . . should make her a lady forever." Soon after McGan also received a visit from "Mr. Hoyte" asking about Maria's whereabouts. Supporters of Monk countered these affidavits with those of their own, contributing to a veritable press war over *Awful Disclosures* and consequently to even greater overall public interest in the controversy.[32]

Monk's defenders kept pace with the growing opposition. An article in the *New York Evangelist* by "One Who Knows" dismissed the Montreal affidavits as "senseless" and "contradictory." *Downfall of Babylon* insisted that the affidavits of "unprincipled profligates" and "ignorant Papists" should be rejected. The bribe Mrs. Monk described, claimed the *Protestant Vindicator*, actually came from Montreal priests who promised Isabella Monk one hundred pounds if she would say Maria "had *not* been in a nunnery at all." Mrs. Monk's character was enough to condemn her as a witness, according to the *Vindicator*. Her "habitual intemperance, coarse impiety, [and] long-indulged hatred and cruelty towards her daughter" demonstrated the "worthlessness" of her testimony. J. J. Slocum, a Presbyterian minister and one of Maria Monk's Protestant protectors, also denounced Mrs. Monk as "unreliable" because of "an extreme backwardness," characteristic of Canadians, and even alleged that Mrs. Monk had "gone so far as to threaten her [daughter's] life." Picturing Isabella Monk as an unfit mother proved enough for many to discount her testimony. Her apparent lack of conformity with true maternal sensibilities rendered her "barbarous," suspicious, and untrustworthy, in the same manner of unmarried priests and nuns.[33]

The second edition of *Awful Disclosures* also responded to the affidavits, clarifying the otherwise suspicious appearance of Monk in Montreal in the summer of 1835. "My readers, I think, will learn from the following pages, that when a nun has merely escaped from a Convent, but a small part of her difficulties and dangers may be passed," read the opening lines of the "Sequel to the Narrative." She considered suicide along the canal because of the overwhelming suffering she endured in the convent. This suffering also caused some "derangement of mind." When Hoyte visited Mrs. Monk in Montreal, he and Maria were there to obtain legal information against the Hotel Dieu. The excitement of this venture might have led "to some appearances" of disorder. After a lengthy description of her mother and the citizens of Montreal being in cahoots with the Catholic priests to recapture her, the sequel concluded in a way that would allow for further tweaking. "I am persuaded, from the experience I have already had, that past scenes, before forgotten, will continue to return to my memory . . . and that many of these will tend to confirm, explain, or illustrate some of the statements now before the public." A number of papers reprinted a version of this extended story, including the *New York Evangelist* and the *New York Journal of Commerce*. As Maria Monk continued making headlines across the country, her true story became more difficult to detect.[34]

Supporting Monk with more than words, Samuel Smith published graphic images based on the scenes in *Awful Disclosures*. The illustrated book *Dreadful Scenes in the Awful Disclosures of Maria Monk*, which also appeared serially in Smith's paper, vividly unveiled "what awful deeds are perpetrated under the cloak of religion." One image portrayed nuns and priests as fiends, taking gross pleasure in the murder of Sister Francis, smothering her under a mattress. Other scenes depicted the credulous nuns' belief that sheet-covered brooms were ghosts, and the morbid death of "Mad Jane" Ray hanging upside down by a rope (Figures 1.2). The public glimpsed the infamous rumored infanticide in another that pictured a nun dropping a murdered infant into a giant well in the convent cellar floor. The gloomy, dark stone room provided a gothic backdrop while the image of the woman releasing her child into the abyss suggested the dangerous inversion of mother-hood that resulted from living as a nun. The publication of these images reinforced caricatures of convent life and nuns while allowing other avenues for profit from the Maria Monk controversy.[35]

FIGURE 1.2. "They All Believed in Ghosts," printed in *Downfall of Babylon* (1836).
Courtesy of the American Antiquarian Society.

In response to the escalating spectacle, six men of Montreal, mostly Protestants, three of them ministers, launched a formal investigation of the Hotel Dieu. Reverend Curry served as secretary of the Home Missionary Society; Revs. G. W. Perkins and Henry Esson were Presbyterian ministers; Benjamin Holmes, Esq., was a cashier of the Montreal Bank and justice of the peace; John Estell, Esq., worked as an architect and surveyor; and John Jones, the only Roman Catholic, was editor of the Montreal paper *L'Ami du Peuple*. Without notice, the men descended on the convent with *Awful Disclosures'* depiction of the premises in hand, conducting a search "from the cellar to the roof." Curry reported that the nuns "cheerfully opened every enclosure" to the investigators. Afterward, he declared he was "unable to find any resemblance whatever between that building . . . and that map furnished by Maria Monk." Perkins agreed that it would be "impossible" for a person "at all acquainted with the internal plan of the nunnery, to have drawn up the map . . . given in [Monk's] book." In a subsequent article entitled "Maria Monk, the Nun-Such," the *Saturday Evening Post* interpreted the results of the investigation as proof that Maria Monk was an "impudent humbug." The *Portsmouth Journal of Literature* likewise confirmed the conclusions of the investigators and the "upstanding character" of the Hotel Dieu.[36]

But "interior alternations have been made!" came the resounding response of Monk's supporters. And they had a second escaped nun from the Hotel Dieu to prove it. Like Monk, Sister St. Frances Patrick, or Frances Patridge, offered a salacious and incriminating narrative of the Hotel Dieu of her own, claiming that she too made a narrow escape from within its walls. According to *Zion's Herald* and the *New York Sun*, Patridge's story would prove the truth of *Awful Disclosures* "beyond all rational doubt," making Monk's accusations appear tame. Reports described Patridge as "tall and graceful" at age twenty-seven, with a "penetrating vivacity" in her eyes. Allegedly based on his interviews with this woman, Samuel Smith wrote *The Escape of Sainte Frances Patrick, Another Nun from the Hotel Dieu Nunnery of Montreal*. The pamphlet-sized narrative, however, was mostly a prop for *Awful Disclosures*. As a corrective to the recent investigation of the convent, Patridge confirmed that the interior of the Hotel Dieu "had been so entirely altered since Miss Monk's escape, that no one could recognize it as the same." Smith upheld the story as "confirm[ing] all that Maria Monk had stated." True to form, Smith published an illustration "representing the escape of St. Frances Patridge." George Bourne confirmed her "additional secrets," which "most amply corroborated all the criminal allegations" brought forward by Monk. Bourne concluded his endorsement of the latest escaped nun, citing a biblical passage: "In the mouth of two or three witnesses, every word may be established."[37]

"The final proof in female form," however, proved to be more of a liability than an asset. Not long after the publication of her story, Patridge "deserted the confederacy," charging her male protectors with "taking undue liberties with her person." Before her retreat from their assembly, she also declared Monk to be an impostor and herself alone as the "authentic escapee from the Montreal nunnery." Despite claims of authenticity, Patridge never achieved the attention afforded to Maria Monk. Only two newspapers, the blatantly anti-Catholic *Downfall of Babylon* and *Protestant Vindicator,* even mentioned her name, and that only in reference to her story suggesting the falsity of Maria Monk's. Later Reverend Brownlee claimed that Patridge was a Jesuit in disguise.[38]

A few months later, John Jones, of the Montreal investigative committee, published his own book-length denunciation of Monk unsubtly entitled *Awful Exposure of the Atrocious Plot Formed by Certain Individuals Against the Clergy and Nuns of Lower Canada.* He deplored Monk's book as a "tissue of ill-constructed lies from beginning to end." Proceeding to correct these "lies," Jones addressed minute and major details. The nuns of the Hotel Dieu were not sometimes called "Sisters of Charity," as mentioned in the book, since they were a different order, the "Sisters of the Congregation." "It is untrue that any of the nuns are veiled," he stated further, "if this implied concealing the face." Moreover, the Hotel Dieu "never sent a 'rich carpet' to the king of England 'as an expression of gratitude for the money annually received,'" as *Awful Disclosures* alleged. The Hotel Dieu had never received funds from the monarchy at all. While Monk wrote of nuns lying down inside a coffin that bore their name during the "veil taking" ceremony, Jones asked, "Is it necessary to say that there is no such coffin?" He corrected a number of other fine points, including disabusing the public of the notion that any of the nuns sported beards.[39]

More significantly, Jones challenged the notion that Maria Monk ever spent time in the Hotel Dieu as a nun. Monk did have some experience with nuns, he argued, but this was during her residence at a Magdalen asylum, a place for the restoration of prostitutes. Like other "houses of correction" during the antebellum era, Magdalen asylums were established to reform prostitutes or "fallen women" by isolating them from society and imposing a strict regimen of daily tasks. Named after Mary Magdalen, who according to the New Testament had been healed from a life of sexual crime, Magdalen asylums were largely run as explicitly religious institutions, both Catholic and Protestant. The Magdalen asylum to which Jones referred was also known as the Charitable Institution for Female Penitents. The daughter of a wealthy merchant, Agathe-Henriette Huguet Latour, opened the institution in 1829 on property owned by her family. The religious affiliation matched that of its Catholic founder, and as the asylum grew it became more entrenched among the other Catholic institutions of Montreal, including the Hotel Dieu.[40]

Jones described how Monk's portrait of the Hotel Dieu matched not the convent but the asylum. Monk attested to fifty girls living at the Hotel Dieu, and there were fifty women in the asylum. *Awful Disclosures* mentioned a few nuns by name, including Jane McCoy and Jane Ray, but these two women were "reformed prostitutes" and residents of the asylum. Agathe-Henriette Huguet Latour, whom Jones referred to as Mrs. McDonnell in reference to the surname of her late husband, confirmed Monk's residency in 1835. In an affidavit of her own, Latour stated that Monk had "for many years, led the life of a stroller and prostitute." After her residence of nearly a year, Latour kicked Monk out for being pregnant. The description of the architecture and design of the Hotel Dieu in *Awful Disclosures*, Latour confirmed, matched her own ward precisely.[41]

Jones used this information to dismiss Monk's character and thus her reliability, repeatedly referring to her as "the prostitute." According to Jones, Latour tried to "restore her to the habits of virtue; but Monk proved a hardened sinner." After leaving the asylum, Jones theorized, Monk "wandered from place to place" until she took up with a "disgraced and cast-off clergyman," Reverend Hoyte. She pretended to be his wife and told him about her experience in the asylum. Out of his "love of lucre," the clergyman suggested a use for this story, and *Awful Disclosures* was born. So too was a love child, Monk's alleged evidence of her rape at the Hotel Dieu. Jones concluded that Monk escaped from the asylum only to run into and share her experience with Hoyte, who altered her story from escaping the asylum to escaping the convent.[42]

If Maria Monk had resided in the Montreal Magdalen Asylum, this would suggest a woman in desperate circumstances. In the early nineteenth century, Magdalen asylums in the US and Canada functioned as a refuge of last resort for prostitutes. While the so-called fallen women found aid and shelter in such facilities, they endured long hours of manual labor to earn their keep. The Montreal Magdalen Asylum depended directly on the manual labor of its residents or "magdalenes" to remain in operation. At the same time, those who ran the facilities constantly reminded the ward of their "guilt in the eyes of their maker." Records show that most women who frequented Magdalen asylums stayed only "long enough to get reclothed and recuperated." Magdalenes commonly challenged the rules, were thrown out, or escaped. Despite having no legal authority to detain residents, asylum authorities took measures to prevent them from escaping, suggesting the regularity of such occurrences. Monk's probable residence in the Montreal Magdalen Asylum would point not only to her desperation but also to her familiarity with toilsome work, stories of intrigue, and creative escapes.[43]

Jones's book sent the Protestant protectors of Maria Monk, into a frenzy. Slocum responded to Jones's critique and the Montreal investigative conclusions with his own book, *Reply to the Priest's Book, Denominated, "Awful Exposure of the Atrocious Plot Formed by Certain Individuals against the Clergy and Nuns of Lower Canada, through the Intervention of Maria Monk."* Slocum's book included a lengthy refutation of the "priest's book," "further confirmation" and "revelation" of *Awful Disclosures*, and multiple testimonies, including one from George Bourne confirming the existence of a "subterranean passage between the Seminary and the Hotel Dieu." *Zion's Herald* declared Jones's examination to be "altogether unsatisfactory" on the basis of Jones being the editor of a "Romish paper." Samuel Smith accused Jones of conspiring with the priests of Montreal to abduct Monk from New York and return her to the convent. Though Jones may have diminished the credibility of Monk's book, the continued amount of energy in the growing debate attested to the interest that surrounded Maria Monk.[44]

The priests of Montreal themselves had little to say in response to *Awful Disclosures*. According to one paper, this was because they considered something as clearly fictitious as *Gulliver's Travels* "beneath notice, belief, or refutation." Monk's supporters, however, pointed to this as further evidence of guilt. "It is not a little remarkable," read an article in the *Protestant Vindicator*, "that no one of all the persons so boldly impeached by her of the most atrocious crimes has even whispered a hint that she was not a nun." In the revised edition of *Awful Disclosures*, Monk claimed that she had anticipated no response from the priests of Montreal to her book because "they feared an investigation" and "further disclosures." The book even stated that the priests felt a sense of relief that her "'disclosures' were not the most 'awful' which they had reason to expect." The *Baltimore Literary and Religious Magazine* criticized the Montreal priests' silence as unmanly. "The way for men to acquit themselves of such charges is at once manly and boldly, to challenge and demand an instant examination into every particular." Likewise, the American Tract Society officially labeled the priests of Montreal void of "manly honesty and virtuous innocence" in their neglect to allow the matter to be "brought to a fair trial." Appealing to long-held anti-Catholic beliefs that priestly celibacy left men emasculated, these responses further cast a veil of suspicion over convent life.[45]

Catholic newspapers in the US spent more time addressing *Awful Disclosures*. A number of them reprinted the Montreal affidavits under the title "Maria Monk's 'Awful Disclosures,' Villainy Exposed!!!" The *Boston Pilot*, a Catholic weekly, accused *Awful Disclosures* of being a "mere copy" from an older European book entitled *The Gates of Hell Opened, A Development of the Secrets of Nunneries* (1731). One of the most scathing attacks against *Awful Disclosures* in the *Catholic Diary* was in a letter to the editor. In March 1836, a US Catholic priest, Father McMahon, referred to *Awful Disclosures* as "the devil's prayer book." He called on all "honest Americans" to consider the "facts" and argued that Catholics had "reason [and] religion . . . in our favor." That same year the *Catholic Telegraph* condemned Monk's book as the "basest [of] lies." The *Catholic Telegraph* printed numerous articles on Monk, keeping up with the affidavits, investigations, and press statements to expose what the paper referred to as "Maria Monkism." While the Catholic response to Monk was swift and undeniably critical, the Protestant press spent more time and energy promoting, criticizing, and arguing about the book. *Awful Disclosures* in many ways was a Protestant creation, reflecting specific fears, fascinations, theories, and values, and exposing some of the internal disagreements among Anglo-American Protestants about their identity vis-à-vis Catholicism, especially regarding the role of women, marriage, and the family.[46]

The following year, William L. Stone, a Protestant clergyman and editor of the *New York Commercial Advertiser*, one of the most prominent Whig newspapers in the country, decisively undercut the claims of Maria Monk. Stone confessed an initial inclination to believe the "fearful revelations" of Monk because of his "prejudices against the Catholic faith." The widespread "excitement" over the book inspired him to inspect the convent himself. If the nuns and priests were "actually guilty" of their alleged crimes, Stone claimed, then "the truth should be known," and if not, "the accusers should be arrested." Taking the work seriously, Stone, along with two other investigators, studied the illustrated version of *Awful Disclosures*, which included detailed maps of the premises as laid down by "Maria Monk's memory." With the book in hand on the day of the investigation, Stone and his cohort set their sights on "nothing short of a minute examination." After days of personally investigating the Hotel Dieu, "in every room, closet, and pantry," Stone denounced the book as "wholly and unequivocally, from beginning to end, untrue."[47]

Of his first visit to the convent, Stone wrote that he "might very well have expected to find it guarded by gorgons, hydras, and chimeras dire, *but it was not so*." After entering a "wide open gate," an English-speaking nun with an "agreeable appearance" led Stone through the building. He was surprised to discover such easy access into the convent and to see that the nuns were not gloomy. The women he encountered looked nothing like those depicted in *Awful Disclosures*. They were cheerful, with "faces wreathed in smiles." His guide conducted him through the apothecary and the hospital wards. Though not permitted into the "inner apartments" of the convent on his first visit without the permission of the bishop, Stone ended the first day of his investigation "having seen nothing of vipers" and hearing "no groans."[48]

On the second day, Stone and his cohort received the necessary permission to search each room. They opened every trapdoor and descended into every vault, discovering that the vaults were merely storerooms filled with hospital supplies.

Stone suspected one door, "leading from the outside directly into the building," of possibly leading to a subterranean passage. But it "merely proved to be the kitchen cellar," a "receptacle of potatoes and turnips." The three men even nosed around the nuns' bedrooms. Of these Stone corrected the assumption that their "cells" were "dark and gloomy places." They were "neat little apartments, containing a single bed, with green curtains and counterpanes, two old-fashioned high-back chairs, [and] a little desk, with a small case for books." While *Awful Disclosures* presented the interior of convents as the opposite of a warm, inviting hearth, the temple of the Victorian wife and mother, Stone felt compelled to correct this. After day two he concluded that "the author had never been within the walls of the cloister."[49]

In response to the repeated accusations of "material alterations" since Monk's time in the convent, Stone reported that "neither an outward wall nor a cellar nor a vault has been whitewashed." The mason work was of "ancient and timeworn stone." He even calculated the likelihood of *Awful Disclosures'* charge of infanticide within the convent. According to the book, seventy-five babies were born and murdered in a year. Stone pointed out, however, that there were only thirty-six nuns living in the Hotel Dieu and that half of them were "past age." This would mean that fifteen of them would have had to given birth to two and half children a year. Stone finally considered the criticism of the Hotel Dieu not opening its doors to the public immediately after the release of Monk's book. He found that if visitors were admitted at any time, the nuns would get nothing done. As each was "constantly employed," their "patients would suffer" from such interruptions. Taken together, the evidence unearthed by Stone convinced him that "Maria Monk was an errant impostor; that she never was a nun . . . and that the nuns and priests were innocent in this matter."[50]

Stone's forceful denunciation unleashed a wave of reactionary responses. The American Tract Society promptly issued a petition against the investigation. Samuel F. B. Morse was among the first to sign. Morse already expressed a penchant for anti-Catholic and nativist conspiracies, articulated in his previously published book, *Imminent Dangers to the Free Institutions of the United States* and *Foreign Conspiracy against the Liberties of the United States*. Articles in *Downfall of Babylon* and *Protestant Vindicator* also unsurprisingly blasted Stone. "Stone has pleased the Papists wonderfully," read an article in *Downfall*. He was part of "Jesuitical hoax," announced the *Protestant Vindicator*. Indeed, the editors made rejection of Stone's conclusions a litmus test of true Christianity, stating that "every devout Christian . . . [stood] decidedly against the humbug of Col. Stone."[51]

As the months went by, the criticisms got more creative. It was because the colonel was "Stone-blind, Stone-deaf, and Stone-hearted" that he rejected the veracity of *Awful Disclosures*. Some papers even employed poetry in their rebuke, likening Maria Monk to truth incarnate and Stone to the rock that was rolled away.

"Maria Monk is still alive . . . For truth will ever live and thrive . . . Though covered by a mighty Stone." The most elaborate criticism satirized Stone's investigation in a volume-length epic poem. *The Vision of Rubeta, An Epic Story on the Island of Manhattan, with Illustrations Done on Stone* appeared in 1838. So popular was the epic that a one-act play based on the poem was published the same year. The American Tract Society resolved that Stone's examination was "altogether unsatisfactory." The society further condemned those who suggested that Monk really resided in the Montreal Magdalen Asylum as "unprincipled profligates [who] call themselves Protestants." This flurry of rebuttals suggests the significance of Stone's critique and revealed the extent to which the controversy of Maria Monk escalated into a press war, with increasing hyperbole and spectacle.[52]

By early 1837, Protestants divided over the story of Maria Monk. The readership of the *Quarterly Christian Spectator*, affiliated with Yale theologians, represented one contingent. In a twenty-page refutation of *Awful Disclosures*, the *Christian Spectator* dismissed Monk as a "liar and fornicator" and criticized the "grotesque logic" put forward by her supporters. According to the editors, not all who questioned Monk's story were "panderers of popery and aids to the devil." The editors also chastised Monk's supporters for the way in which they allowed the controversy to cause a rift within the Protestant community. "With such Protestantism," lamented the editor of the *Christian Spectator*, "we have no communion." The editors encouraged their readers to convert their Catholic counterparts, to remedy their "ignorant, bigoted, and darkened [minds]" through "love" rather than vitriol.[53]

Toward the end of the summer of 1837, Monk suddenly disappeared from New York. Like her unusual visit to the Robertsons' three years earlier, she again found herself on the doorsteps of a medical doctor's home. This time, though, she was alone and in Philadelphia. Dr. William Sleigh must have recognized her or at least the name when he opened his door to Maria Monk around ten o'clock in the morning on August 16. Otherwise he might not have invited her in to hear her story or sent for six other "distinguished citizens" to serve as witnesses. Disheveled and forlorn, Monk related to the gathered men a sad story, seeking their mercy. She told them that she had sailed to Philadelphia from New York in the company of six priests who had artfully persuaded her to leave with them. She also wanted to get away from her Protestant protectors, she explained, who "made well by my book" without proffering any of the rewards to her. "I find I have gone from Catholic Jesuits to Protestant Jesuits!" Monk exclaimed, bursting into tears.[54]

After arriving in the city, Monk told Sleigh that she and the priests took up residence at the Philadelphia Catholic Orphan Asylum. It was from this institution that she fled from the priests after overhearing their breakfast conversation, in which the New York bishop, John Hughes, presiding and providing the rum, slammed down his pint, proclaiming, "Damn her! We've had enough trouble already!" Concerned with whether she had truly been abducted by priests and if her Protestant protectors had cheated her, Sleigh invited J. J. Slocum, one of said protectors, to help clear things up. When Slocum arrived the following day, Sleigh was shocked by his "perfect indifference" and "unaccountable lukewarmness" regarding Monk's welfare. When Sleigh asked Slocum what was to become of her, Slocum reportedly burst out, "I don't know what is to become of her and I don't think she will have anything coming to her!" After his brief encounter with Slocum, who quickly thereafter returned to New York, Sleigh advised Monk to get legal advice.[55]

With raised suspicions, Sleigh conducted his own investigation. The results from this, along with a description of his interview with the runaway nun, Sleigh compiled in a book entitled *An Exposure of Maria Monk's Pretended Abduction and Conveyance to the Catholic Asylum, Philadelphia, by Six Priests, with Numerous Extraordinary Incidents During Her Residence in this City.* Mrs. Davis, "a Protestant lady of high respectability and owner of a boarding house," testified that a young woman giving the name "Miss Jane Howard" arrived at her house on August 15 fresh from a New York steamboat. "Miss Jane Howard," attested Davis, "was Miss Maria Monk. I would at any time recognize the same lady." Sleigh also interviewed the nuns who ran the Catholic Orphan Asylum in Philadelphia. The Sisters confirmed that "a woman who matched the description of Monk came to the Asylum" unaccompanied. The woman, they said, claimed that her husband had left her and wanted to know if she could work there as a seamstress, a domestic, anything. The nuns apparently turned her away, offering her neither work nor shelter. A third witness said he saw Monk alone on the boat from New York. It was he who suggested Mrs. Davis's boarding house. Sleigh systematically built his case against Monk upon these statements, confirming still further that Bishop Hughes was in St. Louis at the time of Monk's visit, and thus never presided over the alleged breakfast in Philadelphia.[56]

Unlike Jones, who dismissed Maria Monk as "the prostitute," Sleigh described her as a victim in need of help. As a physician, Sleigh declared Monk "incapable of taking proper care of herself." He urged "those connected with her" to place her in "some Asylum," where after a few years, "she might become a worthy member of society." Sleigh voiced concern for Maria, her child, and society if she remained free to do as she pleased. "She cannot be more than twenty-one. . . . She is a mother! What is now to become of her?" Sleigh demanded. He warned none could be safe while "such a person is at large." She may next decide to publish *Awful Disclosures of Protestantism*, he warned. The public needed to be protected from Maria Monk and she needed protection from herself.[57]

The last grand effort to salvage the popularity and credibility of *Awful Disclosures* appeared in a second and final book whose title listed Maria Monk as the author: *Further Disclosures by Maria Monk, Concerning the Hotel Dieu Nunnery of Montreal; also Her Visit to Nuns' Island, and Disclosures Concerning That Secret Retreat*, published in 1837. The work represented a mix of the sensational themes present in the first book and a detailed courtroom like defense. The first half of *Further Disclosures* offered an exhaustive, multilayered, and confusing argument in support of Monk's story, with over four hundred pages delineating arguments against Monk followed by rebuttals to those arguments. The book then unveiled "further disclosures" of the crimson corruptions of the nuns and priests of Canada, including a lengthy description of "Nuns' Island." Surely meant to both entice and horrify readers, Nuns' Island, located in the St. Lawrence River, harbored the young and most beautiful nuns who were visited by the priests for "criminal purposes" during their "holy retreat." The island also conveniently operated as a treatment center for the inevitable diseases incurred on such retreats. Despite the salacious details, *Further Disclosures* did not come close to unleashing the type of hysteria created by Monk's first book. Perhaps the public wearied of the controversy; or maybe Monk had simply lost credibility or appeal, a predictable fate of her celebrity.[58]

On the heels of the incriminating investigations of *Awful Disclosures*, skeptics began seriously questioning Maria Monk's authorship of the book. If Monk was a feeble victim who received the rudiments of an education, as her book claimed, could she have published a two-hundred-page manuscript? Could she have published another two hundred pages that same year in a revised edition, meeting every challenge published by her opponents and juxtaposing them with supportive articles and affidavits? The *New Hampshire Patriot* charged Theodore Dwight with being "the actual author of the book." Others pointed to Slocum as the author. Slocum later admitted authoring at least part of the book, though he claimed Monk dictated the content. Later legal procedures suggested a large collaborative effort among Monk's Protestant protectors. In November 1836, Hoyte jointly sued Monk and Slocum for a share of the profits. Soon after, Monk and Slocum brought a case against Harper Brothers. The court ruled in favor of the prominent publishing company, arguing that George Bourne took out a copyright that excluded Monk from the profits. The strong similarities among *Awful Disclosures* and Bourne's own anticonvent novel, *Lorette*, suggest the book was largely his creation.[59]

In 1838 Monk gave birth to her second child. This time she blamed no priests. With her popularity dwindling, only the *Protestant Vindicator* came to her defense, attributing her pregnancy to a Jesuit conspiracy. Updates in the press on her whereabouts mostly disappeared until 1847, when the Connecticut *Morning News* reported that the "notorious Maria Monk, whose gross and scandalous falsehoods [which] made so much noise a few years since," was imprisoned for "grand larceny" in Sing-Sing, the New York state prison in Auburn. A year later the *Barre Patriot* informed readers that Monk's "life of drunkenness" led her into the almshouse in New York. Just before her death in 1849, the Vermont *Weekly Eagle* described Monk as "apparently in the last stages of an ill-spent life." The "abandoned woman of New York," as the author described her, "sunk to the grave" alone and penniless in the "sick ward of the Blackwell's Island Penitentiary" in New York. Within a few months of this article, Monk died at the age of thirty-two. Her conditions strangely resembled those depicted of convent life in *Awful Disclosures*. She was alone, in a gloomy prison cell, under the guardianship of what was likely a callous overseer, a victim of a harsh life.[60]

Despite Maria Monk's quick and decisive fall from grace in the public eye, *Awful Disclosures* continued to sell well throughout the century. With little concern for the real Maria Monk, readers poured over the pages of *Awful Disclosures*, prompting the publication of new editions every year. What one journal referred to as "Maria Monkism" mattered more than Maria Monk. The image of Catholicism, convent life, and nuns captivated the public and forged a caricature of nuns that would last long past the time anyone would even recognize the name Maria Monk. In *Awful Disclosures* the prisonlike convent contrasted with the ideal of a warm inviting home. The nuns of the Hotel Dieu lived unhappy, unfulfilled, and unproductive lives, suggesting that happiness and usefulness were not to be found in a convent but rather in a domestic life of marriage and motherhood. *Awful Disclosures* spoke to society's growing interest in sensational literature and their inclinations toward anti-Catholicism, but resonated most with prevalent concerns regarding female gender roles and sexuality. Presenting a nightmarish world where single women were given to sexual debauchery, torture, murder, and despair only reinforced the burgeoning ideals of domesticity as the happiest and best life for women.

In the meantime, the real Maria Monk remained veiled from the public, who projected onto her the role of victim, villain, harlot, or lunatic. Perhaps Monk played a version of all of these roles. But the popularity and legacy of her book went far beyond her as a person in real time.

To arms!! Ye brave and free. . . . Leave not one stone upon another of that curst nunnery that prostitutes female virtue and liberty under the garb of religion.
—*Posted on the Old Charlestown Bridge*, August 9, 1834

Of all the drones whoever infested the world, none surpass in perfect uselessness . . . vice, and misery as the inhabitants of convents.
—*Female Convents, Secrets of Nunneries Disclosed*, 1834

2

Burning Babylon

THE ATTACK AGAINST MOUNT BENEDICT AND THE BIRTH OF THE CONVENT NARRATIVE

TWO YEARS BEFORE the appearance of Maria Monk's *Awful Disclosures*, Louisa Goddard could not fall asleep. She attended Mount Benedict Academy in Charlestown, Massachusetts. On that Monday, August 11, 1834, she had just returned from a pleasant weekend visit with her family, and she missed them. She got out of her little bed in the large room she shared with over a dozen other girls her age who now slept soundly, and approached one of the tall windows. Careful not to make a noise, she lifted the sill, allowing into the otherwise stuffy room a gentle summer breeze carrying the sweet smell from the fruit trees lining the grounds below. Mount Benedict, a girls' school run by Ursuline nuns, was a formidable three-story red brick structure that sat on top of a large hill in the center of twenty-four acres of well-tended farmland. The thoughts of Louisa that night, whatever they were as she gazed out at the moonlit town, were suddenly interrupted by the shrill howling and whooping of male voices cutting through the night. Among indecipherable huzzahs, she heard the words "Down with the Pope! Down with the Convent!"[1]

None of the other girls stirred in their beds. A few moments passed before the shouts went up again, louder this time. Louisa strained to see where the voices might be coming from in the shadowy expanse. As the voices became clearer, so did dark figures of men. She remembered the rumors of a mob planning to attack the convent, rumors dismissed by the Mother Superior as baseless. Alarmed, she dashed across the room to the bed of the nearest sleeping girl, Elizabeth Williams, shaking her. Just then, a brick flew into a window, startling the other girls awake. Moments later, Sister Mary Austin, a teacher remembered by Louisa for frequently hiding a yawn with a handkerchief, pushed open the tall wooden door into the girls' room. Holding a lantern with a shaky hand, she whispered, "Girls, don't be frightened, but you better dress yourselves." One by one, the drowsy young girls began assembling their clothes, complaining of not being able to find the sleeve of a frock or of a petticoat dropping into a chamber pot. As they floundered in the dim light, careful not to step on broken glass, sounds of gunshots caused some to cry. Stunned, Sister Mary Austin sunk into a chair as her ward continued outfitting themselves. An older pupil then ran into the room and shook Austin by the shoulder. "Did you hear me? The Superior is not hurt. They shot at her, but they did not hit her."[2]

The mob outside the convent walls detested the presence of the Ursulines in their town and held special contempt for the Mother Superior. John Buzzell, the ringleader of the rioters, called her "the sauciest woman I ever heard talk." Their rage boiled over amid growing rumors of imprisoned nuns. In their inebriated state, they called the Mother Superior's name that night, demanding that she show herself and bring with her the "innocent victims" kept locked in "dungeons." As they repeated this demand, "using violent and threatening language," the Mother Superior herself finally threw open the main door of the convent. She confirmed the mob's worst view of her, as she ordered the rowdy lot to "Dismiss immediately!" and warned that the bishop had "twenty thousand Irishmen at his command in Boston" who would "whip all of you to the sea!"[3]

Mary Anne Moffatt, or Sister St. George, the Mother Superior of the Charlestown Ursulines, was a stout and stately woman who carried herself with a "royal uprightness" that "demanded deference from all who approached her." Born in Montreal in 1793 into a Protestant family, Moffatt received an education in an Ursuline academy in Quebec before converting to Catholicism. Her father, a British officer, whose loyalty to the Crown during the American Revolution cost him his business, died in 1810, leaving the family impoverished. Moffatt made a life for herself when she joined the Quebec monastery as a novice two years later, although she had no dowry. With some help from Catholic friends and relatives, she was able to take religious vows in January 1812. She chose the new name of St. George, a Christian martyr and dragon slayer. In 1824, Moffatt left the Quebec convent for New England, likely reluctant to relocate among Yankees whose fathers imprisoned her father during the war.[4]

At Mount Benedict, Moffatt established a reputation for being demanding, stringent, even dictatorial. She was known to speak sharply to the other nuns, who, like servants, always bowed before speaking to her. With impressive administrative skill, she oversaw all facets of life in the convent, from the spiritual well-being of the nuns to the administration of the academy. Moffatt also managed a small crew of groundskeepers and repairmen who performed daily maintenance at Mount Benedict and tended its gardens. She was cultured and intelligent, a lover of the arts, fluent in English and French, but also short-tempered and haughty. She once reported that it would be "a difficult matter for any man to control me." Her lack of submissiveness and domesticity confused some of her neighbors and enraged others, who were already suspicious of the imposing convent in their town.[5]

The Ursuline convent was originally established in Boston in 1820. There the nuns offered a free day school for Catholic girls, mostly from the families of impoverished Irish immigrants. After a number of the nuns died of tuberculosis during an epidemic in the 1820s, Bishop Benedict Fenwick, who had recently arrived in Boston as the city's second bishop, requested the help from the elite Ursuline community in Quebec. Among the nuns who came to aid the fledging community in Boston was Mary Anne Moffatt. She along with the bishop, for whom the convent was named, moved the school to Charlestown, transforming it into a flourishing, elegant academy that catered more to members of the upper class than the previous school in Boston. The city's elite citizens, many of them Harvard-educated Unitarians who wished to secure a European-like education for their daughters, welcomed the new school. The night of the attack against the convent, fifty girls resided at the academy, forty from Protestant families and ten Catholics. The prospect of the city's Protestant girls receiving an education in a Catholic institution made certain Protestants in Charlestown and neighboring towns uneasy. Fear of a Catholic conspiracy, of young women converting to Catholicism, or worse, the possibility of them becoming nuns, forgoing futures as wives and mothers, led prominent ministers like Lyman Beecher to sound the alarm.[6]

Although Mount Benedict occasionally accepted students without charge, by the 1830s, the institution strayed from its original mission as a day school for Catholic girls. Many of the predominantly Irish Catholic families could not afford to send their daughters to Mount Benedict, which charged $125 a year. The highly educated Ursulines themselves were "effective agents in the dissemination of genteel culture," as historian Daniel Cohen put it. Indeed, convent schools like Mount Benedict were among the few places where girls could receive an advanced education in the US. They were taught geometry, chemistry, geography, history, rhetoric, mythology, moral philosophy, and composition. In addition to "useful knowledge," students at Mount Benedict took classes in needlework, drawing, painting, languages, and music—all trappings of female refinement. The academy further required young ladies to enter Mount Benedict with items that assumed a degree of wealth, including "six napkins, six towels, one knife and fork, one silver goblet, one silver dessert and tea spoon, and two pairs of sheets and pillowcase." As the Ursuline community grew in status, resentment among some laboring Charlestown male citizens developed as well.[7]

Inside the academy that August night, Moffatt remained calm, assuming her usual collected, authoritative demeanor as she helped the Sisters corral the young students. She instructed the older girls to take the hands of the younger ones. In neat rows, the schoolgirls followed each other through the broad halls, out the convent's back door, and into the balmy, summer night air of the courtyard. Though understandably scared, the girls stayed silent, arranging themselves on the dewy lawn at the convent's edge in their disheveled clothes. They watched as a series of shadowy figures flooded into their school and their home, following the flash of torches from one window to the next, into the rooms where they learned, shared meals, played, and slept only minutes before. As the mob overtook Mount Benedict, Edward Cutter, a neighbor of Mount Benedict, and a few of his friends who had arrived to help lifted the girls over the railing to safety on his farm while the nuns crawled through an opening in the fence.[8]

The group of men that descended on the Charlestown convent on August 11 consisted of sailors, brick-makers, firemen, and rabble-rousers. While many were poor and uneducated, the mob represented a range of socioeconomic backgrounds. Most of the men performed strenuous manual labor for a dollar or two each day in the brickyards that surrounded the convent while the wealthy members of neighboring towns sent their daughters to receive an expensive education from the Ursulines. They equated their declining status as the area became more industrialized with the growing presence of Catholics and foreigners in their vicinity, and no one stood out as much as the Ursulines of Mount Benedict. Some of the men had either left families behind in search of work or were unmarried. The enclosure of a group of un-available single women, many of a young marrying age, may have further irked some of them. "They were a socially submerged group," wrote a historian of the event in 1934, "leading plodding and monotonous lives with no stake in community welfare." As such, he concluded, they "became reckless and willing tools in the excitement of the moment." But not all of the rioters were laboring bricklayers, and their attack against a particular group of women, not simply a church or the wealthy, suggests a broader impulse than religious or class conflict alone, one that especially reflected gendered concerns.[9]

That night, after throwing back rounds of drinks at a local tavern, the rioters, led by bricklayer John Buzzell, covered their faces in war paint, reminiscent of their "Boston Tea Party" forebears. Entering the convent grounds, they echoed revolutionary rhetoric, "Down with the Pope! Down with Tyranny!" To the sound of these chants, men began tearing down the convent fence, lighting a giant bonfire with the posts and tar barrels. Soon flames that could be seen from miles around lit up the sky. The sounds and the light drew the townspeople out of their beds and homes. A steady trickle of Charleston citizens, an estimated four thousand, emerged to witness the scene. Like the fire itself, news of the event spread quickly in the coming days, moving beyond New England to the rest of the nation and across the Atlantic. Later when a Protestant from Boston visited Pope Gregory XVI, the pope asked him reproachfully, "Was it you who burned my convent?"[10]

As the flames grew, a few firemen arrived on the scene from Boston Engine Company No. 13. One of them, Prescott Pond, had a sister-in-law, Rebecca Reed, who resided for a short time at Mount Benedict as a novice but left before taking formal vows. The firefighters watched motionless as manic men danced around the rising bonfire. According to Louisa Goddard, "they [even] seemed to give the rioters sudden courage." As the firemen stood by, in silent approval, the mob rushed into the academy. None of the firemen turned on their hoses, and some even joined the mob. After selectmen of the town received word of the riot, they deferred to the police. Yet the police force, which consisted of one part-time officer, could do little to stop the unfolding events. As most towns in the early nineteenth century lacked an equipped police force, citizens often responded to social, political, economic, and religious tensions through extralegal means. The majority of towns merely had "watchmen" who looked out for fires and patrolled streets at night with a bell to announce the hour. The complicit engagement in the attack by the firemen and watchmen of Charlestown shows that a broad scope of the town's citizens shared anti-Catholic feelings and suspicion of women who lived communal, unwed lives.[11]

By midnight shadows of men could be seen running back and forth in the flickering light of the building. The men took full possession of the convent, going through private drawers and trunks, pocketing souvenirs, sharing a laugh as they donned the clothes of the former inhabitants, breaking furniture, and tossing the pieces into giant heaps in the center of rooms. This was more than "concern" for imprisoned women. This was punishment for women who so boldly chose convent life, women who audaciously created their own lives and thrived, women whose very existence seemed to insult them. They hurled hand-crafted instruments from the great music room out the windows, guitars and harps landing in dissonant chords along the littered lawn. They even managed to drop a piano from the second story, which "fell with a crash distinctly audible above all other sounds." On top of the large piles of furniture, they heaped Bibles, crosses, vestments, altar decorations, and personal items before torching them all. An hour and a half later, onlookers gazed in wonder as billowing flames engulfed the entire building.[12]

From there, the mob turned from the convent to the cemetery near the garden. Dressed now in the uniforms of the students, the disheveled crew tugged open a trapdoor to the brick mausoleum that housed the bodies of deceased nuns, scrambling down the narrow steps. The gowned men yanked corpses out of coffins, animating them like puppets, and pulled out teeth as tokens to remember the night. They then stormed the bishop's cottage, which sat on the grounds of Mount Benedict. Bishop Benedict was not there that night to watch as a New Hampshire resident of the mob put on a mock auction of his library before tossing each book into a fire that eventually consumed the house. Finally, the mob ransacked Mount Benedict's verdant gardens, trampling the grounds, digging their axes into fruit trees, and uprooting ripening grape vines. The vim and vigor of the pack by this time began to tamper off, after almost seven straight hours of mayhem.[13]

As the sun began to rise on August 12, 1834, ashen men dispersed, but the occasional plume flickered on among the ruins. All the while, hundreds of townspeople stood stunned. The firemen had gone home. The magistrate could not be found. Though many were deeply disturbed by the scene, no one had acted to stop the destruction of Mount Benedict.

Two weeks before the rioters unleashed their wrath against the convent, rumors circulated around Charlestown and Boston of an escaped nun from Mount Benedict. Elizabeth Harrison, known as Sister Mary John, worked as the school's music teacher and as "mother assistant" to the Mother Superior. At the end of July that summer she suffered from "a nervous excitement or fever," as one doctor claimed, from the arduous task of giving fourteen nearly hour-long music lessons a day. The demanding and intimidating temperament of the Mother Superior may have also kept the young woman in a constant state of anxiety. During the school's annual fête, when students performed musical numbers and received awards for their accomplishments throughout the school year, Harrison strenuously labored on top of regular duties in the suffocating summer heat. The event left her bedridden with severe headaches. Days later, the unkempt mother assistant walked out of the convent building, supposedly in a state of delirium. She wandered to the Cutter house, Protestant neighbors of Mount Benedict. Determined and agitated, she told Edward Cutter that she would never return to the convent.[14]

Cutter quickly contacted the Mother Superior and Bishop Fenwick. While Harrison initially refused to talk to either Moffatt or Fenwick, she finally relented, insisting she would only see the bishop. After a long conversation, Fenwick convinced her to return with him to Mount Benedict. Harrison met with a physician, Dr. Thompson, who ordered her to rest as much as possible and refrain from seeing any visitors. Although Dr. Thompson claimed that she suffered from "fever of the brain" and derangement, the city quickly buzzed with rumors that Harrison had gone mad under the harsh rule of the Mother Superior who kept her chained up in the convent's cellar. A number of newspapers in and outside Charlestown reported on the "mysterious disappearance of a young lady at the Nunnery." Some speculated that just as she was finally able to achieve a desperate escape and find refuge, the "powerful bishop" aided by the Mother Superior secured her return through "threats." Some city residents theorized that Harrison was now either imprisoned, removed to another country, or even murdered.[15]

After Harrison's return to Mount Benedict, a number of New England papers ran the story with the intriguingly vague headline: "Mysterious." The *Mercantile Journal*, a local paper, reported on August 8, 1834, that Harrison returned to the convent after being told that she could be "dismissed with honor" after three weeks. When that time passed and her "friends called on her but could not find her," according to the paper, the townspeople became "much alarm[ed]." Two days before the riot against the convent, a series of posters appeared throughout Charlestown echoing the newspaper reports and issuing a warning. One handbill called for an investigation of the convent, stating, "It is currently reported that a mysterious affair has lately happened in Charlestown; now it is your duty, gentlemen, to have this affair investigated immediately, if not, the truckmen of Boston will demolish the nunnery." Another more dramatic handbill enjoined the town: "To arms!! Ye brave and free. . . . Leave not one stone upon another of that curst nunnery that prostitutes female virtue and liberty under the garb of religion. When Bonaparte opened the nunneries in Europe, he found crowds of infant skulls!!" The Mother Superior also received several anonymous envelops with clips of the article "Mysterious" enclosed. Fuming, she ripped them to shreds, refusing to respond to the growing furor against the institution she ran.[16]

From these newspapers and handbills, it appeared people readily believed the worst about the nuns of Mount Benedict. Reports blurring the known with the "mysterious" suggested an inclination to believe that these women suffered, that they were held against their will, that they were sexually deviant, and even that they committed the worst crime it seemed a woman could commit: infanticide. Harrison's "mysterious" disappearance only confirmed deeply held reservations and widespread rumors about nuns. Many Americans could not accept that these single women were okay on their own. Life in a convent could only produce women of deformed femininity, like the Mother Superior, or deranged mental capacities, like Harrison. These women needed to be punished or rescued. And the men were ready for a fight.

The Saturday before Monday's attack against Mount Benedict, a group of Charlestown selectmen visited the convent to investigate the rumors about Harrison's imprisonment. They told the Mother Superior that they wished to "contradict the report generally believed that there were cells under the convent, used for the punishment of refractory nuns, and also secret places of torment and iniquity." Rather than comply, Moffatt became furious. She refused their request to examine the convent and even launched into personal attacks, calling the men "vulgarians" and "plebians." Just before the selectmen awkwardly retreated, Elizabeth Harrison entered the foyer. She pleaded with the Mother Superior to allow her to explain to the men "the facts relative to her illness." As Moffatt presided skeptically, Harrison told the men gathered that she suffered from some "temporary hysteria" and that she was not imprisoned in the convent or tortured. The men appeared to believe her, promising that they would publish Harrison's account in the Monday morning papers. Just as they assured, an explanation of the "circumstances that had led to the story of the escaped nun" appeared Monday, but alongside this report, the selectmen included an account of the Mother Superior's rude reception of them and her refusal to allow an examination of the convent.[17]

On Monday morning, nearly twelve hours before the mob would attack the convent, a lone selectman once more visited Mount Benedict. When the porter announced his arrival, the Mother Superior commanded the young woman to "shut the door in his face." But the man refused to leave, telling the woman at the door that "this convent is really in great danger." "Even this very night," he persisted, "it could be attacked." He asked permission once more to examine the convent cellars to disprove circulating rumors about Mount Benedict. The door woman returned timidly to the Mother Superior, who remained obstinate in her refusal and was now angry with the young receptionist. Moffatt insisted that she was not afraid of anyone and that it was the selectmen's job to protect and not to interrogate them. Again Harrison approached the Mother Superior on the matter, her eyes swollen and her nose red from crying. Through chocked sobs, Harrison pleaded to be allowed to escort the man in his investigation. "He's a friend," she pleaded, a valuable relationship in a "community of enemies." Harrison believed the rumors about an impending attack and, feeling she was the cause, wanted to quell the growing animosity against her Sisters, her students, her only family and community. The two women argued for a few minutes before Moffatt finally agreed to allow the man to examine the cellars. Moffatt met the selectman at the door, thrust a lantern into his hands, and directed him to the cellar door. "There sir, if you want to play spy in my house, you shall do it alone." The man hesitated before the steps leading down into the dark cellar, stepped back, and then hurried out of the building. As he retreated from the convent grounds, the female pupils taunted him from the windows. "He's afraid! He's afraid!" Townspeople soon whispered about the selectman's challenged masculinity, but it would not be long before another group of men asserted their virile authority over this community of insolent women.[18]

Moffatt's "saucy" reaction to the selectmen only further enraged the attackers and many of the townspeople. Her authoritative role, lack of submission to men, and haughty demeanor reinforced the notion that Moffatt was a dangerous woman. Although Moffatt was submissive, at least theoretically, to the male bishop and Catholic hierarchy, most Protestant Americans did not see celibate priests as real men. They believed celibacy fostered an insatiable sexual appetite that soon overpowered even the strongest of men, weakening them. Lacking self-control and the ennobling influences of a wife, priests became degenerate monsters intent on ravaging innocent women in convents. Moffatt inadvertently and sometimes blatantly called Catholic and Protestant men's masculinity into question. She challenged their authority to oversee women, and their power within the community. When the mob on the night of the attack called out her name as they torched the building, they reclaimed their manhood from this unmarried, commanding, childless woman and expressed their desire to "protect" other women from her and "wicked" priests.[19]

Just before Harrison's retreat from Mount Benedict, Rebecca Reed, a young novice who had not yet made religious vows, left the convent. After her departure on January 18, 1832, Reed discussed her experiences at Mount Benedict with an Episcopal priest, William Croswell, and then with many others throughout Charlestown. With Croswell's encouragement and help, Reed published *Six Months in a Convent*. The book become an instant bestseller, with more than ten thousand copies sold in the first week. Although *Six Months* appeared shortly after the burning of the Ursuline convent, rumors about Reed's story and drafts of her manuscript circulated prior to the attack. Reed's allegations, together with rumors about the escape of Elizabeth Harrison, created an explosive environment in Charlestown. Moffatt later accused Rebecca Reed's book of being "calculated and designed to destroy the character of the Ursuline Community." She dismissed the work as a "tissue of lies" that only became popular by manipulating the fears of the "ignorant and unreflecting portion of the people." More than any other factor, she claimed, the "circulation of her stories in manuscript and in conversation" worked to "destroy the convent."[20]

Rebecca Theresa Reed came from a poor family in Charlestown. Her father was a local farmer who barely retained the family's residence on rented property. Although the Reeds appeared to have had enough money to send Rebecca to a private school for a time, when her mother died in 1829, Rebecca quit her schooling to take care of household duties for her father and siblings. In these circumstances, few attractive vocational options presented themselves to her. She could work in a textile factory or in someone else's home as a domestic, but both jobs spelled drudgery and offered little social respect, and without an education, she could not be a teacher.

As a member of the town's Ursuline community, however, Reed would be granted an elite education, have nice things, and, as she might have imagined, avoid a life of drudgery and toil.[21]

Reed had reportedly been attracted to the Ursulines since their arrival in Charlestown in 1826. Although she was raised Protestant, Reed converted to Catholicism at the age of nineteen in June 1831. She made a number of friends within the Charlestown Catholic community, including the town's parish priest, Father Patrick Byrne, and even Bishop Fenwick. When Reed first requested to join the Ursuline community, the Mother Superior flatly refused, seeing Reed as a "romantic and ignorant girl." Byrne and Fenwick, however, assured Moffatt of Reed's good character and urged her to accept her at least as a "charity pupil." Reed also reportedly promised the Superior that she "could and would be able to wash, iron, [and] scrub the floors." Reluctantly assenting, Moffatt likely hoped that Reed could assist the overburdened Harrison, assigning her with music lessons. In her initial days as a novice, Reed reportedly appeared "perfectly happy." But she soon grew disillusioned with the ascetic practices and penances required of her by the Ursuline community, which included waking at dawn for prayers and doing manual labor, all while teaching multiple lessons a day. In her own account, Reed complained to Moffatt, who responded with increasing impatience. The Mother Superior later recounted that Reed "came to our community doubtless in the belief that she would have nothing to do there but to read, meditate and join in our prayers. She found that every hour had its employment, and that constant labor was one of the chief traits of our order." In January of 1832, Reed snuck out the back door of the convent and returned to her old neighborhood. No one chased after her.[22]

After Reed's "escape," she did not give up on the idea of becoming a nun. She met several times with Father Byrne to discuss the possibility of joining the Sisters of Charity in Maryland. Reed also lived for weeks with a Catholic family in town after she left Mount Benedict. Later Byrne reported that Reed abandoned her ambitions to be a nun and the Catholic faith when she realized the Catholic family would not financially support her. In March of that year, Reed turned to the Episcopal Church, where she met Reverend William Croswell. She told Croswell about her experience at Mount Benedict, and he took a vested interest in her story. They began meeting frequently and Croswell eventually encouraged Reed to write and publish her story. In the following couple of years, Reed spread slanderous stories about Mount Benedict in conversation and writings throughout the town. She delivered her story in manuscript form to a number of Protestant congregations and various Charlestown families, and even dropped off copies at boarding houses. As a result, Reed became a popular and respected figure within the town's Protestant community, especially among the clergy.[23]

What became *Six Months in a Convent*, appearing in March 1835, told of tor-
turous penances assigned to feeble women and collusion among the priests and the
Mother Superior to hold women captive, amass a fortune, and extend the pope's empire throughout the city. Reed described a series of severe penances assigned for the
slightest disobedience. If they spoke out of turn, they were made to make the sign of
the cross with their tongues on the floor. Some were starved for weeks. She alleged
that the Mother Superior and the bishop held many nuns in the convent against
their will, including one nun named Sister Mary Francis. When Francis spoke out
against the priests or the Mother Superior, they merely deemed her insane, a reference, no doubt, to the diagnosis of Harrison's insanity. Reed also claimed that Bishop
Fenwick demanded a nun on her deathbed to ask God to send down a "bushel of
gold" so that they might build another convent on Bunker Hill, considered sacred
ground by most Americans at the time and off limits to "foreign" Catholics. As
Reed became more uncomfortable in this "strange prison," explained the book, she
overheard Moffatt and the bishop devising a plan to expel her to Canada to keep
her from exposing their crimes. Before they could whisk her away, Reed managed
to "escape."[24]

While most of *Six Months* proved blatantly fallacious, some of the details in the
account could be confirmed. The nuns of Mount Benedict, for instance, occasionally
"bowed and kissed the floor." In Moffatt's response to *Six Months* she defended the
practice, arguing that it "was not an important or frequent occupation" and that it
was "purely a voluntary act." Other details appeared far-fetched, such as the bishop's
wish for a bushel of gold and the designs to secretly ship Reed off to Canada. The
frequent references to stock anti-Catholic beliefs—that the bishop colluded personally with the pope or that nuns lived imprisoned in convents—also seemed to be
the work of Reed's collaborators, more familiar with and invested in anti-Catholic
arguments. Despite the dubious nature of Reed's work and motivations for it, her
"escape" served as a harbinger for the burning of the Ursuline convent. The subsequent publication of *Six Months in a Convent* solidified the continued American
campaign against convents.[25]

While opposition to convents on a religious basis certainly contributed to the
ready acceptance of *Six Months*, the idea that women were imprisoned, that they
were in danger either as nuns or academy pupils formed the singular intrigue with
this book. The opening lines of Reed's book reflected this concern. "It is not a
question of sects and creeds," read *Six Months*, "but it is a grave question of how
the future ornaments to our refined society, the future accomplished mothers of
American citizens, are to be educated." Although theological differences among
Protestants and Catholics were certainly a significant factor in the tensions between
these two groups, the people, and especially the men, of Charlestown seemed to care

more about the way convents shaped the lives of women and the implications of this for them and their society.[26]

A relatively new publishing house in Boston, Russell, Odiorne & Metcalf, agreed to print *Six Months in a Convent*. Sensing the potential popularity of the book, the publishers ensured its supply "to all principal book sellers," and went to the expense of stereotyping plates of the book for reprinting. *Six Months* surpassed the publishers' greatest expectations. Russell, Odiorne & Metcalf worked tirelessly to keep up with high demand for the book, keeping "two power presses constantly in motion, and about forty persons involved in folding and binding." As it turned out, Rebecca Reed's exposé became the first anti-Catholic bestseller in the US.[27]

The investigative committee appointed to report on the burning of Mount Benedict considered the relevance of Rebecca Reed's story. They dismissed her allegations of extreme penances and the cruel treatment of a dying nun, contending that an overwhelming number of witnesses contradicted her claims. The committee's critical approach to Reed, however, only stirred agitation among the convent's enemies, who rallied behind Reed as a victim of Catholic intrigue. An anonymous author sent an article to the Boston *Daily Advocate* in which he cast the former novice as a "defenseless female" and an "American daughter" in need of protection from "foreign institutions." After Judge Fay, who authored a petition on behalf of the Ursuline community, published an article in the Boston *Courier* specifically accusing Reed of inciting the burning of Mount Benedict, Reed (or more likely one of her male colleagues) responded swiftly. She first apologized for her foray into the public realm (something considered unladylike), writing of her aversion to come before the public if it were not to defend her good name. She condemned Fay's attack as one against a "defenseless female" before promising that her ensuing exposé would "be more full and explicit than was originally intended." Her account, though pale in comparison to convent narratives to follow, contributed not only to the burning of Mount Benedict but also to the burgeoning genre of the convent narrative, paving the way for the likes of Maria Monk, the most famed "escaped nun" in American history.[28]

Anti-Catholic print culture, becoming more prevalent in the early 1830s, created an environment in which the burning of Mount Benedict was possible. In 1830, George Bourne published the first anti-Catholic newspaper in America, entitled *The Protestant*. Among other standard-fare anti-Catholic articles, Bourne condemned institutional celibacy for priests and nuns. In one of the first issues, a letter described a number of "Xaviers" (an order of Catholic priests) "going about, seeking what virgins they might debauch" by convincing women to join convents. In another article Bourne claimed that the "history of monastics" proved that "the convent was seldom productive of a single virtue." In contrast, marriage "was instituted in paradise, before sin entered the world," wrote Bourne, referring to the account of Adam and Eve. It "must therefore be considered as perfectly connected with the most entire devotion to the service of God." Bourne lauded matrimony as "the plainest, most rational, and obligatory laws of nature, morality, and religion," and condemned the "worshippers of the wafer god" for arrogantly assuming that the unmarried state was one of "greater purity and sanctity."[29]

The early years of the 1830s saw other criticisms of celibacy, particularly for women. In the early months of 1834, a New York publisher released *Female Convents, Secrets of Nunneries Disclosed*. While the compilation of "No Popery" essays from a late eighteenth-century Italian cleric, Scipio de Ricci, provided the hook for readers, the introduction to the text by Thomas Roscoe revealed the real agenda for the publication. Roscoe focused on the supposed threat convents posed to marriage and the "usefulness" of women. For Roscoe, nuns contributed nothing to society. "Of all the drones whoever infested the world, none surpass in perfect uselessness . . . vice, and misery as the inhabitants of convents." Living lives of "incarceration in gloomy mansion[s] with no duties to fulfill," Roscoe asked, "what value are those excrescences upon society?" Unambiguously, he insisted that "no woman can be justified for abandoning all the obligations which she owes society." Admittedly a work "with little reference to the theological portions of Romanism," *Female Convents* focused on the alleged practical implications for society if women chose "useless" lives as nuns. Such lives surely threatened the sexual, domestic, and child-rearing contributions of women, without which, as Roscoe more than implied, women served no purpose.[30]

The idealization of motherhood, preceded of course by marriage, provided a basis for understanding what was considered by many at the time to be a woman's highest obligations and most natural role. In the eighteenth century, prominent Americans began to articulate a concept of republican motherhood in which women contributed to the strength and health of the nation by raising virtuous sons. By the 1830s, these views of motherhood were revamped and extended. In Sarah Joseph Hale's widely read *Ladies' Magazine and Literary Gazette*, an 1832 article reported on the establishment of "Mother's Lyceums." No other group could "benefit themselves and the world so much by mutual efforts as mothers," wrote Hale, encouraging membership. When motherhood, or what Hale referred to as the most "dignified office," had been given its "just due," the result would be "a new, a better, a holier world." If mothers were loving, nurturing, and pious, it only seemed logical that their influence would contribute to a more just and peaceful society. On the one hand, this elevation of the role of motherhood elevated the status of women, casting their role as mothers (a role not always appreciated) as a vital one, equally as important, though behind the scenes, as that of lawmakers. On the other, it precluded appreciation or acceptance of other roles for women. It implied a disregard for the way nuns might contribute to society on the basis of their unmarried and childless status. A more explicit *Ladies' Magazine* article, "The Convent of St. Clare," reflected the views expressed by Bourne and Roscoe that a nun was a waste of womanhood. It lamented the "beauty" and "bright forms" imprisoned there. Although nuns contributed to society through schools, hospitals, orphanages, charitable projects, and other un-measurable ways, their inversion of female domestic ideals and perhaps the independence displayed in their life choice delegitimized these women for a public who could not see their use.[31]

Reverend Lyman Beecher reinforced the fear of the growing presence of Catholics in America in a series of anti-Catholic lectures he delivered in New England towns in August 1834. The great revivalist minister and patriarch of the Beecher clan gave hour-long sermons about training ministers to send out to the American frontier, the need for greater religious freedom and collaboration (at least for Protestants), and the insidious influence of the "Whore of Babylon" (Catholicism) before packed crowds. He visited Charlestown on Sunday, August 10, the day before the attack at Mount Benedict. One contemporary source listed his "inflammatory sermons," in which "the Devil and the Pope of Rome were never introduced without the other," among the causes of the attack. Beecher alarmed his listeners with talk of a conspiracy underway by Catholic European powers to topple American liberties. If they were not designing against us, he asked his listeners, why would they "pay the passage and empty upon our shores such floods of pauper immigrants?" Such immigrants provided a veritable "army of soldiers" ready to sap the "property and moral virtue of the nation." The "Romish influence" was especially prevalent in the Mississippi River Valley and in the "gratuitous schools" founded by nuns.[32]

Beecher saved some of his greatest invectives for convents, warning especially against the cunning designs of Catholic education. He questioned why else Catholics would "offer education to Protestant children . . . while thousands of Catholic children [remained] neglected and uncared for." He pointed to the spread of the Sisters of Charity, who operated schools and orphanages in nine US cities by that time. Though they claimed not to proselytize, the fact that they "prohibited free thought," had no "Protestant books," and received funds from Europe suggested otherwise, the revivalist argued. Beecher chastised "reckless Protestant parents" who entrusted their children and thus the welfare of the nation to the care of "Jesuits and nuns." The growing prosperity of some of these institutions, warned Beecher, evidenced the imminent dangers of popery. When his listeners in Charlestown and its neighboring towns heard these words, they likely pictured Mount Benedict. It was time to "wake up!" he roared, invest in Protestant schools (a charge his daughter, Catherine Beecher, would later echo), and regard the "reality of the danger" before it was too late. Beecher's sermon, later issued as a book, *Plea for the West*, was an appeal for the preservation of a particular kind of culture. He feared not only the spread of the Catholic religion but also the related culture of this faith, which for him and many Anglo-American Protestants appeared in direct conflict with republican principles, the family, and female gender ideals.[33]

A few days after the burning of Mount Benedict, local authorities held emergency meetings in Charlestown and Boston. At Faneuil Hall city officials appointed a committee of twenty-eight respected city residents to investigate the burning. Theodore Lyman Jr., mayor of Boston, nominated committee members. At the outset the appointed members expressed reluctance to either "aid in the dissemination of the Catholic faith" or attempt to justify the actions of the mob. By the end of September, the committee interviewed over 140 citizens. In the resulting "report," they denounced the burning as a "base and cowardly act for which the perpetrators deserve the contempt and detestation of the community." The causes they cited included the popular belief that the convent was a place of "cruelty, vice, and corruption" and the rumors about the escape of Elizabeth Harrison. Attempting to dispel these beliefs, the report claimed that none of the nuns were forcibly detained. Likewise, "no penances or punishments [we]re ever forcibly enforced or inflicted." As for the students, they were "wholly unrestrained in their communications with their friends concerning all that transpired in the seminary." Protestant students were not influenced to accept the Catholic faith by their instructors. Finally, the report detailed the events of the burning and calculated the cost of damage to be about $50,000 (over $1,000,000 today).[34]

What turned out to be a very public and sensational trial on the burning of the convent took place in Cambridge, Massachusetts. On September 14, 1834, the leader of the mob, John R. Buzzell, stood accused of arson, "entering with intent to steal," and "entering with intent to burn." Each of the offenses was punishable by death. Citizens of the town quickly mobilized to support Buzzell and the others accused. That Buzzell and his compatriots did not run away before being summoned suggests the degree to which they felt secure in the prospect of acquittal. In a display of solidarity days before the trial, Buzzell's supporters freely passed out handbills threatening anyone who dared to testify against members of the mob. "All persons giving information in any shape or testifying in court against anyone concerned in the late affair at Charlestown may expect assassination according to the oath which bound the party to each other," stated the bill. Later, in a petition on behalf of the Ursuline community, Judge Richard Fay wrote that supporters of Buzzell and the other rioters "considered [themselves] martyrs to the cause of true religion" and "filled their pockets" with subscriptions.[35]

What was supposed to be an examination of the accused turned out to be an interrogation of the tenets of Catholicism and female monastic life. Mary Anne Moffatt was the first called to witness. Her appearance in the court, "in the costume of her order," and her explanation that the nuns sometimes referred to her as "president" likely chafed against the jury's Yankee sensibilities. Upon further questioning, she dispelled rumors that the Sisters ever called her "*divine* Mother" or prostrated themselves in her presence. She also defended the community against accusations regarding the Bible, explaining that indeed the nuns were allowed to read the Bible, "when and where they pleased." In response to the query of whether "two nuns ever slept in the same bed," she offered an exasperated "no." Subject to the same type of scrutiny, Bishop Fenwick explained the Catholic rationale behind the practice of confession and priestly celibacy. By focusing on the Mother Superior's role, Catholic beliefs, and celibacy, the defense attorney deftly redirected the purpose of the trial away from examining the defendants. The outcome appeared promising for the rioters as Catholicism and monastic life stood trial instead of them.[36]

Of the thirteen arrested accomplices in the burning of the convent, only two identified John Buzzell as the leader of the mob. Others equivocated. Henry Buck, a nineteen-year-old accomplice, identified Buzzell and described the attack. With Buck's account as his only testimony against Buzzell and the other rioters, James T. Austin, the prosecuting attorney, faced the jury on the third day of the trial to offer his closing remarks. "You yourselves are now on your own trial," he told the men of the jury. "The events of this transaction will be recorded in the history of the country. . . . It will be ascertained by your decision whether the tribunals of justice are to be temples consecrated to truth, or whether their solemnity is to be influenced and swayed by the dictates of prejudice, ignorance, and popular despotism." Austin expressed doubts that the arbitrators of justice would be able to "separate from your minds preconceived opinions . . . to give an impartial verdict." He then referred to the nuns of Mount Benedict, who were but "feeble women," and the occupation they performed, "the most praiseworthy occupation of educating children." Austin perhaps felt it necessary to appeal to assumed female characteristics of weakness and taking care of children to win the empathy of the jury. He concluded by citing the rights of citizenship, "that guarantees protection to individuals professing every shade of belief" and of their property.[37]

The defense attorney, George Farley, addressed the jury next. He referred to widespread rumors that women there were imprisoned against their will and tortured within the convent. If these rumors were not true, "if the institution had not been corrupt," he argued, then "fifteen or twenty thousand citizens would not have suffered a few individuals to destroy it." Before taking his seat, the defense attorney pandered to popular ethnic prejudice, claiming that his client could only be convicted on "foreign and imported testimony." The next day, the jury voiced their solidarity with the defense in their verdict of "not guilty," and John Buzzell was a free man. At this pronouncement, the courtroom burst into cheers, "and the house for a few minutes resounded with claps and stampings of the assembly."[38]

Apart from one accomplice, the rest of the accused were also acquitted. Marvin Marcy Jr., one of the youngest members of the mob, was sentenced to life in prison. In response, citizens, including Bishop Fenwick, petitioned for this "scapegoat's" release. Moffatt, in an effort to "supplicate the governor for his release," wrote a letter on behalf of Marcy, stating that "he was young, and joined in the riot for *sport*, as many other boys would do." After seven months, city judges released Marcy. The cost in damages to the convent and the personal property of the pupils, however, were never repaid.[39]

Responses to the burning of Mount Benedict in the aftermath of the trial were mixed, but hostility toward the nuns' life would only grow. On behalf of Bishop Fenwick and the Ursuline community, including parents of some of the former residents, Richard S. Fay, a probate judge, presented a pamphlet petition to the court's ruling. Despite being a Protestant himself, Fay took up the cause of defending the Ursuline community because he believed that the accused were "undeniably guilty." Fay sought to move beyond arguments based on "religious or sectarian grounds," presenting his case to "liberal and enlightened members of every religious denomination." He began his argument describing the character of the Ursuline order, praising their efforts in education and charity, and writing that they "have nothing to conceal." The violence launched against them sprung from "a deplorable ignorance and delusion." It was to be presumed, Fay continued, that the Ursuline community was an innocent party. No charges had been brought against them, not even by those who accused them the loudest of criminal deeds before the burning of the convent. They are "good citizens of the Commonwealth, obedient to the laws and paying all taxes and duties levied upon them," and thus "entitled to full protection under the law." In other words, the nuns of Mount Benedict were not shirking their "duties" as women. The government "wantonly violated" the social contract with this community by disregarding their "right to property" and "to be protected." Fay appealed to his readers' "patriotism," urging them not to see their country's beloved laws "degraded and trampled." Though "public opinion was against Catholics," Fay encouraged the state to remember that "the Catholic is as much under your protection as the Protestant." He then closed his argument by lamenting the destitution and poverty the Ursulines suffered when they lost their home and workplace.[40]

A number of others came forward, publicly denouncing the attack. Many cast the burning as simply "uncivilized." Fay wrote that "the scenes of Indian barbarity never succeeded the ferocious conduct of the Convent rioters." One of the parents of a Mount Benedict pupil likewise condemned the "intolerant and lawless spirit" of the rioters, which was altogether "hostile to the spirit of our civil and religious institutions." The Boston *Evening Transcript* quickly condemned the event as "a cool, deliberate, systematized piece of brutality, unprovoked . . . totally unjustifiable, and visiting the citizens of the town . . . with indelible disgrace." These unequivocal reactions, however condemnatory, failed to consider the power of opposition toward women who blatantly rejected marriage and motherhood. This hostility perhaps went deeper than people realized.[41]

The most prominent Catholic response to the burning of the Ursuline convent came from Mathew Carey, a nationally acclaimed publisher and editor from Ireland. In a "Circular," Carey called on Roman Catholics of the US to "serious consideration" of the "atrocious outrage at Charlestown." The event, he claimed, was inspired by "an infuriate spirit of hostility" rooted in "gross and shameful falsehoods and misapprehensions" that prevailed concerning Catholicism and in particular monastic life. To avoid further violence, Carey encouraged "zealous efforts . . . to be made for counteraction." He lamented the defensive position too often assumed by the Catholic community, which he compared with the neglect of Catholics in Ireland to speak out against discrimination by the British. Carey proposed the formation of a society with members in "the four large cities" in the US. Such a society would not only "repel attacks" but also collect dues to publish books and pamphlets to correct misconceptions, which they would distribute "gratuitously to persons of different denominations." Although Carey's call to duty went mostly unheeded, he had not underestimated the intensity of convent prejudice, which would only increase in the following decades.[42]

While the burning of Mount Benedict led some to condemn the culture of anti-Catholicism for fostering violence, others remained firm in their opposition to nuns and convents. Indeed, the burning of the convent represented an inauguration of the American campaign against convents, marked by the subsequent success of Rebecca Reed's *Six Months in a Convent*, the phenomenal popularity of Maria Monk's *Awful Disclosures of the Hotel Dieu* two years later, and a second convent riot in Baltimore one year after the Mount Benedict attack. Opposition to nuns would only continue to grow in tandem with other Anglo-Protestant reforms and Victorian domestic ideals in the decades leading up to the Civil War. Nearly a year after the burning, the Boston *Daily Advocate* commended *Six Months in a Convent* as a true exposé of convent life, and called on American citizens to "protect American daughters" from such a life. The monumental success of *Awful Disclosures*, which took sensational antinun sentiment to new heights, marked the growing impulse to make sure American women did not become nuns.[43]

A near-copycat attack took place in Baltimore a year after the burning of Mount Benedict. In 1835, Presbyterian ministers, Reverends Robert J. Breckinridge and Andrew B. Cross, two outspoken anti-Catholics, established the *Baltimore Literary and Religious Magazine*. From its founding, the paper reserved special contempt for convents. One of the first leading articles announced: "Carmelite Convent in Baltimore—An Outrage Which Was Probably Committed Therein." Based on the testimony of six members of the Methodist Church, located near the Carmelite convent, the article told of desperate cries for help that came pouring from within the walls of the convent one evening. Breckenridge charged Father Gildea with holding young women against their will and torturing them if they tried to escape. "Whereas we once thought they were willing victims," wrote Breckinridge of the nuns, "we are now convinced they are not." Breckenridge alluded to the burning of Mount Benedict, writing that an escaped nun "led to the burning of the 'cage of unclean birds' last summer." It was now left to the archbishop of the diocese, declared Breckenridge, to explain the strange cries that emanated from the convent.[44]

These suspicions, reinforced by the "escape" of Sister Isabella Neale from Baltimore's Carmelite convent, led to a riot. Neale left the convent on August 18, 1839, on a Sunday morning. She wandered the streets mumbling to herself and knocking on random doors seeking shelter. Like Elizabeth Harrison, Neale's story spread quickly and within a day a crowd of angry spectators gathered on the street outside of the Carmelite convent. In the meantime, Mayor Sheppard C. Leakin helped to alleviate some of the crowd's agitation by securing Neale's transportation to a nearby hospital. Although Neale was later deemed mentally unstable, or in the words of the university physicians, a "monomaniac," her departure from the convent set off three nights of rioting in Baltimore. The exact details of Neale's mental health or the reason she left the convent remain unclear, but the non-Catholic citizens of Baltimore had a ready narrative of female captivity and exploitation that allowed them to draw their own conclusions.[45]

The Carmelites established the first convent in the territorial US in Port Tobacco, Maryland, in 1790 before moving to Baltimore in 1831. Unlike later, active communities of women religious, the Carmelites practiced a strict cloistered rule, devoting themselves completely to prayer and contemplation. After moving to Baltimore, the order expanded its reach, opening a school on Aisquith Street.

Their presence, along with the Sisters of Charity in the city, came under suspicion as anticonvent propaganda spread.[46]

On the first night of the riots, nearly a year to the date from the burning of Mount Benedict, on August 17, 1835, a crowd threatened to tear down the convent and free the "imprisoned women." Hoping to avert a repeat of Mount Benedict, Mayor Leakin immediately called on six hundred city guards to protect the convent. In the meantime, the mayor and three other prominent town leaders inspected the building and questioned the nuns about their treatment. Despite a lack of incriminating evidence, the crowd refused to disperse. After a newspaper printed a dubious report that "Miss Isabella Neale was sane," the following day the crowd started launching rocks at the barricade of city guards blocking the convent. The guards' fixed bayonets scared the rioters away, but they returned for a third night on August 20, though considerably fewer in number. The next day, two physicians confirmed that Neal "was certainly deranged." The rioting ceased that evening, as force and "scientific conclusions" seemed to have quieted the rage.[47]

Despite the quelling of the violence, the *Baltimore Literary and Religious Magazine* jumped on the story, reporting that Neale, "a prisoner" of the Carmelite convent for nineteen years, finally "succeeded in getting out." According to the article, the mayor sent Neale to the hospital, not to appease the crowd or to investigate her mental health, but to "protect" her from those who wished to secure her return to the convent. The crowds that gathered outside the Carmelite convent, stated the article, consisted of "indignant" Protestants and shame-filled "papists." Even if Neale was "deranged," as the "papists" attested, this "did not justify . . . keeping a prisoner." Based on a personal interview, explained the author, "she seemed sane enough." The editors concluded that Neale's escape helped the good citizens finally understand the danger convents posed to women and that "we have told them only the truth."[48]

Like the Charlestown mob, the gathering outside the Carmelite convent in Baltimore likely acted out a sense of male duty to "protect" women, anti-Catholic suspicions, and anger and suspicion at the thought of inaccessible, single women who lived beyond the reach of Protestant men, away from the jurisdiction of a father or a husband, behind stone walls where regular men of the city were denied passage. After the quelling of the riot, the *Baltimore Literary and Religious Magazine* referred to the "probable atrocity" at the Carmelite convent. Because the women there lived behind "the carefully closed and curiously grated windows," the men of the town could not be sure what occurred there. They wanted to know. They suspected the worst. And these suspicions justified their demands for a forced entry into the realms where these single women lived, to "deliver" them into lives of marriage and motherhood.[49]

A few years later, Damon Norwood satirized the growing antinunnery craze. *The Chronicles of Mount Benedict: A Tale of the Ursuline Convent* told the fictional story of Mary Magdalen, a resident of the Ursuline convent and witness of its destruction. Norwood depicted outlandish characters, such as a priest named Father Everlust, who enjoyed nothing more than "gin cocktails, dice and cards, and unchaste nuns." In an obvious reference to rumors of Elizabeth Harrison's escape, Norwood described the ill-fated escape of St. Mary Francis Harrison. Her plans floundered when priests discovered her the next day "passed out drunk in a gutter beneath the convent fence." They sentenced her to death after demanding an answer as to "why [she] presumed to go and tell those mobocratic Yankees of our actions." In keeping with the gruesome revelries found in other convent narratives, Norwood described Harrison strung up by a "large hook, with a long chain . . . fastened in her mouth" like a fish. Friars hitched a horse to the chain, "hurrahed and cracked their whips" as "the horse started, and away went Mary Saint Frances Harrison." This produced a "most tremendous excitement among the good people of Charlestown."[50]

Norwood continued satirizing such "ignorant prejudices and narrow-minded belief of thousands of New Englanders." In his novel, the pope himself, "accompanied by his friend the devil, came over the big sea at once" to quell the mounting suspicions of the townspeople against the convent. After the murder of another refractory nun, who was burned to death for her insubordination, the people of the town mobilized against the convent. The "dark and dingy smoke [that] proceeded from the chimneys of the convent" from her "burning flesh" allowed the townspeople to "suspect the truth instantly." From that point, Norwood depicted the burning of the convent, mixing reality with farce. While the mob advanced into the convent, a terrified pope hid beneath the altar as the priests plotted with Satan. "Would that Beelzebub were our governor!" intoned priest Everlust, pledging to the prince of darkness, "If you will save us and our convent, we will owe you eternal gratitude." In the end, "King Beelzebub and his imps" escaped the burning embers while the rest of the "inmates" perished inside.[51]

With this outlandish narrative Norwood gave vent to his frustration with anticonvent propaganda, Charlestown residents' credulity, and the burning of Mount Benedict. He scoffed at the popular belief, portrayed in tales such as Maria Monk's *Awful Disclosures*, that most convents housed a giant pit into which were thrown "refractory nuns and strangled babies." Though the nuns of Charlestown claimed the hole found in their own kitchen floor was for "slop," wrote Norwood in his satirical novel, "the wise people of Charlestown" knew better and also were convinced that an alligator lived in the pit that was not discovered after the burning because "he burrowed so deep beneath the ground." In the preface, Norwood denounced the way in which citizens of "this generation" willingly believed "a bold unvarnished lie . . . as in the cases of Maria Monk and others." Though not a Catholic himself, Norwood criticized popular American culture of the 1830s by which many "found their belief not on the known customs and opinions of the Roman Catholics of the present day, but upon the tales they read of popery."[52]

In 1846, the Massachusetts legislature voted again on whether or not to raise funds of compensation for the ruined property at Mount Benedict. The vote failed to pass and faced defeat again in 1853 and 1854. The hill of Mount Benedict stood as a blackened ruin for years afterward. Scattered bricks and other remnants on the patchy grass likely held different meanings for different people, for some symbolizing a defeat of Rome, the downfall of the Whore of Babylon, and for others representing the extreme implications of religious sectarianism, the epitome of intolerance and persecution. The burning of the Charlestown convent inaugurated the American campaign against convents and represented a key event in American nativism that would culminate with the popular Know Nothing political party's formation of a "Nunnery Committee" in Massachusetts in 1854. Convent exposés by Rebecca Reed and others helped usher in the convent narrative genre. Although no single act of violence would equal that perpetuated at Mount Benedict in August of 1834, prejudice against nuns and convent life would only continue to grow throughout the following decades, permeating larger facets of American society, from abolitionism to politics. The only way to ensure virtue and liberty for American women and the nation itself would be to eradicate the cloister from the republic. And the movement was just getting underway.[53]

Slavery totally annihilates the marriage institution!

—GEORGE BOURNE, *Slavery Illustrated in Its Effects upon Women and Domestic Society*, 1837

Are the sons of freemen required to countenance, nay, asked to build impassable walls around a licentious, lecherous, profligate horde of foreign monks and priests, who choose to come among us, and erect little fortifications which they call nunneries for their protection?

—WILLIAM HOGAN, *Popery! As It Was and as It Is*, 1845

3

Uncle Tom and Sister Maria

WOMANHOOD IN THE ANTISLAVERY
AND ANTICONVENT CAMPAIGNS

A STORY THAT captivated Americans in the years leading up to the Civil War focused on the life of a female fugitive. Emboldened by a mother's desire to protect her child, she risked a dangerous escape. Baby in tow, she dodged her captors, bent on reclaiming their ward. With the help of some concerned northerners, the mother–child duo eventually found safe haven, and their story became symbolic of a larger American struggle. This was not the narrative of the slave woman, Eliza, and her little boy Harry, famed characters of Harriet Beecher Stowe's *Uncle Tom's Cabin*. This was the tale of Maria Monk, an "escaped nun." Although Maria Monk had actually never been a nun and did not write the book that bore her name, *Awful Disclosures of the Hotel Dieu Nunnery of Montreal* became an instant bestseller, second only to *Uncle Tom's Cabin* before the Civil War. By 1860, "Maria Monk" was a household name, her image as iconic as that of Eliza the slave.[1]

Monk's book sparked an "escaped nun" franchise, with over twenty best-selling convent narratives, contributing to a growing movement against convents in the US. Yet *Awful Disclosures* grew out of baseless conspiracy theories, desires to profit from the growing demand for sensational literature, and deep biases against certain kinds of women, while *Uncle Tom's Cabin* was born out of admirable convictions of the evils of slavery. One book prompted persecution of a minority group of women; the other harkened the end to nearly two hundred years of oppression. Moreover, as the allegations against convents could not be collaborated as were those against slavery, the two books could not appear more different in content and significance. So why was *Awful Disclosures* so popular? How had what one newspaper described as a "miserable catchpenny" come to rival *Uncle Tom's Cabin*? The answer in part has to do with some striking yet understated similarities between *Awful Disclosures* and *Uncle Tom's Cabin*, and the way in which both anticonvent and abolitionist literature tapped into troubling questions about female sexuality, marriage, and the family.[2]

Not coincidentally, both the campaign against convents and the antislavery movement began in earnest in the 1830s. The cause for immediate abolition gained momentum in this decade, as more people vocally cast slavery as a moral evil deserving immediate attention. On January 1, 1831, William Lloyd Garrison launched the *Liberator*, in which he called for "the immediate enfranchisement of our slave population." Moving away from moderate antislavery, Garrison did not hesitate in calling slave owners "an adulterous and perverse generation." In explaining his new sense of urgency, Garrison extended the following analogies. "Tell a man whose house is on fire, to give a moderate alarm; tell him to moderately rescue his wife from the hands of the ravisher; tell the mother to gradually extricate her babe from the fire into which it has fallen." The references to home, sexuality, marriage, and motherhood resonated with his readers' deepest values, inspiring a movement. Garrison's paper served as a harbinger for some of the first antislavery societies, with the New England Anti-Slavery Society forming in 1832 and the American Anti-Slavery Society established the following year. By 1837, the American Anti-Slavery Society listed over a thousand affiliate groups, local and regional.[3]

This same decade saw the beginning of the American campaign against nuns, inaugurated on a national stage by the burning of the Ursuline convent in 1834, the publication of *Awful Disclosures* in 1836, and the appearance of three anti-Catholic periodicals. George Bourne published the first anti-Catholic paper in the US in 1830, titled *The Protestant*. The years 1834 and 1836 respectively saw the publications of *The Downfall of Babylon*, edited by Samuel S. Smith, a self-styled "late popish priest," and the *American Protestant Vindicator*. Both papers took anti-Catholicism to new heights, publishing sensational pieces that especially targeted nuns and convents. In his *American Protestant Vindicator*, President of the Protestant Reformation Society William Brownlee declared that convents "should not be permitted to exist for one moment in any civilized land" as the institutions "prevent women from fulfilling those duties as wives and mothers" and serve to gratify the "sensuality of Roman priests." In calling for their immediate abolishment, Brownlee promoted a constitutional amendment. Both papers promoted *Awful Disclosures* and published the work in serialized form before it appeared as a book. In repeated articles, both papers also argued that marriage, female purity, and the family were at stake.[4]

Not all abolitionists opposed slavery for the same reason, and the movement itself was considerably diverse and fractured. Yet marriage and sexuality emerged as significant themes. One abolitionist declared, "Slavery totally annihilates the marriage institution!" Another claimed, "There is no part of the dark and hidden inequities of slavery which so powerfully demands a correct exposure as the . . . prohibitions of the seventh commandment" (referring to adultery). Adultery and the rape of women reigned paramount as abolitionist topics. Abolitionists insisted that masters had no respect for slave marriages or their own, and that slavery shattered female sexual purity. In her famous assessment of American culture, *Society in America* (1837), Harriet Martineau wrote, "Every man who resides on his plantation may have his harem." She blasted what she referred to as "the licentiousness of the South," asking whether "there can be any security for domestic purity and peace" in such a society. For the planter's wife, who must confess to being "chief slave of the harem," and the female slave alike, the peculiar institution entailed the complete "degradation of women" and marriage.[5]

In sentimental and dramatic prose abolitionists described the experiences of slave families being torn apart, husband from wife and mother from child. The *American Anti-Slavery Almanac* included illustrations depicting these separations, including "Selling a Mother from a Child." Here a slave woman reached out toward her baby while her new owner dragged her away. As one white man held back the now-motherless child, another casually counted coins, the crass cost of severing the closest of family bonds. Harriet Beecher Stowe delivered one of the most dramatic depictions of mother–child separation in *Uncle Tom's Cabin*. While aboard a large ship, a slave woman who had only just been sold and thus separated from her husband overheard a trader sell off her ten-month-old child as well. In despair, the woman jumped off the boat to drown in the water. Emphasizing familial bonds allowed abolitionists to humanize slaves in a way that touched otherwise complacent hearts and minds. Such arguments also struck a nerve with a growing number of middle-class northern Americans concerned with proper female gender roles and sentimental visions of the family.[6]

By the 1830s, abolitionists presented slavery as an institution that inflicted a kind of moral decay on the land. Depictions of the slaveholding states reflected a vision of what Ronald Walters called "the erotic South." Violence, laziness, irreligion, and, most important, licentiousness characterized the South in antislavery rhetoric. "The Southern States are One Great Sodom," declared one abolitionist. Another described the Dixie states as "one vast brothel." Allegations of debauchery corresponded with those of violence and savagery. "It is well known that the most savage violences [*sic*] that are now heard of in the world take place in the southern and western States," claimed Martineau. "Burning alive, cutting the heart out, and other such diabolical deeds . . . are heard of only there." George Bourne described the South as a place in which whites "indulged in all the vicious gratifications which lawless power and un-restrained lust can amalgamate." As images of the "erotic South" became standard fare, opposition to slavery among middle-class northerners mounted.[7]

Theodore Dwight Weld's influential *American Slavery as It Is* (1839) extended stories of how all this affected women. Weld described one woman whose master beat her after she refused to have "criminal intercourse" with him. Seeing that her "case was hopeless," she eventually "gave herself up to be the victim of his brutal lusts." An 1835 tract decried the "licentiousness of intercourse" as the most "criminal attributes of American slaveholding." Female abolitionists also spoke up for their enslaved sisters. In 1833, Lydia Maria Child, reflecting a concern for female sexual purity, wrote that the "negro woman is unprotected" and is not allowed to have "a sense of shame." The Ladies Anti-Slavery Society of Canton, Ohio, focused on the plight of women, stating in their group's constitution that "while man is scourged, woman is more than scourged." Indeed, "as a mother her parental feelings are disregarded . . . as a daughter her virtue is wantonly trampled on. . . . Whatever there is of delicacy or dignity in the name of woman, whatever of innocence or helpless-ness in her nature, whatever of purity or loveliness in her character; these are made the . . . prey of the vile."[8]

This type of sexually charged and gendered language represented a new strategy among abolitionists. Descriptions of sexual violence constituted the emergence of what historian, Carol Lasser termed "voyeuristic abolitionism." Such stories "galvanized readers . . . to act against slavery on the basis of both horror and identifi-cation." This voyeuristic content was also "deeply implicated in debates over gender roles." References to the rape of female slaves, prohibition against slave marriages, and separation of mothers from their children spoke about and to women. Responding to what Sarah Grimke called "the bonds of womanhood," women mobilized, forming female antislavery societies and risking public ridicule for out-spoken activism. The charged gendered rhetoric at once empowered some women to act while stirring anxiety over sexuality and the role of women. Unmarried women, sexually exploited women, women who could not fulfill their roles as mothers, and broken families presented a personal, religious, and national crisis deserving of im-mediate attention. In her detailed statistical research, Lasser demonstrated how this type of voyeuristic abolitionism, with its focus on women and sexuality, appeared most prominently in 1836.[9]

Awful Disclosures delivered its own version of voyeuristic Catholicism in spectac-ular form this same year. Perhaps it should be no surprise that Maria Monk's night-mare convent world mirrored that of a female slave, tapping into the same domestic concerns as its contemporary abolitionist literature.

The antislavery writing of George Bourne, an English immigrant to the US and Presbyterian minister, had the greatest influence on immediate abolitionism. As early as 1815, Bourne blasted slavery as "so entirely corrupt that it admits of no cure, but by a total and immediate, abolition." The following year, Bourne published *The Book and Slavery Irreconcilable*, a work that remained mostly unnoticed in the US before Garrison "found it and devoured it." The work argued from the Bible against slavery, referring to the institution as "manstealing" and thus in violation of the Eighth Commandment. Garrison and his counterparts freely quoted from Bourne in their defense of immediate abolitionism. Bourne contributed to Theodore Dwight Weld's *American Slavery as It Is* (1839) with anecdotes from what he witnessed of slavery while living in Baltimore. He also penned other influential antislavery works, including *Picture of Slavery in the United States* (1834) and *Slavery Illustrated in Its Effects upon Women and Domestic Society* (1837). Like Garrison, Bourne did not mince words. "Slavery," he declared, "inflamed slave holders with self-conceit, making them hard-hearted, . . . licentious, unfaithful, and irreligious." He especially highlighted the sexual degradation of female slaves and the humiliation of white wives. When Bourne died in November 1845, Garrison wrote, "He was one of the earliest, most uncompromising and powerful opponents of slavery in the United States." "Next to the Bible," he concluded, "we are indebted to his work for our view of the system of slavery." Not coincidentally, Bourne also served as a ghostwriter for Maria Monk's *Awful Disclosures*.[10]

The thrust of Bourne's antislavery position rested on religious premises. David Brion Davis argued that "while Bourne associated slavery with the very essence of human sin, his main concern was not the plight of Negroes but the corruption of the Christian church." According to Davis, Bourne "was far more interested in the purification of religion than in slavery as an institution." Bourne's religious values were certainly central to his abolitionism, but his antislavery arguments rested as much if not more so on concerns regarding female sexual purity, marriage, and the family. His focus on the way in which slavery threatened domestic relations heightened by the 1830s, as reflected in his book, *Slavery Illustrated in Its Effects upon Women and Domestic Society*. Many of the same domestic arguments that Bourne used for opposing slavery also appeared in his criticism of convents, revealing an integral connection between the antinun and antislavery movements.[11]

As much as he denounced slavery, Bourne extolled marriage. "Since the beginning of creation, the whole order of society," read *Slavery Illustrated*, rested on one principle: "it is not good that man should be alone. I will make a help meet for him." Slavery corrupted the "divine appointment of matrimony," claimed Bourne. In the book's hundreds of pages, he praised the cosmic significance of marriage as the paramount relationship that "preceded all other relations." In his numerated critique of slavery, Bourne listed first: "Slaves can make no contract; not even the covenant of marriage." Slavery not only precluded marriage among slaves but also weakened the skills necessary to be a wife and mother among white women. By relying on the labor of others, "white women of the South," he argued, "are ordinarily disqualified for the duties of wives and mothers when they arrive at maturity." By threatening marriage, slavery produced substandard women. "The prime object" of matrimony was "to preserve the native purity of woman in all its unsullied freshness and primitive vigor." No other subject in reference to slavery proved "more painful and humiliating" for Bourne "than that of marriage."[12]

Bourne upheld "female chastity" as integral to marriage and "the cornerstone of society." The virtues of female sexual purity could not be overstated. "This inestimable attribute," he wrote, "combines the wife's affection and the mother's love . . . in all their energetic purity." In this light, Bourne argued that nothing was worse about slavery "than the constant and universal desolating effects which slavery produces upon women." As with many antislavery works, Bourne disclosed numerous testimonies of sexual assault against female slaves, the details of which likely enticed readers as much as they incensed them. Bourne included one story related to him by a slave woman in which she stated that her master's son "was in the practice of compelling her, whenever he pleased, to go to his bed." Bourne expounded on the helplessness of this woman: "What could she do? Poor girl! She could not flee, for she was a slave!" He mourned this otherwise "pious girl," condemning the "brutal lust" of her captor. Like the "trapped" nuns of the Hotel Dieu, alleged captives of lascivious priests, the female slave had "no means of defense or escape" against her captor's "unbridled passions." With righteous indignation, Bourne concluded, "Slavery! Thou art the mother of harlots and the abominations of the earth!"[13]

Like Bourne and other abolitionists, nun opponents described convents as a threat to female sexual purity, marriage, and family. William Hogan, whose book *Popery! As It Was and as It Is* borrowed its title from Weld's *American Slavery as It Is*, described convents as "little fortifications" ruled by "licentious, lecherous, profligate priests." In a series of anecdotes, Hogan described a number of "helpless females" who became "debauched" in convents. Hospitals overseen by nuns were nothing more, he argued, than homes for the "illicit offspring of nuns and priests." All of this endangered the family. "The family is in question . . . the bosom of society— the family circle," Hogan intoned. *Awful Disclosures* likewise claimed that a nun's chief duty was to "live in criminal intercourse with the priests." Uncooperative nuns faced torture and sometimes death. Like the detailed descriptions of female slave beatings, *Awful Disclosures* related scenes of nuns being "brand[ed] with hot irons" and "whip[ped] on naked flesh." Hogan, Monk, and others explicitly accused nuns and priests of committing infanticide. Such depictions unveiled a nightmarish inversion of ideal womanhood, happy marriages, and family life.[14]

In voyeuristic style, convent narratives and Bourne's abolitionist works offered graphic images of violence. One image in *Awful Disclosures* depicted "the smothering of St. Frances, a nun at the Hotel Dieu." *The Beautiful Nun*, a convent narrative by popular novelist Ned Buntline, featured a kneeling woman in chains looking up helplessly at a priest towering above her posed to strike. Bourne's *Picture of Slavery* included engravings such as "Ladies Whipping Girls," "Flogging American Women," and "Selling Females by the Pound." In "Flogging American Women," a man whipped a woman naked from the waist up while another man leered at her. "Ladies Whipping Girls" portrayed a white woman beating a cowering female slave tied to a fence. It looked strikingly like an illustration in *Sister Agnes*, of one nun whipping another. (Figure 3.1) Each of these images focused on women, portraying the violence they endured on their bodies when outside the protection of husband and home.[15]

Bourne wore the hats of abolitionist, pastor, anti-Catholic, and "Protestant protector" of Maria Monk, finding, as historian Ronald Walters put it, "his careers easily reconciled." Bourne authored one of the first convent narratives in the US, *Lorette, the History of Louise, Daughter of a Canadian Nun, Exhibiting the Interior of Female Convents* (1834), and he came from a long line of Protestant dissidents. Upon his arrival to the US he worked as journalist and writer, eager, as one biographer described him, "to write on any cause that enlisted his temperamental enthusiasm and promised to furnish financial rewards." From his early career to his death, Bourne was burdened by debt and so energetically kept at his trade. His antislavery and anti-Catholic writings likely stemmed from a combination of sincere and mercenary motivations. In the end for Bourne, the plantation and the convent, the planter and the priest, the slave woman and the nun became his greatest obsessions and proved conveniently interchangeable.[16]

Lorette appeared three years before *Awful Disclosures*. It echoed Bourne's antislavery sentiments. In *Lorette*, Canada replaced the South as a location of "profound debasement," and Catholicism and particularly convents supplanted slavery as an institution that threatened female sexual purity and marriage. The book presented Lower Canada as a place given to "dancing, gambling, [and] gormandizing." In the narrative, priests resembled slave masters in their tyranny. The book traced the story of Louise, who found herself captured by a "leering Jesuit." As his captive, Louise became "the slave to [his] will" and endured life in a convent—"the most miserable and guilty life in the world." Although the priest used "every extremity of violence" to retain her, Louise escaped, running away like a fugitive slave. During her time in the convent, however, she discovered the shocking truth that an old nun was her mother and the sly Jesuit her father. In despair, after her traumatic escape, Louise considered suicide, but a young man rescued her just in time. The narrative

"The penitent kneeled down, her shoulders were bared."

FIGURE 3.1. "The Penalties," from *Sister Agnes; or, The Captive Nun.*
Courtesy of HathiTrust.

leaned toward a happy ending as the two decided to marry. But at the ceremony, the same priest delivered the crushing news that the betrothed were brother and sister. Bourne dedicated the book to Arthur Tappan, one of the time's most well-known abolitionists and evangelical reformers and another alleged "Protestant protector" of Maria Monk. He claimed that the book's purpose, like that of abolitionism, was to "enhance the love of freedom."[17]

An enterprising and efficient author, Bourne borrowed material from himself, recycling storylines, characters, and arguments. *Awful Disclosures*, which he likely ghostwrote, and *Slavery Illustrated* incorporated much from *Lorette*. Like *Awful Disclosures, Lorette* was set in Catholic Canada. *Lorette* began with two men discovering a distraught woman about to kill herself by jumping off a cliff. After the men provided her shelter, Louise revealed her shocking story. *Awful Disclosures* likewise related Maria Monk's rescue by Protestant men who intercepted her suicide attempt after her escape from the Hotel Dieu. While convalescing, Monk allegedly unveiled the story that became the basis of *Awful Disclosures*. Rape, violence, and entrapment appeared in all three works, but *Lorette* and *Slavery Illustrated* shared the theme of incest. A result of the tyrannical and licentious priests and slave drivers, two women in these narratives found themselves either impregnated by their brother or about to marry them. In either scenario the promise of love, marriage, and a happy family were shattered.

The similarities between condemnations of slavery and convents reveal something about the tenor of the time. Presenting something—anything—as a threat to female purity, marriage, and family served to legitimize just about any reform measure, from antislavery to temperance to anti-Catholicism. During the antebellum era, many middle-class Americans ascribed to a near-sacred status of the family, becoming more interested in the way the family and domestic piety could civilize America. In her pivotal book *The Christian Home in Victorian America*, Colleen McDannell argued that "the Protestant attitude toward the sacredness of the family developed in the antebellum era" and that by this time "domestic religion and home sentiments had become more fundamental than sectarian concerns." Good women, or what Barbara Welter referred to as "true womanhood," defined by purity, piety, submission, and domesticity, stood at the center of this domestic ideal. In her examination of nineteenth-century anti-Catholic literature, Marie Anne Pagliarini argued that "Catholicism was represented as a threat to sexual norms, gender definitions, and family values that comprised the antebellum 'cult of domesticity.'" It was thus not just religious anti-Catholicism that allowed many Americans to look past evidence pointing to the fraudulent nature of *Awful Disclosures*. Ideals of womanhood, marriage, and family more forcefully compelled people to oppose anything that appeared in conflict with these models. Readers did not seem to care that Maria Monk's stories could not be confirmed in the same way as those of Sojourner Truth's or Harriet Jacobs's. Americans did not need to personally know a priest who resembled the villainous slave driver, Simon Legree, of *Uncle Tom's Cabin* to believe that priests were one-dimensional profligates. They could speculate on their own about what occurred behind closed doors of the "homes" of women who swore off a life of traditional marriage and motherhood, and the images were not pretty.[18]

Harriet Beecher Stowe dramatized the moral arguments of abolitionism in spectacular fashion. More than any other work of literature, *Uncle Tom's Cabin; or, Life*

Among the Lowly, changed hearts and minds about slavery, rendering abolitionism mainstream. The *National Era* hailed the book as "THE STORY OF THE AGE!" Yet as many historians and literary critics have noted, *Uncle Tom's Cabin* was about much more than slavery. Its prominent concerns were marriage, family, and motherhood. Historian Amy Dru Stanley noted, "No abolitionist argument proved more compelling than that testifying to the conflict between slavery and domesticity, as demonstrated by . . . *Uncle Tom's Cabin*." Stowe shied away from voyeuristic abolitionism of the 1830s, suggesting sexual misdeeds rather than graphically describing them. In this way, as Carol Lasser noted, "Stowe's moderate prose allowed the book to enter northern parlors, even while enraging southern readers." Yet the same domestic tropes in earlier abolitionist writings concerning female gender roles, marriage, and motherhood remained prominent, being perhaps most fully and powerfully combined and expressed by Stowe.[19]

Uncle Tom's Cabin appeared first in serial form in the June 1851 issue of the political periodical *National Era*. The timing could not have been better. Months before saw the passage of the Fugitive Slave Act, igniting fierce reaction in the North. Stowe's own outrage against the law along with her recent grief over losing a child provided political and personal motivation for her writing. Later revealing her sorrow over the death of her infant son to a friend, Stowe wrote, "It was at his dying bed and at his grave that I learned what a poor slave mother may feel when her child is torn away from her." The combination of highlighting a mother's grief and the political injustice of slavery in the resulting novel produced a stirring effect. The popularity of *Uncle Tom's Cabin* quickly expanded beyond the *National Era*'s readership. As the tale unfolded with each new chapter release, people responded with challenges, endorsements, and overall interest. By October, one contributor noted, "Whenever I went among the friends . . . I found there 'Uncle Tom's Cabin' a theme for admiring remark—everywhere I saw it read with pleasant smiles and gushes of irresistible tears. Mrs. Stowe is winning . . . love and gratitude . . . by this incomparable story."[20]

That same month Stowe made arrangements with Jewett & Co. to publish a bound edition of the novel. Its appearance on March 20, 1852, furthered the work's spectacular popularity. In its first day, the book sold three thousand copies. By April a second edition went to press, and sales reached three hundred thousand by the year's end. Although he criticized Tom's peaceful acceptance of oppression, Garrison lauded Stowe's "great facility" of "feelings and emotions" to "awaken the strongest compassion for the oppressed." The work drew in many who had previously ignored or remained ignorant of the debates surrounding the peculiar institution, and sales made headlines. On May 13, 1852, the *Independent* described the work's popularity as "without precedent in the history of book publishing in this country." Jewett capitalized on book sales further, issuing an illustrated edition. In response to the criticism the book generated among some southerners, Stowe also published *A Key to Uncle Tom's Cabin* featuring "Original Facts and Documents, upon which the story is founded, Together with Corroborative Statements Verifying the Truth of the Work." The authors of *Awful Disclosures* also published a detailed sequel in response to fans and critics.[21]

Uncle Tom's Cabin opened dramatically with white men tearing apart a slave family. Mr. Shelby, a relatively kind but debt-ridden and cowardly man, reluctantly struck a deal to sell two slaves to a diabolical slave trader, Mr. Haley. While Shelby discussed selling Tom, a loyal, skilled, and religious slave, Eliza, a young slave woman, walked in the room chasing after her two-year-old son. Haley quickly eyed her up, noting her potential profitability in the "fancy trade," but he chose to invest in the youth, offering to purchase the little boy. After leaving the room, Eliza overheard the two men discuss the terms of the sale. Horrified at the thought of being separated from her only son, she planned to escape with him. Eliza later declared to Uncle Tom and Aunt Chloe, her closest friends and fellow slaves, "I'm running away, carrying off my child—Master sold him!" Previously Eliza's husband, George Harris, enslaved on a neighboring plantation, escaped to avoid being married off to another woman. He promised to purchase his wife and son after securing his freedom in Canada, but it was now up to Eliza and Harry to find him. The tragedy of *Uncle Tom's Cabin* was the severing of this family, and the hope of the novel was their reconciliation in a happy home.[22]

The editor of *The Annotated Uncle Tom's Cabin* claimed that Eliza "would have been immediately recognized by Stowe's readers" as "the poor but genteel Victorian heroine." Eliza's elevated feminine status rested on her role as devoted wife and mother. As a mother, Eliza's love and suffering were unsurpassed. "But stronger than all was maternal love," wrote Stowe, describing the source of Eliza's courage to leave the only home she ever knew. Her escape scene quickly became iconic. With Harry in her arms, Eliza crossed the icy waters of the Ohio River, narrowly avoiding Haley, who chased them "like a hound." Eliza found safe haven in the home of an Ohio senator. The senator's wife, also a mother, took pity on Eliza, calming her "with many gentle and womanly offices." But Eliza would continue to face a hostile environment in her quest to keep and save her child and fulfill her role as a true mother. Toward the end of the novel, Stowe extended another dramatic tale of mother–child separation in the story of Cassy, a mulatto woman. In recalling her son's removal from her, Cassy explained to the slave Tom, "The poor boy screamed and looked into my face, and held on to me, until, in tearing him off, they tore the skirt of my dress half away; and they carried him in, screaming 'Mother! Mother! Mother!'" Wiser in the wretched ways of slavery, when Cassy gave birth to another child by another slave owner, she "kissed him, cried over him, and then gave him laudanum." Because of slavery, she could not fulfill her motherly role.[23]

Historians have traced a growing idealization of motherhood in the Victorian era. As an agrarian society gave way to an industrialized one, men and women who used to share household duties split ways. Women frequently took over parenting while men competed for work in the marketplace. This development feminized parent-hood, prompting the development of new concepts of motherhood. As the home appeared in greater contrast to the increasingly impersonal and sometimes dangerous public sector, women became more associated with the ideals of the hearth. Stowe's commitment to nineteenth-century ideology of what some historians have termed "angelic motherhood" shone through many of her leading characters. Rachel Halliday, a Quaker woman who offered refuge to Eliza and Harry, embodied an ideal wife and mother, reigning over an inviting, safe home. When Rachel gently called Eliza "my daughter," the words flowed "naturally from [her] lips . . . for hers was just the face and form that made 'mother' seem the most natural word in the world." Stowe wrote, "Rachel never looked so truly and benignly happy as at the head of her table. There was so much motherliness and full-heartedness even in the way she passed a plate of cakes . . . that it seemed to put a spirit into the food and drink she offered." Her soothing and able care of the runaways elicited her son's remark that "Mother can do almost everything."[24]

Likewise, little Evangeline St. Clare, or Eva, the innocent child friend of Tom, symbolized, as one critic put it, "a spotless motherly Christ coming to redeem the world." Although a child and not a literal mother, Eva exhibited angelic maternal instincts, caring for others above herself. "Always dressed in white," Eva was "the perfection of childish beauty," with golden hair that "floated like a cloud" and "violet blue eyes" that bespoke "deep spiritual gravity." Stowe unsubtly compared Eva with a maternal Jesus, who took on the sorrows of the world. In her death scene, Eva's grief over slavery and humble acceptance of her lot completed her apotheosis. Stowe later commented on the meaning of her novel, stating, "This story is to show how Jesus Christ . . . has still a mother's love for the poor and lowly." Indeed, the symbolism of a female savior appeared throughout *Uncle Tom's Cabin*, her divinity inseparable from her motherhood. Harriet Martineau shared Stowe's deep belief in the redemptive power of motherhood, stating that if the peculiar institution were confided to the mothers' charge, "they would accomplish its overthrow with energy and wisdom."[25]

Marriage, a prerequisite to motherhood, proved central to Stowe's book. *Uncle Tom's Cabin*, as one literary critic wrote, "is thoroughly preoccupied with marriages— broken up marriages, failed marriages, fatalistic and tired marriages; bittersweet, evergreen, surprisingly emotional marriages; hasty, postponed, 'if-only' marriages; in-name-only . . . and doomed marriages." Eliza and George, Uncle Tom and Aunt Chloe, the Shelbys, Cassy and her unnamed lover, the Hallidays, the St. Clares, and other couples filled the book. In the first chapters, readers met Eliza and George, a young couple deeply in love. For their informal wedding, Mrs. Shelby "adorned the bride's beautiful hair with orange-blossoms" and a veil, which "could scarce have rested on a fairer head." "For a year or two," explained Stowe, "Eliza saw her husband frequently and there was nothing to interrupt their happiness." George exclaimed, "I scarcely could believe I was alive, I was so happy." But their matrimony stood on shaky ground because of slavery. After George's master threatened to "marry" him to another woman, George cursed the day he was born. "Don't you know that a slave can't be married?" George asked Eliza. "I can't have you as my wife. That's why I wish I had never been born." For George, Eliza, and Harry, slavery proved to be the greatest stumbling block to their happy ending. Stowe reiterated this sin of slavery in other sentimental passages, asking, "But what needs tell the story, told too oft, of heart-strings rent and broken?"[26]

Stowe along with other novelists of the Victorian era helped create the "happily-ever-after" final sequence that upheld marriage as key to contentment, especially for women. In a sexually charged scene, she described the reunion of George and Eliza: " 'To-night!' Eliza repeated, 'to-night!' The words lost all meaning to her; her head was dreamy and confused; all was mist for a moment. . . . She dreamed of a beautiful country . . . and beautifully glittering water; and there, in a house which kind voices told her was a home, she saw her boy playing, a free and happy child. She heard her husband's footsteps; she felt him coming nearer; his arms were around her . . . and she awoke!" Stowe also presented Rachel Halliday's home as heaven on Earth. "This, indeed, was a home,—*home*,—a word that George had never yet known a meaning for." As George dined in this domestic temple, he attained "a belief in God," and his despair "melted away." Uncle Tom unsuccessfully strained toward this happy ending. As one critic noted, "home and family mattered most to him," and for the sake of his children who might be sold if he absconded, Tom went peaceably with Haley. The loving marriage, the doting children, the peaceful home—this was the good life, an Eden repeatedly illustrated in antebellum literature, graspable if only certain facets of society could be reformed.[27]

Not all women in *Uncle Tom's Cabin* stood as paradigms of perfection. Marie, Eva's mother, exhibited the opposite attributes of her Christ-like child. Surrounded by servants since childhood, Marie grew vain, selfish, and lazy. Rather than the giving, compassionate wife and mother, she berated her husband whose efforts were never enough and rebuffed her daughter's affection, responding to a hug with, "That'll do,—take care, child,—don't, you make my head ache." Ruling their New Orleans plantation, Marie enjoyed torturing her slaves and turned a blind eye to separating the slave woman "Mammy" from her children. Her piety was mere show, focused more on donning "diamonds, silk, and lace . . . to a fashionable church." As one critic noted, the character of Marie "was despicable precisely because she so utterly failed to live up to the Victorian ideal of the loving mother."[28]

If the kind of ideal motherhood exhibited in *Uncle Tom's Cabin* represented America's hope of salvation, and if marriage and family promised happiness, the nuns of *Awful Disclosures* were the most miserable women, and anticipated the nation's ruin. Much like Marie St. Clare, the Mother Superior in *Awful Disclosures* took delight in torturing underling nuns with grueling chores. The unwitting mothers of the Hotel Dieu were not the right kind of mothers, callously committing infanticide without a hint of sentimental remorse. Rather than respectable wives, they lived as priests' concubines. Unlike Eliza, Rachel, and little Eva, whose goodness manifested itself in physical beauty, many of the nuns embodied masculine, repulsive forms. One old nun, "very ignorant and gross in her manners," sported "quite a beard on her face" and acted "very cross and disagreeable." Another had a "large figure," a "wrinkled face," and a "careless dress." In contrast to Stowe's ideal women, Monk's nuns feigned religious devotion, veiling their hypocrisy and superstition. The nuns never read the Bible and they "all believe[d] in ghosts." In short, the nuns of *Awful Disclosures* and the stereotypical nun that emerged in the ensuing American campaign against convents presented the antithesis to the model woman, seen perhaps most explicitly in *Uncle Tom's Cabin*.[29]

Stowe's understanding of a woman's place did not align perfectly with that of George Bourne. Her gender ideology allowed for a more feminist vision in which there was room for unmarried and even proto-career women, but most of the exemplary women of *Uncle Tom's Cabin* embraced what many perceived as a "woman's supreme calling": motherhood. Being a mother fostered a woman's compassion, helping her to raise children "to love, work hard, and avoid evil." Stowe upheld this role as sacred and useful. As historian Nina Baym argued, domesticity was "set forth as a value scheme for ordering all of life" with the goal that "home and the world would become one." In rejecting their "highest calling," nuns threatened the reformer's vision of extending home values into the world. Just as slavery challenged the forging of good wives and mothers and familial happiness, convents blocked these as well, and could thus be seen as a national menace. In *Awful Disclosures* and other convent narratives, nuns lived as "slaves" of a corrupt system. George Bourne, William Hogan, and others claimed that young women were duped into joining convents and found themselves captives after "taking the veil." These "helpless females" faced dire consequences if they did not cooperate in any litany of misdeeds. The liberation of these women from their "captivity" promised the type of domestic happiness Eliza eventually found and the kind of world envisioned by abolitionists in which marriage and motherhood triumphed.[30]

In contrast to Eliza, who prevailed through escape, Stowe described how slavery fostered in other women "gross, unrestricted animal selfishness." These "feeble and discouraged" slaves were "women that were not women." Treated "like brutes," they "sunk . . . to their level." Likewise, brutish nuns appeared throughout *Awful Disclosures* as well, callously torturing each other and killing their babies "without remorse or shame." In obedience to masters/priests, female slaves/nuns became selfish, defiled, and savage themselves. The "homes" of such women were not the inviting hearths of Rachel Halliday. Stowe pictured plantations as "dark places," cut off from society, where no one could "testify if you were burned alive." In the Hotel Dieu, nuns lived in a "prison house of death," "shut up in a place from which there has been . . . but one way of egress . . . the grave." The images of these women who were not women and homes that were not homes helped mobilize a nation against slavery and convents as essential reforms.[31]

The greatest villain in *Uncle Tom's Cabin*, however, was not Marie or any other woman, but a man, the fiendish slave owner Simon Legree. Reflecting earlier abolitionist writings, Stowe depicted slave owners and overseers as the chief antagonists, whose arbitrary powers spawned numerous vices, the worst being lasciviousness. Abolitionists believed that any form of concentrated power led to corruption and that slavery stood as the clearest example of this. Simon Legree epitomized the worst traits of the slave owner. This crude and perpetually drunk bachelor often flew into a rage asserting his authority over his slaves. When Tom refused to whip a female slave at Legree's bidding, the "demonical" man had Tom whipped nearly to death. Stowe hinted at sexual violence, describing Legree putting his "heavy, dirty hand over [Emmeline's] neck and bust" before purchasing her. "I don't mean to make you work very hard," he whispered to her, "only be a good girl." Jealous of Tom's faith, Legree snatched away Tom's Bible, telling him, "I'm your church now . . . do as I say!" Yet "reprobate and godless" as he was, there was a time "when he had been rocked on the bosom of a mother." He lost his soul when instead of imitating this "gentle woman," Legree "followed in the footsteps of his father." Legree's rundown plantation mirrored the man. A long swamp lined with trees from which "hung long wreaths of funeral moss" led the way to the "desolate and uncomfortable house." This "enclosure" spoke of the gloom in which Legree's charge lived.[32]

Simon Legree was cut from the same cloth as priests of the Hotel Dieu. Drunk on their authority, these clerics tyrannized the nuns. Like Legree, these priests kept Bibles out of nuns' hands, teaching them to "receive as truth everything said by the priests." Convent narratives exaggerated the hierarchy of the Catholic Church, describing priests as having total power over congregants and nuns, whom authors described as "slaves." Just as *Uncle Tom's Cabin* linked Legree's sexual appetites with his bachelorhood, anti-Catholic literature suggested that celibacy turned priests "into sexual

madmen, bent on ravaging the purity of innocent women." *Awful Disclosures* confirmed that "every one of [the priests] was guilty of licentiousness." Monk related the
frequent "criminal intercourse" between nuns and priests, claiming "often they were
in our beds before us." Frequent references to nuns as "harems," "priests' prostitutes,"
and "slaves" reinforced growing accusations of sexual violence in convents. Like
Legree's plantation, the Hotel Dieu stood removed from the happiness of companionate marriage, true womanhood, and safe homes.[33]

While scholars cannot deny the success and historical significance of *Uncle Tom's
Cabin*, they have long since debated its literary merits. Critics, including James
Baldwin, have condemned the work for its sentimentality. In his review Baldwin
wrote, "The parading of excessive and spurious emotion, is the mask of dishonesty."
Alfred Kazin offered a similar critique, stating, "Uncle Tom is too good, too simple,
just as the slave traders are too beastly, Simon Legree too awful, Eva too saintly."
While granting that the book was "deeply moving and essentially true," George
Orwell described it as "an unintentionally ludicrous book, full of preposterous melodramatic incidents." Whether *Uncle Tom's Cabin* made the cut as good literature,
it was a book for its time. As one historian recently claimed, "Like most popular
works of art . . . *Uncle Tom's Cabin* was influenced by the cultural modes and tropes
that were fashionable in its day." Stowe's magnum opus reflected a sentimental vision
of womanhood, marriage, and family that were often combined in popular sentimental novels. Albeit with less admirable motives, the same might be said of the
over-the-top content of *Awful Disclosures*. Its melodrama, sentimentality, sensationalism, and one-dimensional characters placed the book in the category of propaganda rather than literature. These features gripped readers, and the presentation
of convents as antithetical to true womanhood and a happy home reflected some of
the strongest messages of antebellum popular culture. In being books of their time,
Awful Disclosures and *Uncle Tom's Cabin* had much in common.[34]

In terms of staying power, Monk's book paled in comparison to Stowe's. *Uncle
Tom's Cabin* has been republished in over six hundred editions. It has appeared
in various manifestations throughout the years, in plays, music, and film versions.
But neither has ever gone out of print, and in its time, *Awful Disclosures* captivated
Americans much like *Uncle Tom's Cabin* did. Readers simply could not resist the invitation to peer beyond the "shroud of secrecy" allegedly enveloping convents. Both
works offered a subtext, juxtaposing two worlds, slave and free, happy and miserable, married and alone, pure and defiled, reflecting the desires and fears that many
Americans had for their country.[35]

In his groundbreaking study of *Uncle Tom's Cabin*, David S. Reynolds contended
that the novel "absorbed images from virtually every realm of culture—religion,

reform, temperance tracts, antislavery writings, sensational pulp fiction, and popular performance." It was Stowe's "immersion in [this] popular culture, that set the stage for her affecting novel." Reynolds might have also included convent narratives in his list of popular culture examples. If it were not for the growing elevation of marriage and family in antebellum America, abolitionist and antinun literature, and their subsequent movements, would have been considerably less energized. As Ronald Walters claimed, "family itself was a matter of both anxiety and hope" in antebellum America. This "anxiety found nightmarish confirmation in the Southern way of life" in antislavery literature. This concern also found confirmation in convent narratives. Antislavery propaganda helped define the South, slavery, and slaveholders as "symbols of negation, opposites against which to measure what was good and progressive . . . [reflecting] firmly held judgements about what man and society should be." In much the same way, convent narratives, and perhaps none more than *Awful Disclosures,* constructed a Catholic identity and in particular a female identity that stood as symbols of negation. As writers pictured Catholic lands and convents as places of abomination, so too did they cast nuns as the inversion of the ideal woman, relegating single womanhood to second-class status. *Uncle Tom's Cabin* and *Awful Disclosures* not only condemned slavery and convent life, respectively, but also provided sure footing for the strictly-defined ideals of true womanhood, marriage, and domesticity.[36]

Every girl who has been educated in an American nunnery has departed from it assuredly with every refined feminine sensibility destroyed.

—*Female Convents*, 1834

The nuns are very skillful in making converts, and their ceremonies well-calculated to captivate the minds of young people.

—*Protestant Girl in a French Nunnery*, 1846

4

Textbook Popery

CONVENT SCHOOLS, THE FEMINIZATION OF TEACHING, AND THE NATION'S CHILDREN

IN 1844, *LADIES' MAGAZINE* published a love story entitled "The Young Music Teacher." In the narrative, Mary, age eighteen, and her twenty-year-old sister, Jane, find themselves "without fortune or home" when their widowed father suddenly dies. A wealthy uncle graciously opens his house to the two young women, an offer Jane eagerly accepts with relief. But Mary hesitates, feeling it her "duty" to "support herself" under a man's roof who has no "natural responsibility" to provide for her as a husband or a father might. To contribute her fair share, Mary becomes a music teacher, a decision that appalls Jane. "Lessons in music! . . . Think, Mary, of how your doing so would affect your station," Jane protests. In embarrassment, Jane ignores her sister in polite society and contentedly attends balls on her own. As an active socialite, Jane soon meets Hartly Cleveland, a wealthy, educated man "of high principles" who courts her. While waiting on Jane in her uncle's parlor one day, however, Cleveland meets Mary. Not realizing she was Jane's sister (as Jane never mentioned her), he assumes Mary is "only a music teacher." But her conversation intrigues him, and soon he cannot stop thinking about the music teacher. Jane's long primping routine allows for other chance meetings, leading Cleveland to ask the uncle about the mysterious woman. When he learns Mary and Jane are sisters, he recognizes the full measure of Mary's "nobleness." His affections turn toward Mary as Jane "was no longer beautiful or interesting in his eyes." By the end of the story, Mary and Cleveland get married in a wedding larger and "more brilliant" than any that had "been given for two or three years." And the story of the "humble music teacher," whose conduct lifted her "to the skies," became legendary.[1]

Stories like "The Young Music Teacher" helped change the narrative on women in the workforce, particularly teaching. The female protagonist's work as a teacher was "noble" and made her even more appealing to male suitors. Although offering her a degree of independence for a time, teaching ultimately prepared her for marriage. The story's triumphal conclusion made no mention of whether Mary would continue teaching. Her wedding and union to a man with the "natural responsibility" to support her suggested her music career was short-lived. By presenting female teaching as a road to marriage, this story contributed to the growing acceptance of teaching for women while reinforcing female gender norms of domesticity.

In the 1840s, teaching became increasingly feminized. While men had dominated the profession since the colonial era, some schools in New England began to hire women as teachers in the antebellum era. Leading reformers for the common school movement, such as Horace Mann, stressed the importance of a moral (rather than merely intellectual) education for children, and consequently turned to women as the natural instructors. Indeed, reformers justified female teaching as an extension of a woman's moral sensibilities and maternal instincts. The prospect of paying female teachers less than men also proved appealing as the common school movement got underway and citizens faced raised taxes. In the coming years, teaching became both ideologically and statistically a female vocation. By 1888, women made up 90 percent of the teachers in cities and 63 percent of all American teachers, rendering the female teacher an iconic image. Yet during the same decades that teaching became feminized, convent schools, where nuns worked as teachers, increasingly became objects of scorn and loathing in anti-Catholic sentiment across the US.[2]

Anti-Catholic literature forged an image of the teaching nun as a calculated conspirator, void of "female virtue," and convent schools as a danger to children. *Female Convents* informed readers, "Every girl who has been educated in an American nunnery has departed from it—either a determined sceptic . . . or a disguised and dispended Papist; and assuredly with every refined feminine sensibility destroyed." One of the most popular convent narratives of the 1840s, *The Protestant Girl in a French Nunnery*, captured the focus on convent schools and the education of girls. Author Rachel McCrindell presented the book ambiguously as "not a work of fiction, but a collection of facts thrown together." The story featured a pious female protagonist, Emily, who steadfastly maintained her faith in the face of "popish" tricks. In the narrative, wealthy Protestant English parents sent their young daughter to a French convent school. Although the nuns promised not to proselytize, Emily confronted daily challenges to her Protestant faith. Fortunately, she knew enough of her Bible to combat these challenges. When she witnessed Catholic pupils kneeling before statues, she mentally recited a passage from Exodus warning against idolatry. When a Catholic student proclaimed "Mon Dieu!" the Protestant girl recalled the biblical invective against taking the Lord's name in vain. And when the nuns praised her for her diligence in the classroom and her high moral conduct, she shrunk back from the applause so as not to claim any "good works" for herself, giving all the credit to "God alone."[3]

Yet in this sentimental and pious novel, the prospect of converting to Catholicism was only the first step down a slippery slope. The real danger of convent schools was in the prospect of female pupils deciding to become nuns themselves. "The nuns were very skillful in making converts, and the ceremonies were well-calculated to captivate the minds of young people," wrote McCrindell. Despite her best efforts, Emily became enamored with the cunning nuns. In the presence of a particularly lovely nun who "spoke sweetly," she "felt that her heart was too much moved, that there was a danger in remaining longer in her society." Meanwhile, the Sisters commonly asked the students "how they would like convent life." Although Emily narrowly avoided becoming a nun herself or converting to Catholicism, others "fell under the spells of popery." Some became nuns, choosing, in the words of the author, "to bury themselves in the living death of the cloister," severing "all the enduring ties of society and the prospect of future usefulness." The easiest prey included "young and thoughtless girls whose minds were naturally fond of novelty." Rather than provide moral training out of maternal instincts, the nuns deceptively "transfixed" their students, placing them under "a spell no sensible soul could resist." Such schools, McCrindell concluded, proved dangerous to a young woman's future, threatening "her reason and her very life."[4]

Unlike "The Young Music Teacher," whose education and teaching prepared her for marriage and domesticity, *Protestant Girl in a French Nunnery* (Figure 4.1) presented a type of education that threatened a young woman's marriage and domestic prospects and a cast of deceptive female teachers devoid of moral virtue. The real threat of convent schools, according to many Protestants, was the challenge they allegedly posed to the ideals of true womanhood. Convent schools were not places that prepared young women to step into the roles of wife and mother. They filled young girls with romantic and superstitious delusions rather than practical domestic skills, at worst "entrapping" them within convent walls. Although works like McCrindell's did not include the type of sensationalism, sex, and sadism that were staples of works like Maria Monk's in the 1830s, they nevertheless enjoyed widespread popularity and offered a similar message: nuns and convents threatened American womanhood. Even as more women ventured out of the home and into

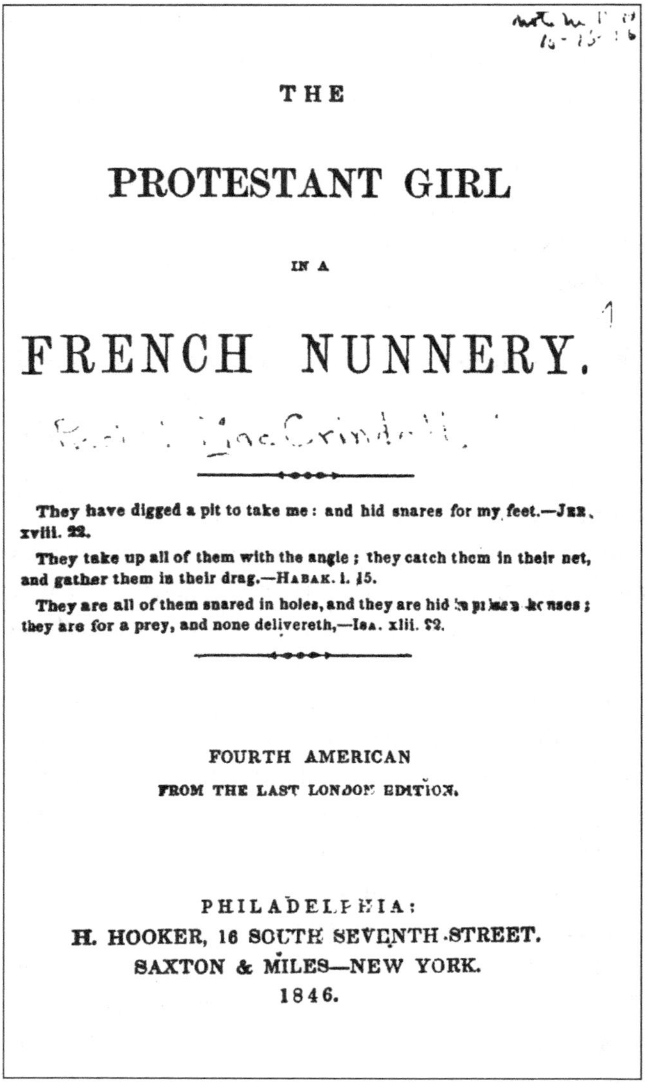

THE

PROTESTANT GIRL

IN A

FRENCH NUNNERY.

They have digged a pit to take me: and hid snares for my feet.—JER, xviii. 22.

They take up all of them with the angle; they catch them in their net, and gather them in their drag.—HABAK. i. 15.

They are all of them snared in holes, and they are hid in prison houses; they are for a prey, and none delivereth,—ISA. xlii. 22.

FOURTH AMERICAN

FROM THE LAST LONDON EDITION,

PHILADELPHIA:
H. HOOKER, 16 SOUTH SEVENTH STREET.
SAXTON & MILES—NEW YORK.
1846.

FIGURE 4.1. *The Protestant Girl in a French Nunnery.*
Courtesy of HathiTrust.

the classroom, nuns who taught appeared dramatically different from the ideal pious women called to raise up the nation's children.

Protestant Girl in a French Nunnery received high praise in the press. The *Episcopal Recorder* lauded the book for extending "excellent lessons on duty," advising its placement "in every Sunday-school library." *The Presbyterian* upheld the book as a true picture of the "arts employed in a French convent to proselyte Protestant pupils" and warned that such methods were "invariably employed in Roman Catholic schools." By 1846, after first being published in London, McCrindell's book went through ten editions. That year its New York publishers reprinted the book with a new subtitle: *A Warning to Protestants Against Education in Catholic Seminaries*. Another version of the book under the title *The School Girl in France* was promoted in the *New York Evangelist* and the *New York Observer and Chronicle*. The popularity of this book reflected the growing suspicion beyond convents in general to convent schools, teaching nuns, and the education of America's young women.[5]

In 1837, *The Presbyterian*, a Kentucky newspaper, published an article warning its readers about a Catholic conspiracy and the important role convent schools played in advancing the purposes of Rome:

> It is well known that the pope and his clergy regard their mission in America as far more important than any others, and that the principal means by which they expect to extend their influence in our country, is the education of youth. And it should be understood by Protestants that their efforts are especially directed to *female education*. In the state of Kentucky they have ten female establishments of which five are conducted by the Sisters of Charity and five by the Sisters of Loretto.

Similarly, the *Boston Recorder* in 1845 cautioned readers against the "loathsome and corrupting influences of nunneries, confessionals, priests, mother abbesses, and the Sisters of Charity" that "young ladies" faced in convent schools. Seeing nuns and convents as conspicuous harbingers of a Catholic conspiracy constituted standard-fare anti-Catholic sentiment, but the explicit focus on convent schools was a new, growing concern.[6]

A flurry of convent narratives published in the 1840s were set in convent schools, including *The Nun of St. Ursula*, by popular novelist Harry Hazel; "The Grey Nuns of Montreal"; and a children's book, *Luzette; or, Good Brought Out of Evil*. These and other works were decidedly tamer in tone than some of the more popular convent narratives of the 1830s, likely appealing to a more respectable, middle-class audience. Ray Allen Billington, in his scholarship on nativism, argued that anti-Catholic literature in the 1840s represented "an earnest effort to win to their standard the religiously inclined sober citizen of the United States." Focusing on children's education, marriage, and the family was a sure way of doing that. Such works mimicked arguments in *The Protestant Girl*. One warned that crafty nuns and priests lured simple, trusting children to attend confession with "sweet meats, pictures, and *bon bons*." Another told of a Mother Superior who lavished praise on pupils, telling them "they were beautiful, fascinating, and they look like angels" until some "decide to be a nun." In each of these stories convent schools appeared as a trap where calculating nuns conspired against young girls, threatening the American family.[7]

Convent school critics both blamed parents for foolishly sending their daughters to convent schools and punished them and their daughters for these decisions in their stories. *Protestant Girl in a French Nunnery* spoke of the "false security" embraced by parents who sent their daughters to be taught by nuns. As a result, "we often see the unhappy father deserted in his old age by daughters" who choose "a living death in the cloister." Authors blamed parents for placing "worldly accomplishments" above their children's "eternal influences." "You must know that it is common for fashionable Protestants to send their daughters to the convent school to get an education, as though their own schools were of an inferior character," expressed the narrator of *The Nun of St. Ursula*. William Hogan, a former Catholic priest whose break from his church in Maryland caused a considerable upheaval in the diocese, criticized mothers especially for being led by "malign influences of fashion" in sending their daughters, "their earthly idols, to a convent academy." In his preface to *Female Convents,* Thomas Roscoe unabashedly demanded that parents "not endanger the virtue and usefulness of your children . . . and especially your daughters [under] the management of Jesuit priests and Ursuline nuns."[8]

Protestant reform associations, which were becoming increasingly popular by the 1840s, forming part of the vanguard of what Ray Allen Billington called "the Protestant Crusade," also rallied against nuns and convent schools, both warning and blaming parents. Members of the American Tract Society scouted out Protestant parents who sent their children to convent schools. In an 1842 tract one woman addressed a mother who sent her daughter to be educated by the School Sisters of Notre Dame in Cincinnati, Ohio. Her open letter, entitled *A Letter of an American Mother to an American Mother,* appeared alongside Tract Number 360, entitled "Roman Catholic Female Schools." Tract 360 warned readers that "the first aim" of Catholics was to "convert our youth to their faith." This religious concern, however, appeared less troubling than the prospect of American girls becoming nuns. After referring to convents as "sealed prisons," the *Christian Parlor Magazine* in 1844 stated emphatically that it was "our own Protestant parents who furnished victims." The author continued, describing a negligent father whose "daughter was buried alive[,] shut up in a nunnery to be his daughter no more!" Schools taught by women who were not themselves wives and mothers threatened the family circle. Whether deluded or "buried alive," the apparent equivalent of taking vows, such education precluded women from fulfilling the "natural" and "God appointed" role of being a wife and mother. Such a fate was worse than death.[9]

Even as authors and entire associations scorned convent schools, advocates for the common or public school movement promoted teachers who exhibited decidedly feminine qualities of gentleness, high morals, and maternal love. In 1840, Henry

Barnard, successor to Horace Mann, claimed, "Heaven has plainly appointed females as the natural instructors of young children, and endowed them with those qualities of mind and disposition, which pre-eminently fit them for the task." Similarly, Mann argued, "the females are incomparably better teachers for our young children than males. . . . Their manners are more mild and gentle. . . . They are endowed by nature with stronger parental impulses." In confronting legislative opposition on religious and economic grounds to public schools, Mann and the Massachusetts Board of Education stressed a woman's moralizing influence in what would otherwise be nonsectarian Christian schools and the female self-sacrificing nature, which suggested her affordability. Similarly, Catherine Beecher, the first proponent of the feminization of teaching, relied on concepts of domestic feminism to argue that teaching was "women's natural vocation." Believing women to be morally superior to men, Beecher perceived them as the most fit to be the moral instructors of the nation's children. In her *Essay on the Education of Female Teachers*, Beecher called for more female teachers "for shaping national morality," especially in the expanding frontier, a place with a growing number of Catholic immigrant communities and convent schools.[10]

Catherine Beecher never married and never had any children, but she nevertheless upheld teaching as the best preparation for marriage and as an extension of a woman's maternal and moral dispositions. By imagining women's employment in schools as a continuation of the work of mothering, reformers justified hiring women as teachers. Horace Mann made a direct comparison to motherhood, writing that a female teacher would lead the nation's youth "as a mother takes her babe, and shields it from harm . . . and trains it to such a glorious [adulthood]." Resting on a particular view of gender that saw women as morally superior to men, a view Mann shared with Beecher, he argued further that "a woman surpasses man in grace, in faith, in affection, in purity," and that while his "nature leads to science and wisdom; hers to love and sympathies." In the promotion of an educational system that would teach morals and the "three R's," no one seemed better suited for the task than women. And their shift from hearth to classroom posed no threat to female gender norms, but rather grew out of and complemented them.[11]

The comparison of the home to the classroom was made manifest by antebellum reformers who conflated the two in this new vision for society. As early as 1838, Samuel G. Goodrich endorsed the common school as "the auxiliary of the fireside." The elevation of the home to sacred levels led others to associate the home with schools and even the church. Horace Bushnell believed in the importance of the home as the location of both educational and religious training. "The house," he claimed, "having a domestic spirit of grace dwelling in it, should become the church of childhood, the table and hearth a holy rite." Overseeing this hearth, women exhibiting "semi-divine proportions of maternity" prepared the "soul's immortality" of their children. Proponents of the common school movement sought to extend the cosmic influence of the home to the school, in which, as historian Redding Sugg argued, "the female teacher might officiate as the mother did at home." Female teachers brought the sacredness of the home to the nation's children, sacrilizing the public school movement and the movement of women into the workforce. Nuns, as keepers of nontraditional hearths, had no place in this burgeoning education ideal.[12]

When Horace Mann died in 1859, his wife Mary Peabody Mann memorialized his attitudes toward the feminization of teaching. "It was his opinion that the divinely appointed mission of woman is to teach," she stated. He saw that a "woman's teaching . . . is more patient, persistent, and thorough than man's." She continued in her elegy of her late husband, lauding him for recognizing that these virtues grew "out of the domestic traits, which are not marred by this use, but only thus directed to the noblest ends." In no way did teaching interfere "with the peculiarly appointed sphere of woman." Indeed, "she is better fitted for the duties of wife and mother for having first used her faculties in imparting knowledge." Earlier, Catherine Beecher wrote to Horace Mann, emphasizing the conciliatory relationship between home, family, and teaching for women. "The great purpose of a woman's life—the happy superintendence of a family—is accomplished all the better and easier by preliminary teaching in school. All the power she may develop here will come in use there." Mann claimed that women made better teachers in part because unlike men, "they never look forward . . . to a period of emancipation from parental control, when they are to break away from the domestic circle and go abroad in the world." Nuns, as women who traveled, never married, and resided over no family were an awkward fit for this model of teaching.[13]

The promise of the female teacher extended by the likes of Mann, Beecher, and Goodrich rested partially on a religious and cultural contest for influence against Catholics. In her speeches to drum up support for female teachers, Beecher lamented the lack of financial and social support Protestant women received in comparison with Catholic nuns. Relating a story of some women teachers who faced opposition, Beecher stated, "Had these women turned Catholic and offered their services to extend that church, they would instantly have found bishops, priests, Jesuits and all their subordinates at hand, to counsel and sustain; a strong *public sentiment* would have been created in their favor; while abundant funds would have been laid at their feet." In the face of the growing number of convent schools, Beecher proposed a Protestant school system where, as her biographer Kathryn Sklar put it, "the family, the school, and the church would form a new cultural matrix within which women would assume a central role." Similarly, while Mann went so far as to praise even single female teachers, or the "Over Thirties," as he called them, because they could "be a mother to all," this approval only extended to single Protestant women. For him convents, or the "harem-monastery," in contrast, "blotted out all the instincts of female purity." Thus, the vision of female-led education rested on Anglo-American domestic feminism that contrasted with a Catholic, European, conventual model.[14]

Although the feminization of teaching began in New England, of special importance to Catherine Beecher and others was the potential influence of female teachers in the West. Fearing the combined influences of lawlessness, Native Americans, and Catholics in the growing frontier, Beecher urged women to enlist as missionary teachers in the West, to form, as Sklar put it, a "vanguard of settlement." The "Christian female teacher," claimed Beecher, would collect "ignorant children around her, teaching them habits of neatness, order and thrift; [and] opening the book of knowledge." In other words, she would instill Protestant middle-class values. Catherine's views reflected the concerns of her father, Lyman Beecher, whose published sermon, *A Plea for the West*, sounded the clarion call for Protestants to combat Catholic influence on the frontier a few years later. The surest means to defeat "superstition" and "despotism," he claimed, was for Protestant education to combat that offered by Catholics. Beecher the elder cited the growing number of convent schools, including those established by the Sisters of Charity, popping up throughout the West, in places such as the Mississippi River Valley, arguing that Catholics won over Protestant parents through cheap or charity schooling. "Can Jesuits and nuns," he asked, "be safely trusted to form the mind and opinions of the young hopes of this great nation? Is it not treason to commit the formation of republican children to such influences?" Beecher pled with his audiences to offer a Protestant alternative. Answering her father's call, Catherine Beecher helped support an organization that by 1847 had sent out over 450 Protestant female teachers to the West.[15]

Nuns established convent schools throughout America in the early nineteenth century. Elizabeth Anne Seton, an American Catholic convert and founder of the American congregation of the Sisters of Charity, established the first parochial school in the US in Emmitsburg, Maryland, in 1809. St. Joseph's Academy and Free School was dedicated to the education of Catholic girls. By 1846, the Sisters of Charity operated parochial schools, academies, and orphanages in Maryland, New York, Cincinnati, and New Orleans, and opened the first hospital west of the Mississippi, in St. Louis. Earlier, the Ursulines, a French order of nuns, had established a school in French New Orleans that continued operating after annexation. In subsequent decades, nuns from a variety of orders made homes in the US, many of them forming schools. Convent schools proliferated in large part in response to the growing number of immigrant communities. The School Sisters of Notre Dame, an order founded in Bavaria, served the growing number of German families moving out into the Midwest and frontier. Communities looked to the Sisters to ensure the survival of the German language and culture and to provide an education among their children. After a group of School Sisters first arrived in New York from Bavaria in 1847, they established schools in Baltimore, Detroit, Chicago, Milwaukee, Buffalo, Rochester, New York, and multiple cities in Missouri, Illinois, and Kentucky.[16]

The Sisters of the Sacred Heart formed in France in 1800 in the aftermath of the French Revolution. The order's founder, Madeline Sophia Barat, sought to fill the "void in Christian education left by the Revolution." In addition to the traditional vows of charity, celibacy, and poverty, the Sacred Heart Sisters also took a fourth vow: "the education of youth." By 1818, Sister Rose Philippine Duchesne set out with several women from the order for the US. After an eventful eleven-week voyage, she wrote back to France: "My dear Mother, As you can see, we are not yet dead." The women first arrived in New Orleans, where they stayed with the Ursulines for six weeks before heading up the Mississippi for Missouri. They built their first houses (also to serve as schools) in St. Charles and Florissant. Duchesne reported on the daily arrival of families coming to settle in what would soon be the twenty-fourth state in the Union. On September 14, 1818, the women opened the first free school for girls west of the Mississippi. By October they opened a boarding school and an "Indian seminary." Dealing with the privations of frontier life, the Sisters not only taught but also "dug in the garden, carried in firewood, tended the cow and cleaned the stable." Under the leadership of Sister Mary Hardy, a pupil in a Sacred Heart convent school who converted to Catholicism and became a nun, the order established twenty-five schools in the US, Canada, and Cuba before the Civil War.[17]

The Society of the Sisters of the Sacred Heart, along with most Catholic religious orders, offered a tiered education. In charity or "free schools," the Sisters taught reading, writing, spelling, arithmetic, and catechism. In boarding schools or academies, they added to this curriculum geography, grammar, music, art, and sewing. They also understood their teaching vocation broadly. Sounding similar to the reformers' rhetoric of domestic feminism, Sophia Barat wrote that nothing was "more pleasing to the heart of Jesus than devotion to the education of children as the most cherished portion of his flock." Yet in addition to teaching in academies, "poor schools," and schools for the deaf and mute (a special project they undertook), the Sisters of the Sacred Heart sought to teach "the adults in their congregations" and even educate "members of [their] communities." Indeed, as part of tightly knit immigrant communities, these nuns did not confine themselves within convent walls, but rather interacted with their communities as active members, understanding their educational vocation communally.[18]

In practice and curriculum, common schools differed little from convent schools. But in theory, Mann articulated a somewhat unique school system built on character training and moral development. "Arithmetic, grammar, and the other rudiments," he claimed in the *First Annual Report*, "comprise but a small part of the teachings in schools. The rudiments of feeling are taught not less than the rudiments of thinking. The sentiments and passions get more lessons than the intellect." Seeing sentiments and feelings as decidedly feminine attributes, Mann believed female teachers could best inculcate this curriculum. His aversion to corporal punishment also led him to embrace female teachers and the feminine ideals of moral suasion. Mann criticized the old mode of teaching under male instructors in New England, a system he claimed was characterized by "Authority, Force, Fear, [and] Pain!" In its place, he promoted instructing through the higher human instinct of love. Drawing on a familial model, Mann suggested that the basis of education should rest on "that powerful class of motives which consists of affections for parents [and] love for brothers and sisters." Mann also believed that public schooling was an "absolute right of every human being" and thereby charged the government with providing it, departing from the private or parochial school model. Mann believed both the pupil and the nation would benefit by an educational system that instilled moral virtue, patriotism, and a good work ethic among the nation's youth. With such a vision there was no room for other educational models.[19]

While common schools purported to be nonsectarian Christian institutions, a decidedly anti-Catholic tone was apparent from the start. Mann promoted a broadly Protestant instruction as a way to provide the nation's youth with the necessary moral and ethical training. He and other common school advocates saw no conflict in requiring the use of the Bible in public schools. "It breathes God's law and presents illustrious examples of conduct," argued Mann. He and his counterparts insisted on the use of the King James Version of the Bible, a Protestant version of the Bible and one they believed every Christian denomination could support. Pennsylvania passed the Free School Act, making the King James Bible a compulsory textbook, with other states following suit. To prevent criticism of using a sectarian text, school boards required the Bibles to be free from "note or comment" that might provide denominational interpretations. This appeased most Protestant groups, but not Catholics, who objected to the King James Version of the Bible and perceived a lack of interpretative commentary as a sectarian approach in itself.[20]

Debates between Catholics and Protestants over the Bible in public schools soon broke out into the so-called Bible Wars in New York and Philadelphia. Convent schools were not available to the entire growing Catholic community in these cities, and the prospect of sending children from Catholic families to public schools led some church spokespersons, such as New York's bishop John Hughes, to energetically object. The kind of Bible used in public schools was not the only thing that put Hughes on the defensive. McDuffy readers commonly used in public schools included anti-Catholic slurs, such as "papists," "popery," and "Priestcraft." One common school text described John Huss as a "zealous reformer from Popery" who foolishly trusted "himself to the deceitful Catholics." Hughes expressed opposition to Catholic tax dollars supporting such schools and requested government funds for Catholic education as an alternative. Perceiving Hughes's criticism of the King James Bible as opposition to the Bible altogether and his request for government funds for Catholic schools as a violation of the separation of church and state, the New York Public School Society dismissed Hughes's complaints, while anti-Catholic groups presented him as trying to rob the treasury to extend Romanism. For New York Protestants, this was just one more example of a Catholic conspiracy, serving to further entrench the idea that two forms of education, one Catholic and one Protestant, were competing for national influence.[21]

These debates coupled with rising tensions among immigrant and native-born groups boiled over into days of rioting in Philadelphia. After heated exchanges between the city's Catholics and Protestants over the use of the Bible in public schools, the Native American Republican Association, a nativist group that would merge into the American Party or the Know Nothings by the 1850s, convened a meeting. The platform of this organization rested on two issues: the restriction of the political rights of the city's growing (and often Catholic) immigrant population, and Protestant control of public schools. As members of the fledging party met on a May afternoon in Kensington in 1844 to specifically address the issue of the school debates, Irish intruders heckled the speakers and the crowd of over three hundred people before attempting to tear down the platform. The nativists retreated, but rescheduled their meeting for the next day. When that meeting, which attracted over three thousand people, was interrupted by a rain storm, members of the crowd ran for shelter to the Nanny Goat Market in an all-Irish neighborhood. The Irish blocked their entrance and the groups started fighting in the streets. The following day nativists returned to Kensington, setting fire to a row of Irish homes as some of the immigrants fired guns from their windows.[22]

While the emerging riot reflected personal, social, and ethnic conflicts among nativists and Irish immigrants who had lived and worked next to each other for years, the nativists soon after unleashed their wrath on the city's Sisters of Charity, suggesting a religious and gendered issue at hand also. They set fire to the fence around the convent school and threw stones into the windows. The Sisters were absent from the convent at the time, having taken up an assignment in Iowa. But when the caretaker, Mrs. Baker, came to the door, someone in the crowd threw a rock, striking her in the head. As the nativists continued to "kindle a fire for burning the school house," they were suddenly "saluted with new halt pecks of Irish bullets." According to one paper, a member of the Irish mob shot a man "through the heart." This precluded further destruction of the convent academy for the moment, but the nativists soon attacked St. Michael's parish. Like the mob that attacked the Ursuline convent in Charlestown, Massachusetts, a decade earlier, the rioters set fire to the building, pulled up shrubbery, and turned over old graves. One man claimed he acted on behalf "of the stars and the stripes." From here, they returned to the convent of the Sisters of Charity, torching the building without hesitation (Figure 4.2). By this time local authorities got involved, with militia units fanning out into the city. Thousands of citizens met in the state house, forming a "Police State" to aid the militia. After authorities dispersed the riots, one onlooker wrote, "Since noon this day one nunnery, one school, seven houses ... and three large Catholic churches have been burned to the ground." Casualties among both Irish and Anglo-American nativists tallied up to at least twenty-four people. Two months after the riots, a nativist-dominated grand jury placed the blame of the violence on poor law enforcement and the attempts of the Irish to exclude the Bible from public schools.[23]

To celebrate their victory, the Native American Republicans put on a lavish parade through Philadelphia's streets on July Fourth. Considered the most impressive

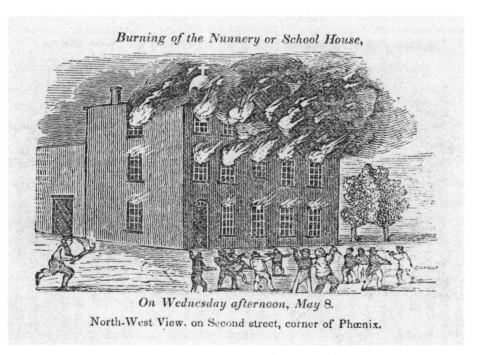

FIGURE 4.2. "Burning of the Nunnery or Schoolhouse," Philadelphia Bible Riots (1844). Courtesy of HathiTrust.

parade in the city's history, the marchers displayed banners and busts and marched to the sound of a triumphant band. One banner portrayed Columbia, the goddess of Liberty, with an American flag draped around her shoulders and an open Bible in her hand, the image symbolizing the school debate among the city's immigrant and native-born citizens. Above Lady Liberty's head perched an eagle holding a banner in its mouth that read "Beware of Foreign Influence." A serpent lay beneath her feet, symbolizing the defeat of Rome, akin to images of Mary with the Satan serpent crushed underfoot. Another banner displayed the face of George Washington's mother, with the inscription "To Mary, Mother of Washington." In opposition to the Catholic elevation of the Virgin Mary, "Mother of God," stood the mother of Washington and Columbia, two women, melded into one, representing the new Mary, the American Mary. Her male followers were patriots, not papists, and her female heirs were wives and mothers, not nuns.[24]

Like the burning of the Ursuline convent in 1834, the Philadelphia Bible Riots in part grew out of the culture created by anti-Catholic literature and sentiment that specifically mocked nuns and convent schools. William Hogan, a particularly notorious anti-Catholic speaker and author, and former Catholic priest, claimed to personally know all convents "to be places of sin, shame, and sorrow." Indeed, it was his "opposition to nunneries" that led him out of the priesthood and the Catholic Church. He published *Popery! As It Was and as It Is, Also, Auricular Confession and Popish Nunneries* in 1845. The book was reprinted at least ten times before 1860. In it, he described convents as "little fortifications" that "licentious, lecherous, profligate priests and monks" formed around nuns. Such places, he asserted, should not be tolerated by the "sons of free men" in America. Hogan also warned parents against sending their children to schools attached to "nunneries," for such schools provided the pathway to become a nun and thus to be "debauched."[25]

Hogan told his readers that all pupils in convent schools were forced to attend confession, a practice that "commences the ruin of the soul." Addressing American mothers, Hogan asked if it seemed at all appropriate for "a young lady, between the ages of twelve to twenty, to be on her knees, her lips nearly close pressed to the cheek of a priest, who in all probability is not over twenty-five or thirty years old." Hogan composed a hypothetical conversation between confessor and penitent, in which the priest, rather than simply listening to the confession of the girl, plants ideas in her mind of new sins. "Do you have any immodest thoughts?" "Do you not like thinking about any men?" "Would you ever like to sleep with them?" Continuing in this way, "day after day, week after week," explained Hogan, the "reptile confessor . . . works up her passions" until she becomes "his easy prey." From that point on, it was a simple decision for the young woman to become a nun, for either she fell in love with the priest or she feared public disgrace in the outside world. Sounding like some of the racier convent narratives from the 1830s, Hogan's book warned that life in a convent threatened female sexual purity. He especially related this fear to the influence of convent schools, warning parents of the alleged dangers of schools taught by nuns who would not protect their pupils from licentious priests. Unlike the ideal school and female teacher as imagined by Horace Mann and Catherine Beecher, nuns and convents according to Hogan represented a grave danger to American women and the fate of the nation.[26]

The publication of *Popery!* included a number of illustrations reinforcing the idea that nuns were the wrong kind of women, devoid of maternal instincts, and that convents threatened female gender ideals, the home, and the family. One image featured a young woman, kneeling vulnerably before the lap of a priest in a private room (Figure 4.3). Their faces nearly touch, as the "reptile confessor" hovers over the "young lady," illustrating his access to women and the precariousness of the situation. In a second image, entitled "Mother Abbess Strangling the Infant," a nun callously pinches the nostrils of a baby, committing infanticide (Figure 4.4). Toward the end of the book, Hogan related a scene in which the father of a young girl tricked into joining a convent tracks down a priest who seduced her. "The Father in Pursuit of the Priest" reflected the common belief that convents threatened the home, breaking up family life and keeping young women from fulfilling their duties to parents, husbands, and children (Figure 4.5).[27]

A YOUNG LADY CONFESSING TO THE PRIEST.—Part II, p. 34

FIGURE 4.3. "A Young Lady Confessing to the Priest," printed in *Popery! As It Was and as It Is.*
Courtesy of HathiTrust.

MOTHER ABBESS STRANGLING THE INFANT—Part II., p. 62.

FIGURE 4.4. "Mother Abbess Strangling the Infant," printed in *Popery! As It Was and as It Is*. Courtesy of HathiTrust.

THE FATHER IN PURSUIT OF THE PRIEST.—Part III., p. 113

FIGURE 4.5. "The Father in Pursuit of the Priest," printed in *Popery! As It Was and as It Is*. Courtesy of HathiTrust.

Nuns in the US were aware of the at times hostile environment in which they lived and worked. In 1836, Philippine Duchesne of the Society of the Sisters of the Sacred Heart wrote to her cousin back in France about the difficulty of establishing convents in the US, where "sects tirelessly [attempt] to make all the Nunneries crumble since, to them, they are houses of the Devil and idolatry." Duchesne continued, describing a "war [against the Catholic Church] evident in newspapers that repeat the absurdities they copy from each other." In reference to the burning of Mount Benedict in 1834, she wrote, "already many churches have been burned in addition to the beautiful Ursuline Convent . . . whose culprits are known but not punished." During the Philadelphia Bible Riots of 1844, Mary Hardy, who served as "vicar general" of the Sacred Heart Sisters, feared for the lives of her Sisters. Writing a few days after the riots, Hardy described the event as "the almost general massacre of Catholics and the destruction of churches." Out of fear of attack against the convent schools, she wrote that "parents withdrew their children," and "for several nights we kept ourselves in readiness." When Hardy traveled between Sacred Heart houses in different cities and states, something she did with remarkable frequency, she always wore "secular attire" and used the title "Mrs." or "Miss" rather than "Mother," so as not to draw negative attention from onlookers who despised the presence of nuns. At a time when the female teacher was becoming immortalized, these nuns knew they were still seen as unacceptable women.[28]

The School Sisters of Notre Dame also learned this lesson quickly. After establishing a school in Wisconsin, one Sister reported that if they went outside, "stones struck them, [and] youths came up from behind and chalked their backs with white crosses." The streets filled with shouts of "Deport the Papists! Parochial schools teach lies! Nuns are slaves and a menace!" We were "bitterly scorned and ridiculed in venomous publications," continued one of the School Sisters, and forced to endure "lewd songs" that "Know-Nothings" sang outside their houses, and the "occasional rock crashing through an upper window." While some nuns were all too aware that some of their neighbors despised them and their life choices and that rumors about convent life circulated in the press and popular publications, the parochial school system nevertheless expanded. Alongside the growing public school system, these represented two visions of education and womanhood in a divided nation.[29]

The hostility that nuns confronted represented a cultural divide between a growing Victorian middle-class model of the ideal home, family, and domestic or "true" woman and a worldview that valued female celibacy and communal living. The lack of association of marriage and motherhood with teaching rendered nuns who nevertheless embraced the feminine vocation of teaching unacceptable. Indeed, marriage and motherhood as portrayed in prescriptive and fictional literature, particularly by the 1840s, achieved divine heights. For a woman not to aspire to this allegedly natural and divinely appointed role posed a problem. *Parent's Magazine*, a publication whose name reflected the growing preoccupation with child-rearing, praised marriage as the "foundation for society, on which the whole superstructure of morality and piety rests." As an institution dating back to Creation, marriage and the subsequent family represented God's greatest design for man. There was nothing more suited to the "general welfare" and "piety and happiness" than the family. *Parent's Magazine* extended high hopes regarding the potential of the well-run family and home. In the right kind of home "no parent, and no child would be found looking abroad into the bustling, out-of-door world, for social comforts, since no terrestrial paradise, occupied by *strangers*, could in the case supposed, at all compare . . . with the charms of *home*." The ideal home largely depended on the mother. While the virtues of home existed in "the whole family circle," they were "most clearly exhibited in those unaccountable emotions of parents, particularly of the mother." In a world of "tribulations," the "domestic fireside" provided a retreat— "a little sanctuary . . . quite on the verge of heaven." In other words, mothers were charged with bringing heaven to Earth. The hope of the female teacher rested on the wife and mother, who might extend her "little sanctuary" to the school room and the world.[30]

The repeated warnings by William Hogan, Rachel McCrindell, Lyman Beecher, and others that convent schools lured women away from this "little sanctuary" rather than preparing them to officiate over it were not completely unfounded. Just as convent narratives warned, sometimes female pupils in convent schools did decide to become nuns themselves. Two young girls raised and educated in an orphanage run by the School Sisters of the Sacred Heart in St. Louis joined the order after living among the Sisters for eight years. The most influential convent school convert was Mary Hardy, whom Sophia Barat called her "first American daughter." Hardy joined the Society of the Sisters of the Sacred Heart after attending the Institute for the Education of Young Ladies run by the Sacred Heart Sisters in Grand Choteau, Louisiana, much to the chagrin of her father. By age forty-one, she assumed the responsibility of "all the American houses" in the order. There were also opportunities for women to contribute to the mission of the Sacred Heart Sisters and other orders if they wished, without taking religious vows. In 1829, the St. Louis diocese approved of the formation of the Confraternity of the Sacred Heart, where women could freely become members. By joining a confraternity, more of a religious association than a vocation, a woman could still marry and have children. Anti-Catholic literature never referenced confraternities, portraying a starker divide between nuns and other women, convents, homes, and schools.[31]

The notion, however, that nuns and priests tricked, duped, and conspired against young, naïve girls, luring them into converting or "taking the veil," pointed more toward the fear among nativists and anti-Catholics than the reality of life in a convent school. Leaders of female religious orders were selective about who they allowed into the club. First and foremost, a candidate needed a "vocation" or signs of a genuine calling to the religious life—a life to which a select few were believed to be called. Sophia Barat lamented the ease with which Mary Hardy admitted new candidates. "For Heaven's sake be more demanding in accepting candidates!" she wrote to her "American daughter." "Vocation first and last." In another letter, she complained of "How many subjects in both worlds [Europe and America] have been accepted without previous investigation, without testing, and—let it be said—without vocation." Barat expressed a strong belief that the society was only as good as its members, and she feared that those not suited to the life of the nun, women who were "like whipped cream, all froth and no substance," would bring down the group. Philippine Duchesne likewise encouraged Sisters to give possible novices "a true picture of the position: inconveniences of every kind, beginning with lodging, and extending to the food that is often disgusting, rigorous cold and oppressive heat." Far from a seduction ploy through flattery, candy, and "calculated ceremonies," nuns intentionally kept their numbers small and were weary of new members.[32]

Perhaps out of concern that female domesticity was being threatened from various fronts in the changing society of antebellum America, some reformers continually reasserted that the purpose of female education was to prepare a woman to run a household. Historian Jo Anne Preston found that women teachers between 1830 and 1860 increasingly called for better wages, greater education, and independence as they continued taking up positions in schools. In response, school reformers stressed the need for girls and young women to be trained to run a household. A *Parent's Magazine* author wrote, "I would have a female qualified for her station as a wife, mother, and mistress of a family." Her "mental improvement," continued the article, "should be associated with a correct knowledge in household affairs. She who is to preside over a family, should be most intimately acquainted with everything that can preserve order or promote comfort." As discussions of female teaching led to questions of what type of education women should receive, *Parent's Magazine* concluded that "all the time must not be given to books." Such an unpractical education "may do very well for maidens, or aunts, but . . . they'll never make *wives*." Continuing in this vein, the article warned its readers (likely female) that a woman who creates a comfortable house and is trained in "cleanliness, neatness, frugality, and order" is less likely to have husband or child "wander from home for comfort."[33]

The opposition to convent schools represented a growing national concern with the education of the nation's children, particularly "the future accomplished mothers of American citizens." As Rebecca Reed argued earlier, the question of convent schools "was not about sects or creeds," but about the training of America's women. The popularity of *Protestant Girl in a French Nunnery*, other convent narratives that focused on schools, and the writings of William Hogan pointed to a heightened fear of the influence of convent schools. The development of the common school movement advanced in response to this fear. As Catherine Beecher called for "female missionary teachers" in the West and the Bible Riots broke out in Philadelphia, Americans fought a contest for cultural influence particularly over the education and vocation of young women. In the midst of the national debate over education, parents received special attention. Parents (especially mothers) were at once praised for their divine role in raising children and warned against dangerous forms of education for their daughters. And the stakes were high. They could either prepare daughters for marriage and motherhood or destroy their feminine sensibilities, send them to a living grave, and tear away at the moral fabric of society.

At a time when stories like "The Young Music Teacher" encouraged teaching as a noble pursuit for women, nuns who taught schoolchildren faced taunts and jeers in the streets. They confronted unflattering portrayals of themselves in books and newspapers. Rather than being lauded as "heavenly appointed instructors of young children," who were most suited to "shape national morality," nuns appeared as coconspirators against the youth, threatening the nation's women. Even as teaching became feminized in the 1840s, nuns remained outsiders, embodying the wrong kind of women. By rejecting a life of marriage and motherhood, the nun in no way conformed to the ideal crafted by reformers who justified the feminization of teaching on the basis of its association with a woman's guardianship of the home. Not being wives or mothers furthermore disqualified nuns from raising up young women when the primary purpose of female education was understood by many to be preparation for a domestic life.

With little nuance or ambiguity, antebellum nativists, anti-Catholics, and reformers illustrated a strict dichotomy between domestic female Protestant teachers and nuns, and the division would only grow into a more political concern in the following decade.

We don't believe in Nunneries, where beauty that was made to bloom and beam on the world is immured and immolated, not to say prostituted.
—*The Wide Awake Gift: A Know-Nothing Token*, 1855

After a brief season of hollow pleasure, . . . she sinks willingly to the lowest type of human degradation—the common prostitute; the pure and gentle woman, capable of all high holy duties and affections as wife and mother . . . goes in utter recklessness of herself and all the world.
—*New York by Gas-Light*, 1856

5

Hidden Dangers

CONVENT CELLARS, CITY HAUNTS,

AND THE RISE OF DARK-LANTERN POLITICS

"NEW YORK BY GAS-LIGHT! What a task we have undertaken! To penetrate beneath the thick veil of night and lay bare the fearful mysteries of darkness in the metropolis," announced the opening lines of *New York by Gas-Light*. George Foster's "story of the underground" promised a sneak peek into "the festivities of prostitution, the orgies of pauperism, the haunts of theft and murder, the scenes of drunkenness and beastly debauch, and all the sad realities that go to make up the lower stratum." While the growing urban centers in America may have appeared as bastions of progress to some, Foster countered with the "terrible secrets" that lurked below the city's shimmering surface. Published one year earlier, in 1849, Ned Buntline's *The Mysteries and Miseries of New York* similarly illustrated "scenes of vice and horror" in the growing metropolis, from "the gambling palaces of Gotham" to the "dens of infamy where thieves and beggars congregate." Both authors also covered a staple of the urban underground: the brothel. Buntline bemoaned "how many a poor, now wretched and degraded female has been driven into the paths of infamy by neglect, when one kind word and one helping hand would have saved her." Only one other type of woman concerned Buntline this much: the nun. Indeed, he also wrote convent narratives, penning *The Beautiful Nun* alongside tales of urban corruption. His and other popular works in the 1840s and 1850s reflected a preoccupation with hidden dangers. In this milieu, city and convent, drunkard and priest, prostitute and nun came to represent similar fears and fantasies brought into relief by ideals of domesticity and true womanhood.[1]

In the face of rapid industrialization and urbanization in the US by the 1840s, city mysteries became a literary mainstay. A flurry of works depicting a corrupt urban underworld appeared with enticing titles such as *Mysteries of City Life*, *The Mysteries and Miseries of New York*, *New York Naked*, and *The Quaker City*. They reflected real concerns about urban centers, including the growing economic gap, anonymity and hypocrisy, and temptations of alcohol, gambling, and sex. In bringing hidden pleasures and dangers to light, authors of city mysteries championed their books as harbingers of social justice and reform. Foster's *New York by Gas-Light* would help Americans "discover the real facts of the actual conditions of the wicked and wretched classes—so that Philanthropy and Justice may plant their blows aright." Buntline dedicated his *Mysteries and Miseries of New York* to the clergy of the city in the hope "that they may see and remedy the evils which it describes." In some ways the writings of city mysteries laid the groundwork for later exposé and muckraking journalism such as that by Jacob Riis, whose *How the Other Half Lives* vividly illustrated the dire conditions of the urban poor.[2]

Yet unlike Riis or Ida Tarbell, city mystery authors blurred the lines between fact and fiction, relying on one-dimensional villains and victims and sensational portrayals of criminal conspiracies, sex, and violence. Some authors openly adopted the title of "romance" for their books and incorporated gothic elements, such as haunted mansions and sinister supernatural beings. Indeed, many of the works fit more comfortably within the category of melodramatic fiction than journalism. City mystery authors may well have desired urban reform, but they also wanted their books to sell. Otherwise, Ned Buntline would have gone by his real name: Judson Edward Zane Carroll. To boost sales, authors interspersed real biographical information and architectural illustrations with lurid fictional narratives of vice and tragedy. Literary critic David Reynolds described the genre as "immoral reform writing," noting that the "hyperbolic sensationalism and voyeuristic eroticism compromise[d] whatever political message it might contain."[3]

City mysteries became instant bestsellers, profiting in part from the recent introduction of the revolving cylinder press used by new mass publishers in large cities. They were part of the first "paperback revolution" in which thrillers and sentimental novels flourished as they could be sold cheaply with paperback covers. Authors basked in the popularity of their wares. "No American novel has ever commanded so wide an interest as this work," announced George Lippard in reference to his own Philadelphia-set book, *The Quaker City; or, The Monks of Monk Hall*. Self-promotion aside, his book nevertheless sold sixty thousand copies in its first year of publication and about thirty thousand each year for the following five years. Likewise, in its first year, *The Mysteries and Miseries of New York* sold over one hundred thousand copies. George Foster's *New York by Slices*, appearing initially in serial form in the

New York Tribune, sold around forty thousand copies in its first year. His follow-up work, *New York by Gas-Light*, exceeded expectations, quickly going through three editions in its first month. Newspapers spoke of the "unparalleled demand" for his book, which went on to sell approximately two hundred thousand copies. Moreover, *Quaker City* shared a position with only one other book as a bestseller before the appearance of *Uncle Tom's Cabin*. That other book was Maria Monk's *Awful Disclosures of the Hotel Dieu Nunnery*.[4]

In some obvious ways, city mystery authors copied previously published convent narratives. Escaped nun tales appeared an entire decade before the publication of the first American city mystery. As early as 1836, Maria Monk's *Awful Disclosures* unveiled a vice-ridden underworld where naïve, vulnerable women became entrapped in a life of debauchery. Disguised villains, a mainstay of city mysteries, appeared earlier in George Bourne's 1832 convent narrative, *Lorette*, which included a cast of seemingly pious, yet plotting priests and abbesses. Before city mysteries depicted the intricate trap set by the mirage of urban glamor that entangled naïve young men and women new to the city in vice and poverty, convent narratives repeatedly delineated the "imprisonment" of young women lured into convents under false pretenses. From their earliest publications, convent narratives also included a perplexing combination of seemingly virtuous calls for reform within pages full of seamy details—a format the city mystery authors later mastered. With his own novels "crowded with lustful priests, secret revelers, and demonic tortures," explained David Reynolds, city mystery author George Lippard was clearly influenced by anti-Catholic literature that came before. While responding to new developments in American society, city mysteries also harkened back to and reinforced old fears and appealed to conventional domestic ideals regarding women and the family.[5]

City mysteries and convent narratives helped drive the growing nativist movement of the antebellum era. Nativist works warned that America's enemies "abound[ed] chiefly in cities" where "they could more easily plot mischief . . . and communicate with foreign powers," such as the pope. Urban tales likewise often cast city vice as something "foreign," championing a return to simple American virtue. In addition to writing city mysteries, Lippard penned hyperpatriotic American histories, such as *Washington and His Men; or, The Legends of the Revolution* and *Blanche of Brandywine: An American Patriotic Spectacle*. His biographer argued that Lippard's "veneration of the Founding Fathers verged on the religious." At a time when nativist fraternal societies such as the Order of the Star Spangled Banner and the Order of United Americans saw new chapters popping up throughout the US, the *Democratic Standard* described Lippard's books as "enduring monuments of National Patriotism and the brightest record of American glory." Although Lippard regularly criticized nativists and poked fun at prominent Protestant preachers in his writings, at times he reflected nativist patriotism, suspicion of foreigners, and anti-Catholic sentiment. In its description of the Five Points District, his *Glimpses of New York* echoed nativist complaints of "other nations . . . daily sending their paupers here." Similarly, Buntline, though a radical Democrat, published anti-Catholic convent narratives alongside city mysteries and became an active member of the Know Nothings. Convent narratives, city mysteries, and nativist screeds alike contrasted an Edenic America with Old World corruption and urban decay, warning of an enemy within that threatened women, family, and the nation.[6]

As city mysteries and convent narratives expounded on the dangers of cities and "nunneries," nativist spokespersons warned that the nation itself was becoming a house of debauchery with the influx of foreigners. In his 1850 address, "American Liberty: Its Sources, Its Dangers, and the Means of Its Preservation," prominent Order of United Americans member Alfred Ely chastened his countrymen for "mak[ing] the temple of our liberties a great charnel house of licentiousness." By suffering "ourselves to be the receptacle of ignorance, superstition, and vice," he lamented, " 'our inheritance shall be turned to strangers and our houses to aliens' and ourselves left desolate in the land of our fathers." Their description of a nation being contaminated by vice sounded much like the warnings against Catholic convents and urban brothels in popular print culture. With reoccurring terms such as "licentiousness," "Whore of Babylon," "debauchery," and "vice," nativist warnings, convent narratives, and city mysteries became interchangeable, prompting Americans to equate foreigner, Catholic, nun, prostitute, and corruption as one looming threat.[7]

Members of the rising nativist fraternal orders reinvigorated and further politicized anti-Catholicism and the movement against convents. Nativist books were littered with anti-Catholic diatribes, evidenced in the title of Thomas Whitney's definitive work on the Order of the United Americans (which he helped found): *A Defense of the American Policy, as Opposed to the Encroachments of Foreign Influence, and Especially to the Interference of the Papacy*. Nativist spokespersons regularly asked such questions as "Can a Papist Be a Citizen of the American Republic?" (answer: no). Leading nativists, such as Whitney and John Dowling, explicitly aligned the movement to "keep America American" with the crusade against convents. Thomas Whitney not only laid out a "code of principles" and a strategy to "release our country from the thralldom of foreign domination" that would come to define the American Party platform but also commemorated Maria Monk's *Awful Disclosures of the Hotel Dieu* as a work "almost everyone has heard of" and promoted the publication of *The Escaped Nun* in 1855 as a book "the Jesuits cannot suppress." He reported not only on the increasing number of "aliens" in America but also on the growth of convents in the US, citing with alarm that "In 1808 there were but two Female Academies . . . [while]

in 1855 there are *one hundred and seventeen* Female Academies." The object of such, he told his readers, "is to obtain Protestant young ladies as scholars" in the hopes of converting and confining them. Dowling likewise described convents as "dark prison houses of slavery, corruption, and despair" hidden by a "veil of concealment." As the nativist movement took on more of a definitive shape and as city mysteries began to flourish in the 1840s and '50s, the campaign against convents only swelled.[8]

Popular literature and nativist rhetoric of the antebellum era revealed a preoccupation with exposing a hidden enemy within. City mysteries and convent narratives paraded a cast of disguised villains before readers. Supposing that some of the worst dangers to American life assumed the appearance of goodness, convent narratives frequently referred to the "cloak of religion" under which priests and nuns hid their inner wickedness. Things were never as they appeared: seemingly respectable priests harbored harems, Mother Superiors were anything but maternal, and the nun, who told the world she was contented in her chosen vocation, lived as a captive slave. References to a priest's robe, the Jesuit's "mask," and a nun's veil all conveyed the idea of costume, a covering of one's true identity. *The Escaped Nun*, appearing in 1855, elaborated on the deception of the Mother Superior who "excelled in the art of hypocrisy," luring the unassuming into convents. "Oh how these Superiors are enveloped in artifice." As with a spell, "she lulls you into tranquility, she decoys you into her snares, she fascinates you." *Sister Agnes* confirmed "the depth of villainy which lurked below their polished and dignified exterior." The character of "Friar Anselmo," explained Benjamin Barker, in his book *Celia; or, The White Nun of the Wilderness*, "was merely to illustrate how the deepest and most detestable villains may be covered by the assumed cloak of religious sanctity."[9]

The scope of Catholic deception extended beyond convent walls. Some books described nuns and priests as enemies who infiltrated American homes and families as confessors, teachers, and domestic servants. *The Female Jesuit*, published in 1851, described a Catholic domestic servant and tutor who was actually an authentic "spy-nun" for Rome. The "Jesuitess" traveled "from convent to convent, from country to country," carrying out a "perfect system of espionage." Having pledged "obedience, absolute and unconditional, without question to the consequences," she unwaveringly earned the confidences of her wards, particularly Protestant children, the object being conversion, family division, and increased membership of the Sisterhood. Like convent narratives of the 1840s, which focused largely on the threats faced by young girls in convent schools, *The Female Jesuit* warned Protestant parents against sending their children to convent schools—"the very heart of popery"—and against employing Catholic female domestics, who could be spies. Some of the female spies with their deceptive abilities even preyed on the sympathies of Protestant families by pretending to be escaped nuns in need of asylum. No one was safe against these women, "always at work, plotting and counterplotting." In an obvious slur (and inaccurate appellation), Thomas Whitney claimed that all the convents in the US fell "under the management of Jesuitical nuns." If there was anything worse or more dangerous than a Jesuit, "it was a Jesuitess." The deceptive witchlike characteristics of these nuns reflected the belief that such women were not true women, not women to be trusted, not women who might contribute to the virtue of the republic, but ones who threatened it.[10]

With repeated use of words like "mystery," "hidden," "exposed," and "unveiled," city mysteries displayed a near obsession with deception as well. The development of urban centers contributed to a growing rate of geographic and social mobility as people flocked to the cities for economic opportunities, novelty, and a new life. In contrast to the more personal smaller towns, cities allowed for anonymity, which could be welcomed or feared. In this "urban social world where many of the people who met face-to-face each day were strangers," explained historian Karen Halttunen, "the question 'Who are you really?' assumed even greater significance." Advice books, conduct manuals, and city mysteries warned against hypocrites on the city streets who deceived the trusting. They often focused on two deceptive archetypes of the city: "the confidence man" and "the painted woman." Painted women, or prostitutes who posed as respectable ladies, enticed naïve male city-goers. While he would have otherwise avoided conversation with women of ill repute, he willingly gave his attention to the painted lady who only at the opportune time revealed her true identity. *New York by Gas-Light* exposed readers to the women who "passed for virtuous and respectable wives, mothers, and daughters," while their true "licentiousness had not yet been discovered." As such women feigned respectability, they mocked the good wife and mother, endangering the family and home life that centered on true womanhood.[11]

The confidence or "con" man first appeared in Buntline's *The G'hals of New York*, published in 1850. Conmen displayed the outward signs of Christian virtue to win the trust of unsuspecting strangers for subversive purposes. The most often cited example of this was the conman asking a stranger if he had the "confidence" to lend him his watch. After the trusting stranger not accustomed to the impersonal ways of the city lent his timepiece, the conman would chuckle at his theft as he walked away. The conman could also just be someone who presented one image by day and another by night. Hidden under his "gentlemanly dress," wrote Buntline, existed a character "black, vile, and devilish." In *The Quaker City*, George Lippard told of "goodly citizens, whose names you never hear without the addition of 'respectable,' 'celebrated,' or 'pious,'" who nevertheless clandestinely reveled in brothels, gambling dens, and saloons. Indeed, in Lippard's book just about every character donned a cloak of deception in what he described as a world of "deceits and confidences." While a uniquely American ironic character, the conman also grew out of portrayals of priests, especially Jesuits, so often depicted in convent narratives, who hid under the "cloak of religion," assumed a pious reputation, and preyed on the trusting.[12]

Fear of a deceptive, internal enemy was a quintessential facet of nineteenth-century nativism, driving the formation of nativist fraternal organizations underground before they eventually united and emerged as the American Party. As the numbers of Catholic immigrants piling onto American shores swelled, nativist spokespersons sounded a warning. In his address before the Order of United Americans, Thomas Whitney described "Romanism" as a "treacherous enemy lurking in our midst, under the mantle of feigned sanctity." After providing statistical information on the growing number of Catholics and Catholic institutions in "Protestant America," he described the creeping influence of Rome as "pervading" and "subtle." If not detected and rooted out, such an enemy could destroy "the independent, prosperous, powerful, and happy" character of the country. This view of a secret enemy inspired nativists to be covert themselves, embracing "dark-lantern politics," complete with secret meetings, passwords, handshakes, and a refrain members offered inquiring outsiders: "I know nothing." Whitney described the birth of the Order of United Americans this way: "Silently, deeply, beyond the headless gaze of the self-confident partisan, and the more wary wiles of the scheming Jesuit, the Order of United Americans moved onward . . . and like a subterranean streamlet" undermined political "groundwork" and "papal encroachment." "Its watchword was passed from city to city and from state to state, and its influence, like the wind, felt though still unseen, accumulated at every step." The fear of hidden dangers prompted a counterinsurgency among nativists who took to the underground to spread their roots and grow. The harvest of American Party electoral gains by 1854 was sown in part by repeated warnings against the secret dangers of Gotham and Rome and visions of a republic made virtuous by true women.[13]

Fear of a hidden enemy presupposed a certain level of vulnerability. In contrast to the calculating confidence man or the jaded painted lady stood young, naïve, country-bred men and women new to the city. Such vulnerable youth wilted before myriad novel temptations and deceptive strangers. Lippard's *Quaker City* described oyster cellars as places where "Hope, so young, so gay, so light-hearted has gone down and come up transformed into a very devil, with sunken cheeks, bleared eyes, and a cankered heart." In the city, "many a young man is ruined," explained *Glimpses of New York*. The innocent youth simply could not resist the glittering façade of the gambling halls or saloons. Here the promise, health, and piety of a young man eroded after he became trapped in the city's snares. He got into debt over his head and spent his energy and youth fighting or whoring in a drunken state. One author described how a "gentleman from Ohio" came to New York to sell "flour, bacon, and hams," only to be "taken in and done for by a set of sharks." After asking for directions, the "sharks"—a man-and-woman team—directed the Ohioan to a party, whereupon they got him drunk and robbed him. In explaining the deception, the author lamented, "They can spot a countryman forty rods."[14]

Despite expressing scorn for prostitutes, city mysteries often depicted "fallen women" as vulnerable victims who lost their virtue after being seduced. In 1831, the first New York Magdalen Report claimed that many prostitutes were the "daughters of . . . respectable and pious citizens." With "promises of marriage," villainous men lured them from their homes, "deceiving them into a brothel." Imprisoned there, the "unhappy girls . . . gave themselves up to intemperance and crime." "Multitudes of young creatures are continually deluded, inveigled, enticed, or surprised into the path of ruin, by means of the vilest artifices," related the report. City mysteries reflected this conviction that prostitutes had been tricked into their lives of vice and then became stuck there. In *Mysteries and Miseries of New York*, Buntline portrayed prostitutes as victims of monstrous men. "I do not, with all the world, condemn, upbraid, and curse the poor, hapless courtesans of the town," he wrote. "I *pity* more than I condemn, for two-thirds of them are driven to that life by the perfidy of men, and not by their own evil passions." Foster described women "still young and fresh and fair, with the bloom of womanly innocence" passing a brief transition "between the purity and peace of virtue and the swinish hell of filth and abomination into which the victim hastens to plunge." The perception of prostitutes as victims elevated the social status of these women in a sense by not blaming them for their lifestyles. It also supposed that such women were vulnerable, in need of saving and male protection, and that female virtue and domesticity were in danger.[15]

Similarly, nuns appeared as defenseless, desperate women who had simply been duped into taking religious vows. After posing the question as to why any woman would place herself "in a living, loathsome, and impure grave," such as a convent, William Brownlee, president of the Protestant Reformation Society, blamed youth, inexperience, delusion, and romanticism. "Like little thoughtless children," he wrote, such women were "misled by the arts of priests and nuns." Hypnotized by "baubles and ceremonies," the "young and imaginative" became infatuated with convents "as they would upon any other delusive and theatrical spectacle." Such women, he continued, needed "care," "counsel," and someone to "warn and convince them of their danger." *Nuns and Nunneries* likewise explained that priests and Mother Superiors "beset" young women susceptible to "romantic and sentimental impressions," convincing them of the "heavenly state of a nun" and that being a wife and mother were "dangerous [to] the soul's health." Like city mystery descriptions of prostitutes, convent narratives offered a sharp contrast between the youthful, beautiful, innocent woman and the degraded, miserable, old nun. Convents hid, "immured," and "prostituted" the beauty of women, claimed one book. Much like real prostitutes, these writers cast nuns as vulnerable victims either beyond help or in need of rescue, suggesting a vulnerability of women and the belief that life in a convent could never be one of a woman's own and unmitigated choosing.[16]

Even if she was tricked into a brothel or a cloister, popular literature often made the prostitute and the nun suffer greatly for their choices. Not being married and not having male protection rendered these women susceptible to some of the worst tortures and deaths authors could describe. One of the most shocking scenes in *Awful Disclosures* was the murder of St. Francis Patrick, who was trampled to death under a mattress. In Buntline's *The Beautiful Nun* (Figure 5.1), Sister Ursula "suffered

FIGURE 5.1. *The Beautiful Nun.*
Courtesy of HathiTrust.

all that human existence could endure." Her body was "stretched upon the accursed rack," her "white and polished arms . . . fastened to a steel bar" by a cord that "cut through flesh, muscle, and nerve to the very bone!" As she spun "thick clots of gore fell on the stone." Buntline elaborated on the "fair and half-naked form" of the woman, "its symmetry convulsing . . . the bosom palpitating . . . and the exquisitely modeled limbs enduring all the pain of dislocation."[17]

In a rather bizarre scene in Buntline's *Mysteries and Miseries of New York*, a mother's dream of her daughter's death foreshadowed the real fate that awaited her after becoming a prostitute. The dream depicted a young woman encircled by a snake until "her tongue stuck out from her mouth, and the blood streamed down from bursting veins upon her bosom." Before long, she was "a crushed, blackened, and shapeless mass." Not as gruesome, but equally dismal, a prostitute in Foster's *New York Naked* died an early death from "drink, disease, and starvation." She breathed her last breath all alone "on a wretched pallet in a filthy garret." Such brutal descriptions of the torture and death of beautiful women reflected at once what Karen Halttunen has referred to as the "pornography of pain" and what Daniel Cohen has described as the "beautiful female murder victim" motif, both popular in nineteenth-century sensational literature. In this theme, it was always a particular type of woman, an unmarried woman who embraced nonnormative gender roles and lived in a community of alleged sexual deviance, who endured excruciating suffering.[18]

Whether victim or villain, in early nineteenth-century print culture, nuns and prostitutes stood as archetypes of the wrong kind of woman. Motherhood (preceded by marriage) promised a better society, while nuns and prostitutes anticipated the nation's ruin. *New York by Gas-Light* made the contrast for society clear, describing a prostitute as the "lowest type of human degradation" who "goes in utter recklessness of herself and all the world," compared to "the pure and gentle woman capable of all high, holy duties and affections as wife and mother." The nun-prostitute single woman threatened the ideals of marriage and motherhood, and as such, the republic. She imperiled patriarchal society, a man's exclusive rights to a woman's body, the unpaid though valuable contributions of women in the domestic economy, and the promise of a safe, warm, and loving home. "With no duties to fulfill, no motives to activity," as one male reformer in *Female Convents* asked, "of what value [is the nun] to society?" In convent narratives and city mysteries alike, women who shirked these duties debilitated rather than contributed to society. And they suffered dire consequences for their choices.[19]

Members of nativist fraternal orders extolled the characteristics of the ideal American woman, as one who contributed mightily to the health of the republic. In *The Wide-Awake Gift: A Know-Nothing Token for 1855*, one chapter lauded "American Women." "In all the world are there none so gentle and brave," it read. The author attributed the nation's "wealth and fame" to "the race of noble American mothers," noting that "the stamina of a nation depends on the character of its women." "Good mothers!" chanted the author. Such was the country's greatest asset and greatest need. "If the mothers are intelligent and virtuous . . . poverty, bondage, and shame can never come upon the land." While the author praised such women, encouraging the "emulation" of their virtues, he also warned against a movement away from the ideal American woman. Without virtuous mothers, he claimed, "the sap begins to dry at the nation's root, and the most vital element of our endurance and strength will gradually pass away, leaving the tree of Freedom . . . rotten in the trunk." To avoid rotting from the inside out, the author urged the cultivation of true womanhood. "Teach her to love home and country, to honor parents and old age, to practice industry, and to respect sacred things; in short, educate her as a daughter fitly to become the wife of a freeman and the mother of freemen." In a similar vein, Sarah Joseph Hale's popular *Ladies' Magazine* described motherhood as the most "dignified office" for women. Through their influence, mothers could bring about "a new, a better, a holier world." On the one hand, this elevation of the role of motherhood elevated the status of women, casting their role as mothers (a role not always appreciated) as a vital one. On the other, it precluded appreciation or acceptance of other roles for women. Believing the health of the republic to be resting on virtuous motherhood, no alternatives could be tolerated.[20]

City mysteries, nativist rhetoric, and convent narratives presented worlds of darkness and light, contrasting Christian gentlemen and conmen, fallen and true women, alien and native son. Perhaps the most striking contrast was between the Victorian home and the city or convent. Against the warm, inviting, safe hearth stood seedy underground hovels and gloomy convent cells. George Foster told of "rats [that] gnawed the wainscot along the thick, old walls" of a city bawdyhouse. Although nuns lived in convents as their homes, authors spurned the title for such abodes, opting instead to refer to them as "prisons," nuns as prisoners or "inmates," and priests as criminals. In his 1853 book tellingly titled *Priests' Prisons for Women*, Andrew Cross, a Presbyterian minister and coeditor of the anti-Catholic *Baltimore Literary and Religious Magazine*, called for public protection of "imprisoned" nuns. Cross even compared convents to debtor's prison, writing, "Our state has abolished imprisonment of men for debt . . . ere long we shall ask them to abolish the imprisonment of women who are not in debt to the priests." References to cells, bars, locked doors, and gloomy stone walls solidified the idea of convents as prisons. Reimagining the convent "grate" often used in European convents for cloistered nuns, *Sister Agnes* described its title character "screaming wildly" from behind bars for someone to save her (Figure 5.2).[21]

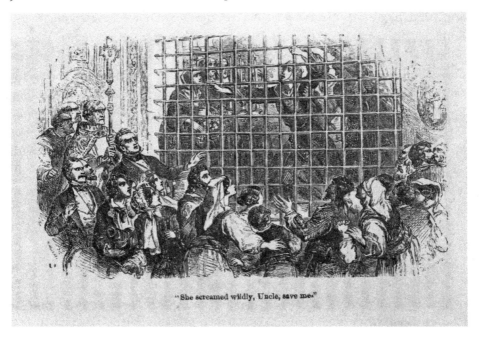

"She screamed wildly, Uncle, save me."

FIGURE 5.2. *Sister Agnes.*
Courtesy of HathiTrust.

At a time when the ideal home appeared as a haven if not a sacred sanctuary from the outside world, the convent emerged on the page as disorderly and dangerous. Mother Superiors could not keep a house the way the moral mother figure described by Catherine Beecher could. *The Escaped Nun* described a "very plump" Mother Superior, "carless of decorum," with one eye larger than the other and a stutter. This so-called mother either "supplied [her ward] with profusion or starved [them] to death." "The economy of this house is thrown into confusion," concluded the narrator. A poem entitled "Horrors of a Nunnery" put the juxtaposition to verse:

Then gloom, dread, and horror my bedside attend, / O then, above all things, I long for a friend, . . . / O, would my past freedom and peace might return! . . . / Vile priests, at their summons, compel me to bow, / My father and guardian, O where art thou now? . . . / Noble brothers, sweet mother, come to my aid, / Believe not the falsehoods, the wretches will tell, / When they say I am happy and chose this dark cell, / Haste, open my prison, delay not to come, / Unbolt my damp dungeon and carry me home![22]

Perhaps even more, city mysteries capitalized on the growing distinctions between "private and public sphere," contrasting a violent, harsh world with a nurturing, safe home. In *New York by Gas-Light*, Foster illustrated a sorry scene of men who forfeited the cozy homes of their families for "cold, narrow, grave-like bedrooms" in boarding houses where they received "'the comforts of home' for five dollars a week." City mysteries detailed the sordid conditions of decaying hovels and shanties in New York's infamous Bowery and Five Points Districts. While the decrepitude of such abodes was off-putting, the alleged debauchery and secrecy that surrounded these antihomes made them at once frightening and enticing. Lippard led readers through "the secret life" of Philadelphia in *The Quaker City*, behind brothel doors where "the devil is played under a cloak, and sin grows fat within the shelter of quiet rooms and impenetrable walls" (Figure 5.3).[23]

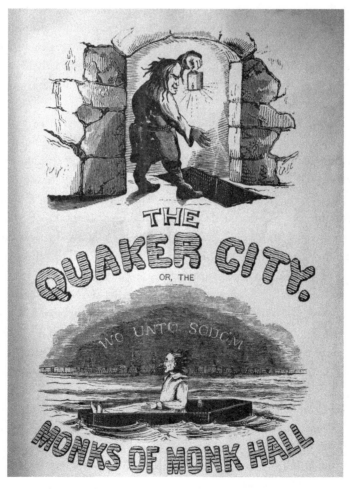

FIGURE 5.3. *The Quaker City, or, The Monks of Monk Hall.*
Courtesy of HathiTrust.

The book focused on a particularly concealed and exclusive venue, "Monk Hall." A mysterious house, built by "a foreigner" before the Revolution, with three stories above ground and three below, wherein "midnight orgies" were rumored to be held, Monk Hall represented a gothic haunted house repurposed for still yet more sinister purposes in the modern city. Like descriptions of convents, Monk Hall was a labyrinthine building complete with "subterranean passages" and trapdoors. Indeed, Lippard wrote that in the past, Monk Hall had been "occupied as a Nunnery." "Mass had been said within its walls; its subterranean chambers converted into cells." As a throwback to its past, urban dwellers who occupied the old mansion referred to themselves as "monks" and kept up an old portrait of an abbot "whose long black robe fell drooping to the floor." Beneath the hood of this imposing figure "glared a fleshless skeleton, with orbless [sic] eye sockets." The current-day "monks" maintained the utmost secrecy, donning robes themselves and holding their late-night meetings "underground." The members were not "ruffians" and "outcasts," but rather respected members of society, lawyers, doctors, and judges, members of Bible and tract societies, and merchants. When they congregated in their "home" they were liable to commit the worst crimes, transforming into something resembling fiends more than men.[24]

Despite their self-given titles, the monks of Monk Hall were anything but austere. As the men drank, "all disguise was thrown aside." The men quickly descended into a drunken revelry and commenced "the ruin" of young women they tricked into the confines of Monk Hall. When the brother of some such unlucky girl tried to rescue her from the hall, he became a captive himself, threatened with death by a prominent "monk." Similar to the cellars and inner chambers of Maria Monk's Hotel Dieu convent, Monk Hall held the corpses of past victims and myriad dark secrets, kept hidden from the light of day. The overseer and doorkeeper of Monk Hall, "Devil-Bug," was "something distinct from the mass of men, a wild beast." He had one large "solitary eye," stacked "rows of bristling teeth," and hair all over his body matted with sweat. This subhuman creature had been "born in a brothel, the offspring of the foulest sin." His condition reflected his lack of a traditional home. "No mother had ever spoken words of kindness to him; no father had ever held him in his arms." Unlike humanity, moved by compassion or benevolence, only "cruelty" warmed the Devil-Bug's heart. "He loved not so much to kill as to observe the blood of his victim, fall drop by drop." The Devil-Bug embodied all the corruption of the city. While a unique villain, his wickedness resembled that of priests in convent narratives. As Reynolds put it, he "seem[ed] a monstrous various of the leering priest" of convent narratives, "while his helper, Long-haired Bess, [w]as like a bedraggled abbess, luring young novitiates into sin." Monsters, and not men, reigned as heads of these dark, underground "houses."[25]

References to domestic ideals proved plastic enough to be used for a variety of purposes. Just as abolitionists argued that slavery threatened the home, urban mystery authors weighed city denizens against the family to bolster reform. Domestic rhetoric also played a role in advancing the growing nativist movement. Nativists often used the language of homeland, purity, and protection to refer to the nation and American citizens. Just as female purity needed protection to ensure domestic happiness, nativists claimed that the purity of the national "home" required safeguarding. Alfred Ely in his speech before the Order of United Americans warned further that "admittance of foreign influences . . . will turn our great and glorious temple of Liberty into a political Black-hole of Calcutta." Instead of a strong temple or pure home, another nativist warned that America was becoming a "receptacle" of the "depraved." The Order of United Americans and other nativists called on "true" Americans to defend their homeland against such intrusion. In describing the rise of the Know Nothings, Thomas Whitney noted the "awakening" of American men, who after being spoken to "in the language of *home* and *country*," "sprang up to the rescue" and "came forth like an army." In this view, foreigners threatened the nation the way convents and brothels threatened women. The purity of the nation, of women, of the home was at stake. If not protected, the nation could become a "Black-hole of Calcutta," looking much like Monk Hall or the Hotel Dieu.[26]

The idea that corruption itself was "foreign" united and strengthened nativism, criticism of cities, and the movement against convents. City mysteries and convent narratives drew on allusions to the foreign, reinforcing nativists' attacks against all things un-American. The foreign foe appeared in the form of the Old World convent, the immigrant, and exotic city venues. City mystery authors alluded to the "Orient" and the Middle East—decidedly nonwhite and non-Christian places— in emphasizing the decadence and debauchery of city life. *Glimpses of New York* compared city residents' worship of the "silver dollar" with "idolatry equaled only by a faithful follower of Mahomet." Foster likened a city saloon to "Aladdin's cave," and prostitutes to "Pariahs." One title that stuck was the new reference to Boston's upper classes as "Brahmins," a term referencing the Indian caste system. Buntline used distinctly foreign language to describe his villainous character in *Mysteries and Miseries of New York*, writing, "His eyes are lustful far more than Tarquin . . . his soul darker that Iago's." Descriptions of certain men as "Turks" suggested their lack of self-control, especially with women. Lippard described a swindler and pimp as a "fervent Turk" clad in a "scarlet Turkish jacket and blue trousers." These foreign allusions served to distance American values of piety, homespun virtue, and democracy from the growing presence of vice, luxury, and social divisions appearing in the nation's cities.[27]

Foreign imagery in city mysteries allowed Americans not only to distance themselves from urban corruption but also to be entertained and enticed. Vivid descriptions of glittering, tempting places and people fascinated readers. Rather than depicting Wall Street as a place of calculation that would likely bore those unfamiliar with it, George Foster likened it to "the valley of riches told of by Sinbad, where millions of diamonds lay glistening like fiery snow, but which was guarded on all sides by poisonous serpents." He transformed an oyster cellar into "Aladdin's cave," complete with "many-colored glass, damask curtains and shaded lights, and a long row of mirrored arcades." Brothels became "Islamic paradises," prostitutes "nymphs," and rich men "Caliph[s] at a masquerade ball." Readers could enjoy a foray into a hidden, exotic world while not endorsing or feeling part of it.[28]

From their first appearance, convent narratives associated convent life with the foreign. Often set in Canada, Spain, Cuba, France, or Italy, convents represented a relic of a distant time and place. Priests resembled "Turks" of the city mysteries in their indulgence and licentiousness. *Rosamond,* set in Cuba, unfolded the horrifying misadventures of rape and cannibalism, with the most sordid details written in Latin or Spanish. A distressed mother in *The Nun of St. Ursula* compared her daughter's decision to become a nun with converting to Islam. *Awful Disclosures'* description of "Nun's Island," which housed the young and most beautiful nuns for the priests' "criminal" visits, sounded strikingly like descriptions of "Islamic paradises" or brothels in city mysteries. One narrative situated a convent in "the desert of Sinai," while another, emphasizing the removal from civilization, placed a convent in "the wilderness." Still more referenced past times and places, comparing alleged torture in convents to that seen in medieval Europe. Like city mysteries, foreign allusions in convent narratives rendered convent life as "other" and dangerous while providing a brief respite from moral standards and gender norms. Like city mysteries, they also kept readers turning pages.[29]

Perhaps no other author capitalized on the drama of foreign allusions more than Harry Hazel. A popular author of both city mysteries and convent narratives, Hazel wrote *The Nun of St. Ursula; or, The Burning of the Convent: A Romance of Mount Benedict* (1845) (Figure 5.4); *The Burglars; or, the Mysteries of the League of Honor, the Belle of Boston* (1844); *Jack Wade, the Cobbler of Gotham* (1856); and, most famously, *Sweeny Todd; or, The Ruffian Barber: A Tale of the Terrors of the Sea and the Mysteries of the City* (1865), among other works. Hazel's fictional account of the real burning of the Charlestown convent appeared among a number of similar stories. Two decades after the burning of Mount Benedict in 1834, anti-Catholics took to mythologizing and commemorating the event as a victory over Romanism. Justifying his foray into the genre of convent narratives, Hazel merely stated that the

FIGURE 5.4. *The Nun of St. Ursula.*
Courtesy of the American Antiquarian Society.

mystery surrounding the burning of the Ursuline convent made it a "good theme for the writer of fiction." Although an imaginative work, Hazel noted that the story "may stumble upon some stubborn truths."[30]

In his rendition of the story, a strapping Yankee, Jack Melville, instigated the burning. Recently returned from an overseas trip, Jack set out to avenge his lovely, young sister trapped within the confines of the convent. Jack had been shipwrecked and washed ashore in Turkey, among "strange looking men with jewelry and long beards." While there, the Ottoman Navy enlisted him, which he led to victory against Greece. After being awarded by the sultan for his victory with "lots of gold," Jack fell in love with Zillah, a Turkish princess who was taken away by a Spanish captain. Jack then received a letter from his mother back home, informing him of his sister's entrance at Mount Benedict. Jack then faced two objectives: to free his sister from the "living grave" of the convent in Massachusetts and to rescue his lover from "Spanish slavery." With the aid of an entire Turkish fleet, he accomplished both in spectacular fashion. Although the Turkish foreigner in this instance was more friend than foe, the allusions to the foreign only reinforced the view of the Catholic as "other" and also rendered the story of the burning of the Ursuline convent a dramatic American victory over an internal enemy.[31]

By having unfamiliar traits, certain places, people, and ways of living were easier to despise. City mystery authors' use of foreign allusions suggested the extent to which the city loomed unfamiliar and frightening if also enticing and exciting. By drawing analogies between American cities and foreign lands often seen as less civilized or virtuous, these works suggested the dire situation in America and revealed real fears Americans had about immorality, vice, and economic disparity in the growing urban centers. Anti-Catholic literature likewise drew on foreign analogies to present convents as un-American and dangerous. If not geographically distant, Catholicism represented a symbolic "dark age" that haunted an American, Protestant present. City mysteries, convent narratives, and nativist groups wrestled with questions of identity, as writers and speakers desperately asserted what it meant to be an American. Real Americans were not swindlers, drunkards, gamblers, brawlers, prostitutes, or profligates. They were not priests or nuns. They were something other than the hordes of illiterate paupers pouring onto American shores. Just as nativists warned against "foreign influence" diminishing "the purity and intelligence" in America, city mysteries and convent narratives provided glimpses of such ruination.

Months before the political takeover by the Know Nothing or American Party, Charles Frothingham published two convent narratives that wedded nativism with the campaign against convents. *The Convent's Doom*, dedicated to the "K.N. Fraternity," told of a woman imprisoned in a convent before being liberated by a "secret society" of men symbolic of the Know Nothings. The priests in the novel boast about not only their control over their female "inmates" but also their influence over American politics. After learning of a "wily Italian" priest luring a young woman into the convent, the secret society took action. With "no laws to help them," the fraternal order raided and burned the "female prison," meant to resemble Mount Benedict, helping "the inmates escape." Patriotic duty legitimated the vigilantism as one brave arsonist explained, "Do you suppose our fathers fought to give their country to Priestcraft and nunneries?" Another of Frothingham's novels with a similar plot, *The Haunted Convent,* also published in 1854, described an unscrupulous candidate for governor in Massachusetts who traded his daughter to a convent in return for the Catholic vote. Although the candidate formally belonged to the "Native American Party," he compromised his dedication to this cause for political gain. Like city mysteries, these novels included mysterious elements, deceptive villains, women in distress, and virtuous male heroes. By presenting convents as foreign fortifications beyond the law that threatened female virtue and the nation, Frothingham melded political, domestic, and religious arguments against convents and advanced the Know Nothing campaign.[32]

Convent narratives like Frothingham's and city mysteries both presented a dystopian American future, leading the way for the political rise of the Know Nothings. In the 1854 congressional election, the Know Nothing or American Party stormed the political arena. For over a decade members of fraternal organizations had met secretly "underground," in homes and lodges, discussing disturbing changes in America, such as the rise of immigration, "foreign influence," "Romanism," urban vice, the changing economy, and political corruption. The sudden coalescence of these groups into one powerful political party surprised the nation. "Who was so wild, or so enthusiastic, as to dream that a party unheard of at the last election, operating through invisible agencies . . . would suddenly spring up . . . [and] absorb the elective strength of the State?" asked William Lloyd Garrison after the Massachusetts state elections. Throughout the country, voters elected forty-three representatives and five senators from the American Party. Some expressed foreboding at the nativist triumph, such as Garrison, who blasted the party for "burrowing in secret like a mole in the dark" and focusing entirely on one's place of birth and religious faith. Others looked on joyfully, including William Brownlow, who exclaimed that "the hand of God is visible in this thing . . . to purify the land." Although the rise of the Know Nothings relied on a variety of factors, including sectional strife and party confusion before the Civil War, it also could not have triumphed without appealing to pervasive anti-Catholicism, nativism, and fear of growing issues wrought by modernization and urbanization, issues and views the convent narratives and city mysteries helped to publicize.[33]

City mysteries, convent narratives, and "dark-lantern politics" all reflected and incited opposition to women who did not fit the domestic ideal of being wife and mother. By presenting this woman—either the prostitute or the nun—as vulnerable, corrupt, foreign or under foreign influence, dangerous, or in need of saving, city mysteries and convent narratives reinforced the need for women to be wives and mothers, the value of the family unit, and the virtue and stability both promised to the republic. Descriptions of a deceptive foe and a foreign conspiracy made the call to action more convincing and urgent. Depictions of women being exploited, tortured, and sometimes murdered played on fears of what happens to women who deviate from certain gender roles and what could happen symbolically to the nation without virtuous womanhood. Nativists capitalized on these various depictions of corruption, womanhood, and foreign influence, proclaiming what it meant to be an American and what it meant to be an outsider, providing a unifying theme around which Americans might coalesce in a time of change and confusion. Their ascent, though brief, would formalize the campaign against convents at the government level.

I have consented, after careful consideration, to expose to the world the horrors, the abominations and wickedness of Mormonism.
—*Awful Disclosures of Mormonism*, 1866

Our institutions would not tolerate the practices ... of the Mormon, with his libidinous licentiousness nor the Romish Church.
—*A Defense of the American Policy as Opposed to the Encroachments of Foreign Influence*, 1856

6

Awful Disclosures of Mormonism

CONVENTS, POLYGAMY, AND THE FEAR OF FEMALE SEXUAL DEVIANCE

IN 1866, A new captivity narrative gripped readers. It told of a young woman seduced by a handsome and charming Mormon man. He convinced her to convert to the recently founded Church of Jesus Christ of Latter-day Saints, intentionally keeping the practice of polygamy a secret, and travel with him to Utah, where he promised to marry her. Once in Zion, however, the man abandoned the young woman, who was then placed on an auction block to be chosen by another Mormon man. After poking and prodding her naked flesh, a decidedly less appealing Saint selected the young woman to join the number of his many wives. She subsequently lived a disillusioned, miserable life, trying and failing both to escape and to kill herself. Finally, when her much older husband died, she stole away to her childhood home and wrote her story as a cautionary tale for "innocent women." Echoing the title of the previous best-selling captivity narrative by Maria Monk, *Awful Disclosures of Mormonism* (Figure 6.1) sounded remarkably like a convent narrative. With themes of threatened female beauty, purity, and usefulness, an underground world of vice and licentiousness, and precarious liberation, anti-Mormon tales mirrored and reinforced the underlying messages of female domesticity and Protestant nationalism found in the heart of the campaign against convents.[1]

Alongside convent narratives, anti-Mormon literature flourished in the 1850s. The formal recognition of polygamy in 1852 by leaders of the Church of Jesus Christ of Latter-day Saints inspired a spate of pamphlets, exposés, and novels fixated on

FIGURE 6.1. "The Escape," *Awful Disclosures of Mormonism.*

the Mormons' "peculiar institution." In 1853, John Russell's *The Mormoness; or, The Trials of Mary Maverick* appeared. The next few years saw the publications of *Female Life Among the Mormons; The Prophets; or, Mormonism Unveiled*; and *Boadicea, the Mormon Wife*, among others. The novel *Mormon Wives* sold over forty thousand copies in the 1850s. By the turn of the century, over fifty anti-Mormon accounts were in circulation. Captivity narratives, the most popular form of anti-Mormon literature, featured stock characters, including villainous Mormon men given to violence, lust, and eccentric beliefs, alongside helpless, captive women. In shaping these familiar characters, anti-Mormon works took cues from anti-Catholic print culture. As historian Terryl Givens noted, the tradition of "sexual bondage," "routine infanticide," and "secret passages," reminiscent of Maria Monk's *Awful Disclosures*, flowed "seamlessly into the Mormon realm." Indeed, convent narratives "paved the way for anti-Mormon writers," who would likewise exploit fears and fascinations with the seemingly unorthodox while upholding American Protestant domesticity.[2]

Alongside public harassment, prohibitions, armies, and militias, popular fiction provided a strong front against the growth of the so-called Mormon menace.

Mormon captivity narratives served as a barometer for the hostility toward and interest in this new faith. They also revealed, as Givens argued, "any number of anxieties and contradictions involving a vast readership's sense of self and nation." Just as convent narratives implicitly asserted who and what Americans were and were not, the abundance of anti-Mormon tales offered a strong statement as to what it meant to be an American. Not able to cast Mormonism as Old World, as the faith grew out of American soil, critics fixated on polygamy as an exotic, un-American, barbarous practice. Indeed, the closed communities, eccentric beliefs, and alleged sexual practices of Mormons provided plenty of fodder for sensational exploita-tion and "othering." Following a similar pattern seen in convent narratives and city mysteries, Mormon exposés typically traced the life of a sympathetic young woman seduced into an alien world of debauchery, who either narrowly escaped or became a lost cause. Focusing on the lives of women, Mormon captivity narratives contrasted a familiar domestic ideal with female ruination and family dysfunction, providing strong undertones as to the implications of a woman's deviation from true wom-anhood for society. As with convent narratives, these tales suggested a sense of na-tional vulnerability represented by and related to women, and imminent danger in the form of a deceptive outsider.[3]

Joseph Smith Jr. was an unlikely prophet. As the fourth son of a poor farming family with less than two years of formal education, he was hardly exceptional. Like many poor New Englanders in the early nineteenth century, the Smiths moved incessantly in search of better conditions for their farming ventures before settling in Palmyra, New York. It was there in 1820 that Smith, as he later narrated, received his first revelation. As a young adult coming of age during the latter half of the so-called Second Great Awakening, Smith became obsessed with religion, and specifically, which church was the true church. Rather than hail the revivals that swept through his town as God's work, Smith wrote critically of a "scene of great confusion," where churches competed for converts, "so that all good feelings, one for another, if they ever had any, were entirely lost in a strife of words and a contest about opinions." In perhaps true American fashion, he sought no authority figure on this matter, but rather retired to the woods by himself in search of answers. Here God told him none of the existing churches was the true one, "for they are all wrong." Later Smith and his followers would continue to draw a sharp demarcation between "Jesus Christ's true church and all others." One, as the Book of Mormon would state, "is the church of the Lamb of God, and the other is the church of the Devil" or the "mother of abominations."[4]

After this, the revelations kept coming. In 1823, a dazzlingly white angel, whom Smith later identified as Moroni, appeared before him, telling him of ancient golden plates containing "the fullness of the everlasting gospel." A few years later, Smith uncovered the plates along with two "seer stones" that would enable him to translate the script. In March of 1830, after three years of translating with the aid of close family and friends, and by "the gift and power of God," the Book of Mormon, or what newspapers would describe as the "Golden Bible," appeared in print, with E. B. Grandin's small print shop in Palmyra publishing five thousand copies. In that year, the twenty-four-year-old Smith counted his parents, his wife, and a few of his closest friends among converts to what he initially called the Church of Christ. By 1853, however, the Church of Jesus Christ of Latter-day Saints numbered over 64,000, and that number would only rise to over 146,000 by 1882. People from a variety of religious backgrounds converted in droves to the new church, perceiving Smith to be a true prophet, seer, translator, and apostle of Jesus Christ.[5]

Many converts, expressing exasperation with the rampant religious sectarianism of the day, were attracted to the idea of absolute authority of continuing revelation and the tangible faith that came with sacramental ritual. The prospect of a literal American Zion also prompted Mormons to travel with a sense of mission. After Mormon missionaries baptized converts in Ohio, Joseph and Emma Smith moved there, where the church continued to grow. Upon new revelation, the Mormons sought the "Promised Land" in western Missouri, the "place for the city of Zion." Here the Saints set about building the New Jerusalem in preparation for the Second Advent of Jesus. The church prospered in Jackson County, Missouri, a site Smith claimed had been or near the Garden of Eden. Their growing numbers, however, stoked opposition, and in 1833 mobs chased the Saints out of Jackson. By 1838, they had been expelled from the entire state. The Mormons trudged on, settling in Nauvoo, Illinois. They enjoyed a few years of peace in Nauvoo, building their community, anticipating the expansion of the Kingdom of God, and naming Smith "Prophet, Priest, and King." Orson Pratt, an early convert to Mormonism, described the early days of the church's growth as "the greatest moral and physical revolution which the inhabitants of this globe ever witnessed." Pratt's analysis rang true, at least in America, as Mormonism quickly became the largest and most successful religion of American origin.[6]

Yet just as quickly as Mormonism grew, opposition mounted to what many saw as a false gospel. Fear of assimilation of Americans to this peculiar new religion prompted swift and unequivocal reaction. It is difficult to overestimate the significance of anti-Mormonism in American history. "With the possible exception of twenty-first century Islam," argued historian Chris Beneke, "no other American religion has inspired such a riot of epithets, such a profusion of calumny, as Mormonism." Beneke might have also added nineteenth-century Catholicism to that comparison. As with Catholics, critics derided Mormons for their seemingly superstitious and un-American beliefs and practices. They pointed to bloc voting, theocratic government, new revelation, secrecy, hierarchal organization, extra-biblical texts, communal living patterns, self-proclaimed prophets, and, of course, polygamy. All of these disturbing developments coalesced in the minds of detractors as "the Mormon problem." Displaying their disapproval, critics harassed the Saints, tarring and feathering some, threatening their lives, and essentially driving them from state to state. Days before a group of recently released prisoners fatally shot Joseph Smith as he sat in a Carthage, Illinois, jail cell, an article in a nearby paper declared, "We hold ourselves at all times in readiness to cooperate with our fellow citizens . . . to exterminate . . . the wicked and abominable Mormon leaders."[7]

No single belief and practice upset outsiders more than polygamy, especially after Smith's Utah successors publically acknowledged and defended the practice in 1852. More than a new Bible or a theocracy, anti-Mormons pointed to polygamy as proof, as historian Sarah Gordon put it, of the "fraudulence of Mormon leaders, the gullibility of their followers, and the irrepressible conflict between Mormonism, on the one hand, and democracy, freedom, and marriage, on the other." Popular culture and politics became inundated with the antipolygamy crusade after the church's public announcement regarding the practice. The idea of plural marriage colored Utah territorial matters, challenging the promotion by Stephen Douglas and his ilk of popular sovereignty for states and territories. The 1856 platform of the newly established Republican Party explicitly asserted the "right and the duty of congress to prohibit in the territories those twin relics of barbarism—polygamy and slavery." With the issue of polygamy as a backdrop, writers crafted an image of Mormon society as a male paradise for the most profligate of men and as a female hell, where only the duped and the coerced lived as captives, much like the popular view of lecherous priests and confined nuns in convent narratives. Plural marriage stamped Mormonism as un-American, un-Christian, and entirely other. In his book on early anti-Mormonism, J. Spencer Fluhman wrote that so much focus rested on polygamy in the nineteenth century that "an alarming number of Americans to this day have trouble articulating what makes a Mormon a Mormon beyond that single practice."[8]

Anti-Mormonism quickly caught up with anti-Catholicism in tone and reach. In his classic article comparing the two, David Brion Davis pointed to "fear of internal subversion" as the energizing source of the reactionary movements. Using surprisingly similar arguments, Protestant authors and spokespersons denounced Mormons and Catholics as deceptive enemies conspiring to overturn American values, replacing them with superstitious religion, unorthodox sexual practices, and theocratic government. Coinciding attacks highlighted the close relationship between anti-Mormonism and anti-Catholicism during the antebellum era. In 1844, a year Beneke described as "the bleakest in the history of American religious relations," violence against Saints and Sisters reached a high point. That year saw the Philadelphia Bible Riots in May and July in which nativists burned a Sisters of Charity convent and a Catholic church in an Irish immigrant neighborhood. That same year in June, Joseph Smith was assassinated as he sat holed up in an Illinois jail cell. A few years later, suspicion of convents culminated in the state-sponsored "Nunnery Committee" in Massachusetts. Near the end of that decade, the nation found itself at war with the Mormons. While the "Utah War" of 1857–1858 proved mostly bloodless and ended relatively amicably, the tensions that led to war reflected the fever pitch of animosity against the Mormons, the only religious group hated as much as the Catholics.[9]

In more than one instance, those who led the campaign against convents also worked to crush the "Mormon Menace." William Hogan, famed ex-priest and author of sensational anti-Catholic exposés, such as *Popery!*, grouped "Mormonites" with "papists" and "popish nunneries," vowing that "all will have their day, and so will common sense." Thomas Whitney, an anti-Catholic writer and the cofounder of the nativist group the Order of United Americans, declared that the institutions of the United States "would not tolerate the practices of the Mormon with his libidinous licentiousness nor that of the Romish Church." Albeit less hyperbolic, Harriet Beecher Stowe engaged in anti-Catholicism and anti-Mormonism. Stowe's *The Minister's Wooing* served as a critique of New England Calvinism, but it also advanced the anti-Catholic trope of vulnerable women seduced into convents at their own peril. Likewise, in a preface to *"Tell It All": A Story of a Life's Experience in Mormonism*, Stowe compared the "chains" bounding "thousands of our sisters" in plural marriage to "the [former] slave-pens of the South." Another woman, Orvilla S. Belise, wrote best-selling anti-Mormon and anti-Catholic novels. In *The Archbishop; or, Romanism in the United States,* published in 1854, she depicted women begging for release from convents. In *The Prophets; or, Mormonism Unveiled,* she described the "bitterness, shame, and despair" that entered the hearts of women caught up in the "brutal barbarism" of polygamy. As American spokespersons took to the page and the podium to denounce what they saw as superstition, female captivity, and worlds of vice, they consigned "Mormonites" and "papists" to the periphery of accepted culture.[10]

The parallels between anti-Mormonism and anti-Catholicism may appear obvious, but as some historians have asked, "What sort of prejudice was this? Was anti-Mormonism about religion or something else?" As with anti-Catholicism, and especially the campaign against convents, anti-Mormonism was about many things in addition to religion. The obsession with polygamy reflected deep-seated concerns about women, sex, gender, and the home, and the subsequent consequences for the nation. Authors of both Mormon captivity narratives and convent narratives not only highlighted these fears but often profited from offering readers "equal measure of righteous indignation and titillation in both genres." As "disclosures of sexual depravity sold well," more than one author easily elaborated on the alleged deviance within Mormon households and Catholic convents. The anxiety over losing "our" women and the horror and fascination with what happened to women who deviated from the script of traditional matrimony and republican motherhood created a thriving market for convent and Mormon captivity narratives while shaping American Protestant identity.[11]

Mormon captivity narratives swelled with a cast of female renegades who looked a lot like Maria Monk, Rebecca Reed, and Josephine Bunkley. Escaped nuns set the mold for runaway wives from polygamist marriages. Perhaps no fugitive wife captured the attention of Americans more than Ann Eliza Young, billed "Wife No. 19" and "The Rebel of Harlem." As a former plural wife of Brigham Young, Mormon prophet and president in the wake of Joseph Smith's assassination, Ann Eliza Young's criticism of what she called her "life in bondage" struck a blow to the top echelons of the church. *Wife No. 19; or, The Story of a Life in Bondage, Being a Complete Expose of Mormonism, and Revealing the Sorrows, Sacrifices and Sufferings of Women in Polygamy* described the disillusionment and heartache plural marriage delivered to women. Writing her story "for the sake of all the unhappy women of Utah," Ann Eliza described "women [who] died of broken hearts" when their husbands took other wives. Men thought "no more of taking a wife than of buying a new cow," she explained, and felt no remorse or sympathy when their distraught first wives tried to commit suicide in despair. According to Ann Eliza, polygamy ran rampant throughout Zion, with "the ceremony of sealing literally going on day and night." Women brushed aside any hesitation, being essentially coerced into polygamous marriages as the practice "was not only advised but commanded" by the "counsel of the priesthood," which "no one dared to neglect." She shared a variety of anecdotes of quarreling wives when one became the "favorite" and of family disorder when mother and daughter married the same man. "They were not happy women," Ann Eliza noted. "No women in polygamy are happy, however loudly they may claim to be."[12]

Allegedly, Ann Eliza caught the attention of Brigham Young, already the husband of eighteen wives, who persistently "tried every way to win" her before resorting to "coercion." After briefly enjoying life as the "favorite wife," Ann Eliza and her son were cast aside, and she became a neglected drudge in her own house. "How I hated my life!" she exclaimed. "It was dull, joyless, oppressed." *Wife No.*

19 described Young's formidable yet disordered home, a large stone building with multiple apartments for the wives. Here bickering women obeyed the commands of a single male master as their children came of age estranged from their father. After encountering the "happy household" of a neighboring Gentile family, Ann Eliza found herself "ready to renounce my religion and leave my home." She carried out her plans "before they could be detected by Mormon spies," retreating from Zion with her only son, resembling the image of Maria Monk retreating from the Hotel Dieu with her son, the alleged offspring of one of the priests. Unlike Monk, who never spent time in a convent, however, Ann Eliza had been the wife of Brigham Young. She sued him for divorce in 1873. Granted the divorce, but not a substantial alimony, she embarked on a crusade against the church, eventually taking to the lecture circuit and publishing to "unveil the horrors of the Mormon religion." As one historian put it, *Wife No. 19* was more of a "personal vendetta" than an actual exposé of life for Mormon women. In a final note in the book, she addressed the American public, "And it is in your own country that these outrages against all womanhood occur, under your own government, upheld by your own chosen legislators," before challenging the government to "eradicate this foul blot upon national purity and honor."[13]

Wife No. 19 drew inspiration from convent narratives. With the same themes of brutish men lording over servile, trapped women; hidden licentiousness; female disillusionment; loss of female purity; loneliness; drudgery; a cut-off society; lack of camaraderie among women; a fateful escape; and subsequent revelations to the public, the narratives were essentially interchangeable. As in convent narratives, the Mormon polygamous household contrasted sharply with the traditional, happy domestic sphere, where one wife wed to one husband lived comfortably and piously, watching over her house and ward. For Young, polygamy was a poison, directed at the heart of the domestic realm, spoiling a woman's "maternal instinct." Summing up the domestic threat polygamy posed, Young's book declared, "Incest, murder, suicide, mania, and bestiality are the chief 'beauties' of this infamous system." As with convent narratives, *Wife No. 19* focused on women—their natural role, what would make them miserable and what would make them happy, and the effects of their domestic arrangements on the nation's virtue and strength. Just as convent narratives claimed the republic had no use for "foolish virgins," Ann Eliza's exposé charged the government with "eradicating this foul blot upon natural purity and honor," maintaining a woman's traditional married role for the sake of the country.[14]

In 1853, during the height of the anticonvent movement, publishers released John Russell's *The Mormoness; or, the Trials of Mary Maverick*. Russell, less of a vitriolic anti-Mormon than most, tried to extend a measured, though critical, representation of the faith. This "narrative of real events," set in a small town of Sixteen Mile Prairie, presented the growth of Mormonism as a natural extension of religious freedom. Russell illustrated violence against Mormons, depicting the brutal murder of the husband and child of a woman, the book's title character, at the hands of an American mob. As a widow and bereft mother, the Mormoness converted to Catholicism and joined the Sisters of Charity to live as a nun. Meanwhile, the man who killed her family met and fell in love with her. After discovering her true identity, however, he lost his mind and died alone.[15]

This melodramatic novel, although condemning violence against Mormons, extended a critique of Mormonism in the subplot. Before the violent outbreak in Sixteen Mile Prairie, the Mormon faith spread in the small town like a contamination by the work of a traveling Mormon preacher. James Maverick, then-husband to the future Mormoness, at first resisted the Mormon mission, committing himself to keeping his community from falling into "the fatal snare of Joseph Smith." But his wife, Mary, attended the minister's meetings and was soon taken with his "ingenious sophistry." One by one, James lost his wife, his best friend, and close neighbors to the new prophet's religion, until he finally converted too. The conversion of the town resulted in violence, including the murder of Mary's family, and her resignation to a convent, a decision presented as a final option in the wake of dashed domestic dreams. Although the novel focused less on polygamy than other Mormon captivity narratives, it highlighted the seductive strength of Mormonism, suggesting that women were most susceptible to the Mormon allure. The pairing of Mormonism and convent life in this unhappy conclusion, moreover, united being a Mormon woman and a nun as undesirable and perilous female vocations. The repercussions extended beyond any single woman's misery to a national crisis with the slow chipping away of female contributions of domestic production and virtue in the larger society.[16]

When followers of the late Joseph Smith followed Brigham Young in a flight from the US to the Utah territory, the Mormon question became one embroiled in a larger conversation about the fate of the West, national character, and the march of civilization. In a sermon echoing Lyman Beecher's "Plea for the West," delivered days before the burning of the Charleston convent in 1834, Congregationalist pastor Horace Bushnell described what he considered the "great problem" of the West in 1847. Where "Romanism" and "barbarism" already threatened the expanding frontier, Bushnell pointed to the further disturbing development of Mormonism. In the wake of Mormon expansion, Bushnell called on true Americans to pour their efforts into civilizing the West, spreading a "new Christian Empire" to the glory of the republic. He enjoined the American Home Missionary Society, for whom he delivered the sermon, to tirelessly fight back against the inroads of popery and polygamy for the sake of the nation's future. For the Home Missionary Society, concerns about civilization in the West often centered on women. One of their published sermons spoke of Catholic "female seminaries" or convents filled with "Protestant patrons" as they "contend for the prize . . . of influence over this land." Mormon women in plural marriages, in their distress and defilement, could not ensure the virtue of the republic. Nor could nuns, who in greater numbers were founding schools for the growing communities in the expanding frontier. "With women functioning as representatives of civilization's march or decline," argued historian J. Spencer Fluhman, the focus on women in anti-Mormon and anti-Catholic print was perfectly natural.[17]

The women of Mormon captivity and convent narratives symbolized the perceived vulnerability of the West—an impressionable, undeveloped terrain—to the alleged influences of barbarism, heterodoxy, and nontraditional domestic arrangements. Critics of Catholicism and Mormonism believed that both faith traditions lured the vulnerable, especially young women, into their group through pageantry and emotional and sensory appeal. Pointing to similarities among anti-Catholics and anti-Mormons, David Brion Davis contended that for opponents, "Roman Catholic sacraments and Mormon revelations were preposterous hoaxes used to delude the naïve." The Saints and the papists seemed to have a variety of intoxicating smells, bells, and ornamentation at their disposal. Why else would they attract so many converts? Opponents saw the forms of these religions, contrary to the abstract faith of "true religion," as tools that led the unenlightened (especially women and children) astray. Like the impressionable children in convent narratives, young women easily found themselves caught up in religious pageantry and the charming façade put on by the Saints in Mormon captivity narratives.[18]

Mormon captivity narratives reinforced a crisis of vulnerability of young women and the nation, a concern well established in the campaign against convents. The opening lines of *Awful Disclosures of Mormonism* alerted readers to the "thousands of beautiful innocent girls who stand in danger of succumbing to the wiles of the Mormon apostle." This warning reflected a common speculation among Mormon opponents that a German peddler had taught Smith the secrets of "magnetic influence," which he used to grow the church and lure women. *The Mormoness* traced the fall of a town to Mormonism to an initial female conversion. Cunning Mormon men, claimed the author of *Awful Disclosures of Mormonism*, lured naïve women with "beautiful visions of happy married lives" along with "dreams of prosperity and honor." To their horror, however, the innocent women found only "misery" in the place of happiness and "ruination, both moral and physical" in the place of prosperity and honor. The villainous Mormon man in the novel charmed the trusting protagonist with his "fascinating manner and pleasing tongue." He was cultured, "having visited every country beneath the sun," regaling his female prey with "stories of his travels." Being "young and inexperienced," the female protagonist fell for the handsome villain. Like the young country, and especially the inexperienced West, such women could be easily fooled, seduced, and ruined by cunning scoundrels.[19]

Maria Ward's *Female Life Among the Mormons*, published in 1855, also emphasized a woman's "powerlessness to resist" the seductive ways of Mormons. In this book, she described her own seduction by Joseph Smith, complaining that "he exerted a mystical magical influence over me—a sort of sorcery that deprived me of the unrestricted exercise of freewill." Not the only one to fall under the spell, Ward calculated that "countless others" came under the "singular and fascinating power, which [Mormon men] practiced on all that came within their influence." Such men "pretended to cure disease and work miracles." To the untrained eye, such miracles proved irresistible. The *New York Herald* echoed Ward's explanation in an article entitled "Mormonism and Mesmerism." "Joe is a magnet," claimed the author, attracting followers by unwittingly dabbling in animal magnetism or mesmerism. James Gordon Bennett, the paper's editor, likewise pointed to Smith's "powerful magnetic influence" as the source of his appeal. Such claims sounded remarkably like the repeated accusation that nuns, "like little, thoughtless children," were easily "misled by the arts of priests and nuns" into joining convents. At a time when mesmerism, hypnosis, and spiritualism attracted thousands, and when charlatan and genuine evangelist alike sought converts, Americans worried about the possibilities of being duped, taken advantage of, and humiliated. The themes of weakness, vulnerability, attraction, innocence, and naivety ran throughout these narratives, prompting a defensive posture for the protection of women and the nation.[20]

If women unwittingly entered the Mormon faith and Catholic convents, as these narratives alleged, then their conversions were not real, their choices nonconsensual. Historian Sarah Barringer Gordon described antebellum antipolygamists as all arguing that "women were duped, hypnotized, or brutalized into polygamy. . . . Never were they voluntary participants." Similarly, references to chains, cells, and conspiracies in convent narratives negated the idea of choice among nuns. As the nineteenth century, sometimes dubbed "the age of the contract," saw an increasing value of consent in marriage, work, and government, the portrayal of Mormon women and nuns as captives (and often sex slaves) justified opposition to Mormonism and Catholicism. The choices of Mormon women and nuns were not their own, and thus they were not the right ones, not in keeping with enlightened society, and not American. Such rhetoric allowed for comfortable distancing for many Americans feeling uncomfortably close to the expanding Mormon faith and Catholic presence. By rewriting conversion and choice out of Mormon and Catholic history, detractors could frame their campaign against Mormons and convents as a liberation movement from the "relics of barbarism."[21]

Mormon prophets and other high-ranking male members embodied predatory barbarism in Mormon captivity narratives, resembling priests of convent narratives, slave drivers of abolitionist literature, and indulgent city dwellers of urban mysteries. Priests had long been portrayed as enemies of the American political tradition. Just as the "wily" priest in Charles Frothingham's 1854 *The Convent's Doom* offered up the "Catholic vote" in exchange for an ambitious politician's daughter being placed in a convent, Mormon men in captivity narratives wielded their political sway over members. The Mormon prophet, according to *Mormonism Unveiled*, surrounded himself with uninformed followers who would vote according to his whims. "Serfs from the old world, and aliens of every nation and clime, with no other naturalization than that of a Mormon baptism, [were] permitted to vote, and even . . . to make laws to govern free-born Americans," claimed the book. Both priests and Mormon men appeared effeminate, self-indulgent, and uncivilized. Illustrations of the Utah War featured Mormon men ducking behind rows of their wives. At a time when self-control reigned as a hallmark of masculinity and civilization, Mormon men gave into lusts for women and power, taking pride in "ruining the greatest number of innocent girls."[22]

According to *Awful Disclosures of Mormonism*, all Mormon men were "carnal-minded, blood-thirsty monsters . . . fiends in the guise of manhood." Anti-Mormon literature picked up on perhaps the most iconic anti-Catholic images—that of a priest leering suggestively at an innocent young woman. In *Female Life Among the Mormons*, a young woman stood in a humble posture before a seated, robed Brigham Young as he informed her of his revelation that she should be his bride. The image, like that of *A Beautiful Nun,* featuring a cowering woman beneath a priest posed to strike, or of the woman kneeling before a priest for confession in William Hogan's *Popery!*, related ideas of threatened womanhood, unbridled male power, and corruption. In this way Mormon men and Catholic priests represented a throwback to tyranny and savagery, the antithesis of worthy American men, and a danger to American women and the republic at large.[23]

Poor choices, even coerced ones, led to unhappy endings. Critics presented life in a plural marriage or a convent as something utterly undesirable, leading women to be miserable, ruined, and scorned. The protagonist of *Awful Disclosures of Mormonism* lamented her transformation from "an innocent, pure-minded girl to a broken-hearted, ruined, and despised woman." *Wife No. 19* detailed myriad unhappy outcomes for women in plural marriages, including one who "became a raving maniac and died in an insane asylum." This trope was old hat for convent narratives, which contrasted the promise of domestic felicity with the "gloom, dread, and horror" of a "nunnery." Even if nuns "were pure," granted one author, "they could not possibly be happy," being made for "social and domestic enjoyment." In contrast to her unhappy fate as a plural wife, *Awful Disclosures of Mormonism* held up the childhood home of the female narrator, the paths to which wove as "roads to Heaven itself." Traditional domesticity promised happiness for women, not the twin extremes of polygamy or celibacy.[24]

When prompted, however, many Mormon women rejected the notion that they were captive victims of profligate men. Eliza Snow, a widow of Joseph Smith, an outspoken plural wife, and the church's most noteworthy nineteenth-century poet, protested forcefully against proposed antipolygamy legislation. "Our enemies pretend that in Utah woman is held in a state of vassalage—that she does not act from choice, but by coercion—that we would even prefer life elsewhere, were it possible for us to make our escape," she stated. "What nonsense!" As she spoke, over three thousand Mormon women gathered in Salt Lake City in solidarity against government attempts to legislate against plural marriage through the so-called Cullom Bill. At their self-styled "indignation meeting," woman after woman stood to speak on behalf of her faith, including the practice of polygamy. If they send our husbands to prison, challenged Phebe Woodruff, they would need to "make their prisons large enough to hold their wives, for where they go we will go also." A female convert from England asked whether this was really "America, the world-renowned land of liberty, of freedom, [and] equal rights." Newspaper editors scratched their heads at the nearly four thousand Mormon women in attendance, remarking on the significance, as a writer from the San Francisco *Evening Bulletin* put it, that "American born and raised, Anglo-Saxon women" could support a system so seemingly demoralizing to them. From the antebellum era until the eradication of the practice, Mormon women largely supported plural marriage. Their support not only ran counter to Mormon captivity narratives but also served, as historian Gordon argued, as "a lightning rod for concerns about women's political participation and marriage that affected the country as a whole."[25]

After the 1857 murder of Parley Pratt, a respected elder of the church, newspapers described him according to conventional stereotypes. The "hoary old villain" met a just fate, claimed one article. Another summed up the story of his murder, describing his seduction of Eleanor McLean, who left her husband to become his "concubine." After tracking down Pratt, Hector McLean acted justly when he killed the man who stole his wife. Eleanor McLean responded to these accounts, offering a written statement that Laurel Thather Ulrich described as "reading like a pro-polygamy novel that never got published." McLean countered the image of Pratt as a seducer, herself as a fallen woman, and her husband as an aggrieved victim. Even before she converted to Mormonism, her husband had been a drunk, she wrote, who had driven "happiness from our home." She had been a long-suffering wife attracted to Pratt as a virtuous apostle of true religion. Eleanor McLean, like Eliza Snow and other Mormon women, openly defended polygamy, challenging negative stereotypes of their husbands and their faith. Nuns in antebellum America faced a similar challenge, with some coming forward to dismiss accusations of being seduced into convents, held against their will, and tortured by lascivious priests. While Mormon women likely harbored a range of emotions and opinions on polygamy not evident in public statements, their responses reflected a level of agency regarding plural marriage negating the caricature of the female captive perpetuated throughout the era in popular print culture.[26]

Mormon women expressed a range of opinions on polygamy. Emma Hale Smith, the first wife of Joseph Smith, was a vocal critic of plural marriage. Emma looked on with disdain as her husband married or was "sealed to" over twenty other women in the early 1840s. Although she gave a partial blessing to a few of the marriages, Emma became more frustrated with her husband, eventually desiring "to be revenged on him." In part to convince his first wife of the righteousness of the practice, Smith presented her and the other Saints with written revelation. The revelation, in the voice of Jesus Christ, confirmed eternal and plural marriage before addressing Emma personally, instructing her to "cleave unto my servant Joseph, and to none else" unless she "be destroyed." Yet Emma remained unconvinced. Her continued resistance showed that not all Mormon women happily accepted polygamy. Yet, even Emma was no captive victim, remaining a willful, vocal member of the church until her death.[27]

The campaign against convents and Mormonism thrived in the midst of the women's movement. Activists poured their energy into the cause of equal rights for women, championing female suffrage as the most important object of this agenda. Some women's rights advocates believed that female suffrage would spell the death of polygamy. What woman, if given the choice, would vote in favor of such a blatantly patriarchal tradition? Thus, it was perhaps one of the biggest blows to anti-Mormonism when Utah became one of the first places to offer women the franchise in February of 1870. Fifty years before the constitutional amendment, Utah unanimously and without debate passed the Female Suffrage Bill. "Was there ever a greater anomaly known in the history of society?" asked one writer for the *Phrenological Journal*. "That the women of Utah, who have been considered representatives of womanhood in its degradation, should suddenly be found on the same platform with John Stuart Mill and his sisterhood, is truly a matter for astonishment." Some activists reluctantly acknowledged the stride for women's rights in the most unlikely of places, with Susan B. Anthony and Elizabeth Cady Stanton visiting Utah to both congratulate women there and push other reforms. But if they hoped female suffrage would lead to the eradication of polygamy, they were disappointed. When the practice was finally abandoned, it was not because of the woman's vote.[28]

Some Mormon men were reluctant practitioners of polygamy. If they had any leadership ambitions, they felt considerable pressure to conform to polygamous doctrine. As converts to the Mormon faith, women and men needed to accept "celestial marriage" as a matter of divine revelation, a mandate by God, an edifying practice that reflected a heavenly state above the laws of man. While 40 percent of Mormons had plural households in 1860, most—about two-thirds—had only two wives. Only a few high-ranking members of the church counted four or more wives. And adherence did not come without a cost. Dozens of church elders experienced imprisonment for their practice of polygamy. Nor did Mormon men rule over their wives with complete sovereignty. Women could bring complaints about their husbands before the church hierarchy and had greater access to divorce than women in the rest of the Union. Agnes Hoagland, for instance, stood before the presidency of the Twelve, charging her husband with "not pay[ing] enough attention to her" and not providing for her sufficiently. She soon after received a divorce, remarried, and remained in Utah and the church. While men in some obvious ways reaped the benefits of plurality, they too resisted easy conformity to caricatures in Mormon captivity narratives.[29]

Despite the uneasy fit of Mormon men and women into the images presented of them in anti-Mormon propaganda, plural marriage still rested uneasily with women's rights. Similarly, the idea of women living under a decidedly male hierarchy in Catholic convents did not exactly appear as a liberal alternative to the Protestant domestic model. And yet women in both traditions bucked conventional standards, traveled, took risks, and chose to live either in female communities or in marriages that were themselves experiments in communal living. Women displayed their volition in leaving the safety of their homes, husbands, and legal families to embrace the Mormon faith. If their statements can be taken at face value, it appeared that many of them acted in sincere accordance to the dictates of their conscience. Eliza Snow defended plural marriage as a reflection of a heavenly state in which all souls were "bound" in an ennobling practice that fostered a "holier feeling" than friendship. As in convents, Mormon women formed not only extended family networks but also female community. As Ulrich noted, "Women banded together to spin, weave, and care for the sick, but also to participate in sacred rituals. The defining concept was not plural marriage but *gathering*." Moreover, the theological approach to the practice "transformed lust into responsibility" and gave "every woman an opportunity to marry and become a mother." Likewise, nuns, while theoretically under the auspices of men, could opt out of marriage and motherhood, live in community, pursue intellectual and social vocations outside of the home, and exercise control over their expenses. During a time known for the heralding of both the ideals of true womanhood and women's rights, Mormon women and nuns fit in neither camp and perhaps defied the simple dichotomy of oppression and liberation. Resistance to plural marriage and convents revealed a lack of knowing what to do with women who lived outside the bounds of traditional marriage and the belief among reactionary conservatives and liberal activists alike that a certain type of woman ensured a more ideal society.[30]

Despite Mormon women's support for polygamy, resistance to the Saints mounted, reaching the halls of Congress. Representatives pointed to polygamy as the chief issue of contention with the Latter-day Saints. To build a case against this peculiar institution, Congress needed to present plural marriage as something exotic, barbaric, Old World, and utterly at odds with American values. Fictive caricatures of Mormonism advanced such an endeavor, allowing the government to become embroiled in the attempt to stamp out the "Mormon menace" on the eve of the Civil War. Authors and Congress helped bring about what historian Givens referred to as an "Orientalization of Mormonism," with references to the "harems of the elders" and "the American Mohammed." One author denounced plural marriage as something that only "belongs now to the indolent and opium-eating Turks and Asiatics, the miserable Africans, the North American savages, and the Latter-day Saints." In 1857, state representative Justin Morrill of Vermont accused the Saints of perpetuating "a Mohammedan barbarism revolting to the civilized world." Others refused to categorize Mormons as white, describing them as a "new racial type" with common "physiological features." *The Women of Mormonism* depicted a "Turkish Scene," featuring a reclining Mormon elder in Middle Eastern dress, inviting a young woman to join him for a sumptuous meal. Just as convent narratives cast nuns as harems, Catholicism as Old World, and priests as savages (and sometimes Turks), critics poured energy into "othering" Mormonism, obsessing over both the sexual and gender nonconforming practices of women. By relegating polygamy and convents to the realm of something pagan, Oriental, and uncivilized, critics could advance a campaign against them. The politics of the 1850s, which included the Mormon War, antipolygamy bills, and convent investigations, proved the effectiveness of such a strategy.[31]

Congress also gained traction against Mormons by equating plural marriage with slavery. In 1856, Republicans vowed to wipe out "those twin relics of barbarism—Polygamy and slavery" in the territories. Even in the midst of the Civil War, legislators managed to outlaw polygamy in 1862, a ruling church leaders defied. "Among the most persistent and most effective of the charges leveled against Mormons," claimed one historian, "was the claim that Utah's peculiar domestic institution, like the South's, was evidence of disloyalty to the national government." In rejecting traditional American values, Mormons became "rebellious," "nullifiers," and "anti-republicans." Like Southerners whose state loyalty ran up against national allegiance, Mormons were loyal to church over country, the test being their commitment to plurality. Just as abolitionists often focused on the way in which slavery threatened marriage, female purity, and family cohesion, critics of the Saints castigated polygamy as the enemy of traditional domesticity. With their concerns for rights—the right to marry, the right to wage labor—the Republican Party rendered domestic arrangements inherently political. The strong backing of middle-class reformers in this party, with their lauding of true womanhood and mainstream Protestant values, only reinforced the party's opposition to slavery, Mormonism, and convents as dangerous and un-American.[32]

Antipolygamy legislation and rejection of it by the Latter-day Saints heightened tensions among church members and the federal government. While celebrating the ten-year anniversary of their arrival in Salt Lake City, in July 1857, Brigham Young received word of the advancement of troops toward the territory. President James Buchanan was ready to prove the federal government's authority in the face of perceived territorial insubordination. Although he ordered the army not to shoot unless in self-defense, he neglected to relay this information to residents in Utah. Having been forcibly run out of their homes before, church members had every reason to expect the worst. With tensions high, and under Brigham Young's direction, the Saints prepared defenses. To block the oncoming soldiers' line and prevent bloodshed, Mormon rangers torched prairie grasses, monitored various points of entry into the territory, and took to the road to keep watch. They evaded combat in a kind of stand-out throughout the following months, until Buchanan issued a Peace Commission in June 1858. But the hysteria of the bloodless war contributed to the actions of renegade Mormon guerilla fighters who tragically massacred a wagon of West-bound immigrants traveling through Mountain Meadows. This disastrous yet isolated event served to reinforce the image of Mormon men as savages so often seen in anti-Mormon propaganda.[33]

Despite a peaceable end to war, the government continued to resist Utah residents' requests for statehood. When it came to the "Mormon question," anti-Mormon legislators often relied on the polygamy card as reason enough to deny admission. The idea that plural marriage fell outside the bounds of acceptable American customs proved convincing enough for the majority of Americans to block Utah's entrance into the Union. As Fluhman put it, "Mormons swam against the cultural and political currents when they assumed that polygamy would be protected as a religious practice" under the separation of church and state. Significantly, it would not be until leaders of the church moved away from the doctrine of plural marriage, encouraging the Saints to follow the law of the land, in 1890, that Congress opened the doors of the nation to Utah. On January 4, 1896, Utah entered the US as the forty-fifth state.[34]

A common concern of the antebellum era, and perhaps a perennial one in American history, was the vulnerability of liberty. Fear that liberty could lead to license or licentiousness prompted politicians, pastors, writers, and community leaders to embrace defensive postures toward outsiders and perceive conspiracies. Increasing religious pluralism in the aftermath of disestablishment, growing ethnic and religious diversity spurred by immigration, and the seemingly untamed and impressionable frontier created environments in which new faiths and traditions could at once flourish and become deeply suspect. These developments saw a revival of old and a pioneering of new roles and ideals for women, from celibate communal arrangements in convents to plural marriage, free love, and civil equality with men. The concurrent advance of true womanhood, the celebration of the Victorian home, and the growing tenor of civil religion that trumpeted a peculiar mixture of Protestantism and patriotism represented a backlash against these changes. Focusing on women—their vulnerability, their ideal role as wife and mother, and the consequences for their alleged poor decisions—reflected deeply held notions about the proper place for women in the republic and latent concerns about the fate of the young nation. Historian Terryl Givens contended that the depiction of Mormons in captivity narratives was ultimately about "American identity," depicting who Americans were in contrast to the other. Their portrait of Mormons, he claimed further, offered a "sensationalistic, exploitative, and ultimately reassuring" message to readers. Distorting the experiences of Mormon women reassured readers that their opposition was well intended, their fear well founded, and their way of living the only way to preserve equality, liberty, and justice of the republic.[35]

Touted as a book "absolutely necessary for the sake of the honor and virtue of womanhood," *Awful Disclosures of Mormonism,* like its predecessor, *Awful Disclosures of the Hotel Dieu,* presented womanhood as hanging in the balance. Mormon captivity narratives and convent narratives offered strict dichotomies between true and fallen women, legitimate wives and harems, contributing female citizens and wasted womanhood. While such works championed "saving" such women from feared dismal fates, they disregarded the independence of them to make decisions for themselves, to pursue their own idea of happiness. After their debut in the 1850s, Mormon captivity narratives continued to sell well during and even after the Civil War, only waning after the church abandoned polygamy. Convent narratives provided the template and momentum for these narratives. Although Mormon women and Catholic nuns lived dramatically different lives, the opposition they faced stemmed from the same domestic ideology that equated true womanhood with being a true American and the role of women with the fate of the nation.[36]

I am persuaded that our welfare as a nation will be greatly jeopardized if Popish institutions ... are suffered to spring up extensively among us, and were it possible I would urge every American to exert the whole vigor of his intellect, in checking the spread of tenets and principles which may undermine our liberties and corrupt the sources of our strength and greatness.

—*The American Nun*, 1836

Are convents then so essential to the constitution of the state? Did Christ institute the orders of monks and nuns? What need has the bridegroom for so many foolish virgins?

—*The Escaped Nun*, 1855

7

The Nunnery Sleuths

CONVENT INVESTIGATIONS AND THE MASSACHUSETTS KNOW NOTHING PARTY

AT THE NOTRE DAME ACADEMY for girls in Roxbury, Massachusetts, Caroline Crabb lay sick in bed. The young boarder held still as Mary Aloysia, the Mother Superior at the academy, "applied remedies" to relieve the "bad humors." As she performed this delicate task, two coaches of Know Nothings recently elected to the Massachusetts legislature along with sixteen of their friends and associates arrived at the house unannounced. Piling around the entrance, one of them asked the woman who opened the door if she objected to a visit by a "committee of the Massachusetts legislature." The group then shuffled into the building, fanning out into the halls, stomping and shouting as they poked into various rooms. Some of the young pupils became alarmed, one shrieking, "Oh! The house is full of Know Nothings!" Mary Aloysia rose from her patient's bedside, assuring the girl that all was well, and left the room.[1]

Joseph Hiss, the "Grand Worshipful Instructor" of the Massachusetts Know Nothings and newly elected member of the House, sauntered into the academy's small chapel, interrupting the prayers of one Sister. The startled woman got up to leave the room, but Hiss followed her, cornering her in the hall as other men turned over chairs, peering suspiciously beneath them. Placing a hand on her shoulder, Hiss asked sardonically, "How do you like living in a convent? Wouldn't you enjoy going out into the world again?" The woman offered no reply to the stranger, who fondled the rosary that hung from her waist. Between winks and leers he asked what punishments she suffered and whether she would like to go with him to Montreal, alluding to Maria Monk's best-selling, salacious (and fraudulent) convent exposé, *Awful Disclosures*. Declining the offer and referring him to the Mother Superior, the woman finally ducked away from the Grand Worshipful Instructor.[2]

Meanwhile, two members from the committee entered the bedroom of the sick girl. Feigning sleep, Caroline Crabb lay perfectly still as strange men huddled into the small alcove. She later recalled smelling cigars on their breath as they hovered over her. From there the investigators poked into every chamber, classroom, and closet in the academy and even inspected a sink used for the disposal of "foul water." Using a lantern to light the way, a few Sisters led their demanding examiners through the cellar. As they crept through the damp basement, the nunnery sleuths repeatedly asked their guides whether there were "any boys in the house" or imprisoned nuns. After finding no abominations, and offering no explanation for their abrupt interruption of the day's tasks at the academy, the band of investigators left just as swiftly as they had arrived. They then convened with a larger group at the Norfolk House, a fashionable Roxbury hotel, for a night of fine dining and copious libations (Figure 7.1).[3]

Seven Sisters from the Order of Notre Dame de Namur operated the Roxbury School on Washington Street. Women from the order originally arrived to the US

FIGURE 7.1. "Norfolk House, Roxbury, MA," *Ballou's Pictoral Drawing-Room Companion.*

in 1840 by way of Belgium, where the order was founded. They first operated schools in various Ohio cities before expanding into the Boston area in 1849. By the time the Nunnery Committee launched their investigation, they had been in Massachusetts about one year, coming at the behest of Boston's bishop, John Bernard Fitzpatrick. Devoted specifically to teaching, the Notre Dame Sisters operated a tuition-funded school open to all who wished to enroll. At the time of the investigations, the school counted twelve pupils between the ages of twelve and fifteen. In an old but well-kept schoolhouse they went about their daily routine with the aid of one Irish maintenance man. In addition to running the academy, the Sisters also operated a charity or free school in Roxbury that served over two hundred children, mostly from local poor immigrant families. The Sisters allegedly got along well with their neighbors, never causing "any sort of suspicion."[4]

When the women arrived in Roxbury on May 8, 1854, they found their house, which would also operate as the school, in disarray and promptly began cleaning. Starting from scratch with what would be their chapel, the Sisters received from a local priest a small table "from his own home" that would serve as their altar. With their preparations completed, the community had their first mass "in our own little chapel," as one Sister proudly wrote, and shortly thereafter received their first pupil. By May 22, forty students had enrolled in the school. In the early days of the foundation, the Sisters put out a fire (started accidentally by the hired man) and endured a chaotic carriage ride pulled by a frightened horse that had not been broken. They relied little on the bishop, who was in Europe when they first arrived and kept a busy schedule. After his return he visited the Sisters occasionally but did not mettle in their affairs. The women showed him deference, however, inviting him to dinner and having a few select pupils play the piano and sing for him before "addressing him four little compliments."[5]

The Notre Dame Sisters also operated a school in Lowell, Massachusetts, and traveled frequently between the schools and from state to state depending on the needs of each institution. Both schools opened their doors to the public periodically for their "distribution of prizes" ceremony, a French custom in secondary schools, where students received awards at the end of each term. They also interacted with the community through charity, receiving "into our classes the girls who found themselves without work and who wanted to come and get a little education." In a town where lots of factory or "mill girls" came to work in the growing textile industry and where the rate of Irish immigration climbed each year, the number of women in need of "a little education" was likely high.[6]

Despite cries to protect women in convents and assertions that nuns lived miserable lives of submission, these women and nuns elsewhere exhibited a relatively high degree of independence. Many experienced grand adventures, traveling from their homes and all that was familiar in Europe, with little financial support or social connections, to establish communities in the US and the growing frontier. Joining a religious order offered women a ticket to see the larger world unencumbered by domestic obligations. Life in religious communities also afforded some ambitious women the opportunity to establish and administer large institutions, such as schools, charity wards, and hospitals. Women religious owned property and made business decisions. The Sisters of Notre Dame de Namur in Roxbury and Lowell taught, studied, traveled, oversaw their houses, and engaged with the wider community.

In their records, Sisters at both Lowell and Roxbury reported hearing rumors about "a society called the Know Nothings" who possibly planned to "burn us down." They expected a visit "any day." It was not far-fetched for the Sisters to fear their school being burned down by outsiders. They had heard of the 1834 attack against the Ursuline convent and academy not far from them, in Charlestown, Massachusetts. How could they be sure a disgruntled group might not burn down their building, leaving them homeless, humiliated, and without compensation, like the Ursulines who ran the Charlestown convent? They passed by booksellers peddling convent narratives that romanticized the burning of the convent as a patriotic victory and were handed tracts warning against "popery." Remnants of the old Charlestown convent still stood among patches of unkempt grass just a few miles away from the schools of the Notre Dame Sisters, a sober reminder of what could be.[7]

Although the burning of Mount Benedict occurred two decades before the formation of the state's Nunnery Committee, a steady stream of popular convent narratives along with the rise of nativist books and speeches kept Americans abuzz with fantastical stories about tortured nuns, deviant priests, and the alleged threat of convent life. Nativists aligned their aims to shield the country from "foreign influence" with a vow to protect the nation's women. Founder of the Order of United Americans Thomas Whitney traced the growth of the nativist movement alongside the growing number of convents in the United States each year. A prominent nativist and Presbyterian minister, Andrew Cross, published a series of letters in 1853 calling for the public protection of "imprisoned" nuns. In *Priests' Prisons for Women*, he focused on the story of Olevia Neal, who left a Carmelite convent in Maryland in 1839. "What has become of Olevia Neal?" he asked, suggesting that she was likely "immersed in mortar up to [her] neck." Cross demanded that Baltimore legislators "abolish this imprisonment of women." Nativists targeted not only immigrants and Catholics but also convents, holding them in special contempt as the epitome of foreign licentiousness and demanding government action against them.[8]

To guard "home and children," nativists vowed to enact "such legislation that none may be imprisoned in a convent." This promise reflected constituents' sentiments in various states by the 1850s. Massachusetts, for one, was flooded with petitions to abolish or at the very least investigate convents. The Boston *Christian Watchman and Reflector* surmised that "if half of the [convent] scenes could be known to the community," the people "would long since have arisen and swept these establishments from the face of the earth." Only the "enactment of a law to open the nunneries and give liberty to every captive" could solve the problem. In 1854, the *New York Observer* stated, "we must have laws in our several States by which the practice may be broken up of confining young women in nunneries." The article went on, estimating that "scores of young ladies in conventual establishments in this country [are] prisoners, in peril of body and soul." Supposing the secret nature of convents and convent schools—a common theme in anti-Catholic writings—the article asked, "If these establishments are not full of abuses, why are they so scrupulously concealed from public observation?"[9]

If the doors were opened, went the common mantra, if convents were exposed, if the veil was lifted, then the public would realize nuns were really slaves, prisoners, unwitting prostitutes, and drudges. Only an investigation would prove to the unbelievers what everyone else already "knew." As the slave question threatened to engulf the country in conflict, some pointed to convent life as worse than chattel slavery. Nativist spokesperson John Dowling argued in 1853 that under their "veil of concealment," all convents were "dark prison houses of slavery." Andrew Cross asked rhetorically whether "unmarried, foreign priests" should be able to "compel [women] as slaves to submit themselves to their will." In Boston-published *Life in the Grey Nunnery*, the female protagonist lamented being a nun. "I was literally a slave," she claimed, "and of all kinds of slavery, that which exists in the convent is the worst." Continuing in this vein, the author wrote, "You pity the poor black man who bends beneath the scourge of southern bondage . . . but you have no tears, no prayers, no efforts for the poor helpless nun who toils and dies beneath the heartless cruelty of an equally oppressive task master." If the "secrets" of the convent were "made known," then the American people would rise up against these institutions. The narrator concluded, calling on "the strong arm of the law" and mighty "Sons of America" to "demand these convent doors be opened and the oppressed allowed to go free."[10]

The Massachusetts Know Nothing legislators rose to the occasion. Convening in the early days of January 1855, the Bay State General Court busied itself "with a batch of new Know Nothing movements," reported the Pittsfield *Sun*. Among them, the government ordered the removal of hundreds of mental patients and Irish paupers to Liverpool, amended the Constitution to deny naturalized citizens and Catholics the opportunity to hold public office, disbanded the Irish militia, and mandated the reading of the King James Bible (as opposed to the optional Catholic Bible) in public schools. A suggested though not adopted measure proposed "requir[ing] Catholics, on being naturalized, to renounce allegiance to the Pope." The men also addressed a flood of petitions requesting nunnery investigations from twenty-seven different towns, including Foxboro, Ludlow, Milford, Oxford, and Marlboro. Wasting no time, the Speaker promptly named a committee for the task.[11]

The "escape" of Josephine Bunkley in 1854 from St. Joseph's, a Sisters of Charity House in Maryland, energized much of the demands to investigate convents. The *New York Observer* included an excerpt from a Virginia paper about "Miss Bunkley's escape," entitled "A Nunnery Law Wanted." Hailed as the "Maria Monk of the 1850s," Josephine Bunkley purportedly escaped from St. Joseph's in Emmitsburg. Later the Mother Superior there freely acknowledged Bunkley's residence at the convent as a novice but alleged that she had never taken vows, that she appeared content during her time there, and that her "escape" was unnecessary as she was free to leave whenever she wished. Despite the Mother Superior's testimony, Bunkley's story made national news and her subsequent book, *The Escaped Nun*, (Figure 7.2) became an instant bestseller.[12]

The book extended a conglomerate of recycled motifs from previous convent narratives, including references to lecherous priests, tyrannical Mother Superiors, insane nuns, subterranean passages, Protestant male heroes, and desperate fugitive nuns. Bunkley's account also likely appealed to a northern, middle-class readership as it unfolded scenes of breaking the Sabbath, gambling, drinking, and prostitution. "The occupations of the nuns and priests in the convent on Sundays, were such as would hardly be thought possible by the people in the States," Bunkley reported. The nuns "amused themselves with games of chance," while priests wiled away the afternoon "gambling and drinking beer and wine." These corruptions rendered convents unfit for "an intelligent and free Protestant country," where a growing number of people championed temperance, Sabbath regulations, and antiprostitution reform. Yet the day would arrive, the author promised, "when Americans would be convinced" of the evils of the convent system, and "it will no longer be necessary . . . to publish books like the present." For the citizens of Massachusetts, at least, that day had arrived with the state's formation of a Nunnery Committee.[13]

Josephine Marguerite Bunkley was born in 1834 and raised Episcopalian. At the age of sixteen she converted to Roman Catholicism and at twenty entered the Sisters of Charity at St. Joseph's Central House in Emmitsburg, Maryland. According to the official admissions log of St. Joseph's, Bunkley stayed in the convent for seven

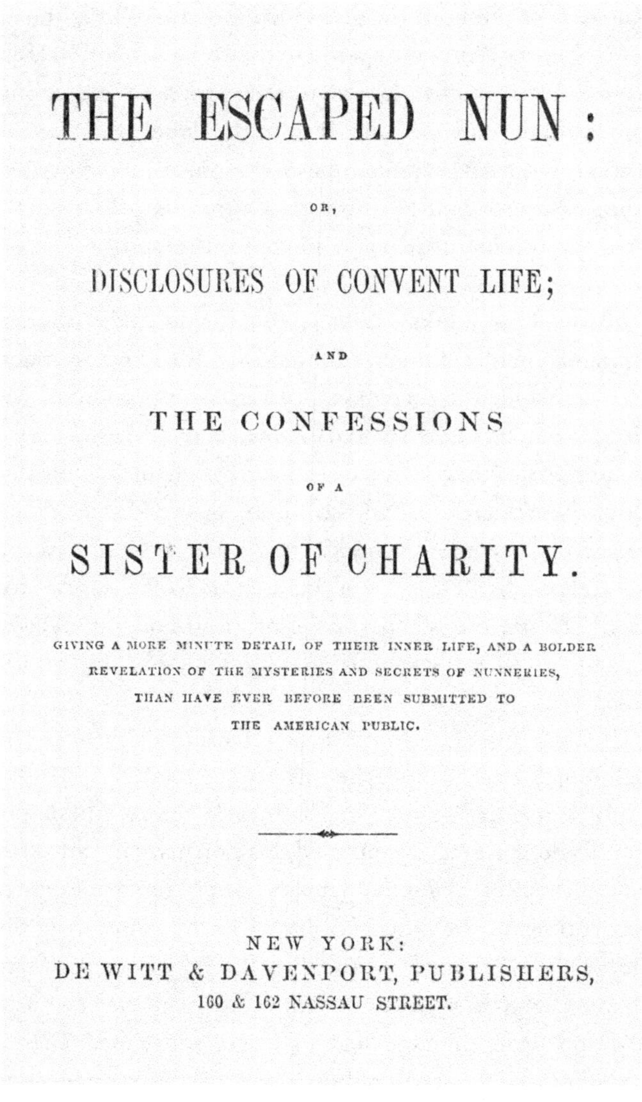

THE ESCAPED NUN :

OR,

DISCLOSURES OF CONVENT LIFE;

AND

THE CONFESSIONS

OF A

SISTER OF CHARITY.

GIVING A MORE MINUTE DETAIL OF THEIR INNER LIFE, AND A BOLDER
REVELATION OF THE MYSTERIES AND SECRETS OF NUNNERIES,
THAN HAVE EVER BEFORE BEEN SUBMITTED TO
THE AMERICAN PUBLIC.

NEW YORK:
DE WITT & DAVENPORT, PUBLISHERS,
160 & 162 NASSAU STREET.

FIGURE 7.2. *The Escaped Nun.*
Courtesy of HathiTrust.

months before voluntarily leaving in November 1854. While Bunkley certainly
resided at St. Joseph's and was familiar with life in the convent, significant portions
of her book proved impossible to collaborate. Some of the seamiest details appeared
in short stories, authored by others, within the book, such as "Confessions of a Sister
of Charity," based on "sources collected by a New York gentleman." Of equally unclear authorship, "Coralla, the Orphan Nun" drew attention away from Bunkley's
story while detailing a series of "startling" revelations about convents. According

to the *Metropolitan*, the "escaped nun," who was really a novice and may or may not have had to "escape," contributed no more than 20 pages—mostly bemoaning long prayers and manual labor—to the 338-page manuscript.[14]

Even before its release, a controversy ensued over the authorship of *The Escaped Nun*. Claiming to be Bunkley's agent, Charles Beale signed with De Witt & Davenport, a company that printed many nativist works, including Thomas Whitney's *A Defense of the American Policy*, to publish *The Testimony of an Escaped Nun*. Although Beale named Bunkley as the author, in reality he and Mary Jane Stith Ushur wrote the bulk of the manuscript. Perhaps for this reason, Bunkley applied for an injunction to keep De Witt & Davenport from publishing the book under her name. Yet before she could obtain the order, the publishers stereotyped the book, printing four thousand copies. Harper & Brothers, operating prosperously in New York at the time and known for predicting bestsellers, quickly caught wind of the story, publishing their own edition with Bunkley listed as the author under the title *The Testimony of an Escaped Novice*. For $1, readers could buy Harper's latest convent exposé by the latest escaped nun.[15]

Various papers reported on the escape of Bunkley alongside other current events. "As an illustration of Romanism and an exposé of convent life, we cheerfully recommend it," read *Zion's Herald and Wesleyan Journal*. Under the title "The Jesuits Cannot Suppress It," the *Western Reserve Chronicle* reported "De Witt & Davenport have the pleasure of presenting a fuller and more detailed account of the inner life of convents or nunneries" and promoted it for anyone not yet fully convinced of "criminalities practiced in convents." "Unlike many [books] of similar character," concluded the *Methodist Quarterly Review*, Bunkley's book "carried conviction of its truth to the mind of the reader." A letter printed in the *New York Herald* written by "A Know Nothing" claimed that "as long as there is an American Party in these United States," Bunkley, "a fugitive from a Roman Catholic Institution," should never want for "friends or money."[16]

Most of the Maryland residents readily accepted the story as truth. A stronghold of nativism punctuated by a riot before a Carmelite convent there in 1839 and the organization of the American Republican Party in Baltimore two years later, Maryland proved good breeding ground for *The Escaped Nun*. Outspoken ministers and editors, such as Andrew Cross and Robert J. Breckinridge, stoked the flames of the anticonvent movement with their *Baltimore Literary and Religious Magazine*, informing readers that convents served as prison houses for women, and that a Catholic conspiracy was underway in the American West. By the time of its publication, Bunkley's book flew off bookstore shelves throughout the state, including the popular shop of W. S. Crowley, a member of a nativist lodge, on Baltimore Street. In the 1855 elections, Know Nothings gained control of Maryland's lower house, occupying fifty-four assemblymen positions and eight senatorial seats. Yet, while Maryland's legislators voted consistently on nativist resolutions, including raising the requisite residence for citizenship, they sharply disagreed on the question of state nunnery investigations. Although referring to nuns as "female prisoners" and receiving multiple requests for the release of these "inmates," the delegates concluded that the writ of habeas corpus provided such women sufficient protection and precluded investigations.[17]

Unlike Maryland, no one in the Massachusetts General Court voiced opposition to the formation of a "Joint Special Committee on the Inspection of Nunneries and Convents." As Boston's *Zion's Herald* praised Bunkley for having "escaped from her prison house," the Bay State selected a committee, charging them with the task of investigating "convents and nunneries" where "women are forever barred from leaving." Before assigning members to the committee, the Speaker read a petition sent to the House attesting to the belief "that acts of villainy, injustice and wrong are perpetrated within the walls of said institutions." He then appointed members to right such wrongs, including John Littlefield of Foxborough, Joseph Hiss of Boston, Nathan King of Middleborough, Joseph H. Lapham of Sandwich, and Stephen Emery of Orange. The following day the president of the Senate named two additional members: David K. Hitchcock of Newton, and Gilbert Pillsbury of Ludlow. After Hitchcock declined the task, the Senate appointed Streeter Evans of Salisbury to the committee. Five representatives and two senators, all new members, thus completed the group.[18]

At the time Massachusetts formed a Nunnery Committee, only a few convents existed throughout the commonwealth. The Sisters of Charity had one house in the state. The Notre Dame Sisters resided on Lancaster Street in Boston and had schools in Roxbury, Lowell, and Salem. That was it. It was perhaps easy to believe the descriptions of convent life presented in accounts such as *The Escaped Nun* with few houses around to challenge such descriptions. The repeated charge to "protect" women from convent life and perhaps the curiosity stirred by such literature also prompted ready support for investigations. In an effort to avoid the accusation of religious bias, delegates broadened the task of the committee, to search "all Theological Seminaries, Boarding schools, [and] Academies," in addition to "Nunneries [and] Convents." Under this order, the committee could have investigated at least a thousand Protestant establishments in the state. Yet they never searched any Protestant institution, singling out Catholic ones, and convents in particular.[19]

The Massachusetts Nunnery Committee first visited Holy Cross College, a Catholic institution in Worcester. After finding nothing objectionable, they ventured to the Roxbury School operated by the Sisters of Notre Dame. A number of "friends" joined the seven committee members. As a result, concluded one critic later, "the party ceased to be a committee, and assumed the character of a mob." Three days later, on March 29, the committee visited the Sisters of Notre Dame School at Lowell. This time, a group of twenty-four men—four from the Nunnery Committee, four other members of the legislature, and sixteen "friends"—traveled twenty-six miles to get there and performed a similarly swift investigation before staying the night in the nearby Washington Hotel.[20]

Before the Know Nothing visit to the Lowell school, the Sisters there felt so alarmed that they "went several nights without getting undressed" and kept their belongings "packed for more than two weeks." A local priest, Father Timothy O'Brien, set up a "guard of sixty men to surround the house" and "all the Irishmen were on alert with their weapons." Curiously, the Sisters did not record the actual visit of the Know Nothings, moving on in their *Annals* to discuss the daily activities of the school. This could point to the dissipation of their fears or perhaps a reticence to focus on unpleasant topics. Yet clearly they felt threatened by public sentiment against them. Word reached the women that the state legislators suspected them of crimes and might investigate or worse at any time. Their preparations for attack indicated high tensions among the small community of nuns and the larger society in which they lived.[21]

After visiting the Lowell school, the Nunnery Committee halted their investigations. Fierce criticism pouring from the pages of the Boston *Daily Advertiser*, edited by Charles Hale, demanded an explanation from the legislature. Hale had been an avid critic of the Know Nothings for some time, and believing that the Nunnery Committee's actions violated the Constitution's Fourth Amendment, he found ready opportunity to voice his disapproval. In a series of articles he presented the investigation as an "unwarranted search" and a "violation of privacy." Casting convents as "homes," Hale asserted "the right of the people to be secure in their persons and houses, against unreasonable searches and seizures." Hale concluded that the committee, having no warrant or concrete justification for the search, violated one of the most precious rights held by the people of the US and especially those living in Massachusetts. Hale contended further that a man's house "is his castle; in which he reigns supreme . . . without hindrance from the State government." Hale's equation of convents with homes struck a new chord. Anti-Catholic rhetoric presented convents as the opposite of homes, describing them instead as prisons, brothels, and dens of vice. Nuns too appeared as the opposite of the ideal guardians of the home. True women, wives and mothers, made a home a home, not captive women, "foolish virgins," and childless drones. The comparison of convents to homes likely never occurred to the legislators or most of their constituents.[22]

Hale also accused the nunnery investigators of violating the gentleman's code. No true gentleman, he argued, "would venture to call upon any lady with whom he is not acquainted," let alone peep around her bedroom. Entering the bedchamber of a lady who was a stranger was an "act so gross, so repulsive to all notions of refinement, that no gentleman can perform it." Defining a true gentleman as one who exhibited "Respect for Truth, Respect for Woman, [and] Respect for Religion," Hale condemned the Nunnery Committee and their supporters as violating all three. Ironically, however, the Nunnery Committee formed as a response to what appeared to be a very gentlemanly call: to defend allegedly helpless women in the face of oppression. The rhetoric of male protection of defenseless females provided the basis for convent investigations. The dual interpretations of gentlemanly conduct, thus, revealed the malleability and strong importance of the concept in antebellum America. Perceptions of the social obligations of men could be used to both justify and condemn the anticonvent movement.[23]

Charles Hale, coeditor with his father of the staunchly Whig *Daily Advertiser*, was a recognizable name in the community. He specialized in Massachusetts political commentary, writing such works as *Journal of the Debates and Proceedings in the Convention of Delegates* (1853) and *Debates and Proceedings in the Convention of the Commonwealth of Massachusetts* (1856). Hale possessed no fondness for the Catholic Church, but he disagreed with Know Nothing policies that discriminated against Catholics and other minorities, perceiving such tactics as a threat to civil liberties everywhere. He skillfully exploited divided opinions on the nativist agenda with his forceful censure of the Nunnery Committee. The publication of his criticism even helped him achieve a seat in the state house in 1855 for which he ran as a member of the newly formed Republican Party. While he truly disapproved of the dealings of the Nunnery Committee, he likely saw the botched investigations as a chance to hasten the decline of the nativist party and build his career.[24]

Hale's condemnations encouraged other critics, who satirized the investigators peeking around corners like dogs, dubbing them the "Smelling Committee." The title caught on, inspiring anti–Know Nothing cartoons of the nunnery investigators sniffing their way around convents, checking out the most benign objects, such as chairs, bowls, and wagon wheels (Figure 7.3). "The investigator discovers a dilapidated cart-wheel, and is heart sick at the thought of the poor victims who have been broken on it," read one caption. Another pictured a man peering under a bed with a caption reading, "What was here discovered has not yet been revealed!" While the cartoon highlighted the ridiculous mission of the Nunnery Committee, the suspicion that medieval torture devices were used in convents and that there were other hidden crimes there had saturated popular literature and rhetoric for two decades,

FIGURE 7.3. "The Convent Committee, better known as the Smelling Committee."
Courtesy of the Boston Athenaeum.

leading many to doubt the dealings of female religious houses and see nuns as captive women.[25]

Ridicule of the Massachusetts Nunnery Committee spread. "The extraordinary movements of our legislature in reference to nunneries" has been "a general topic of newspaper comment . . . throughout the United States," reported the *Barre Patriot*. The *Commercial Advertiser*, a prominent New York paper, condemned the committee for displaying "religious intolerance and persecution." Presenting the matter as an issue of religious freedom, the *Advertiser* argued, "It is not safe to introduce religious questions into our popular elections, for the moment you make religious majorities in the legislature, you practically make religion a state matter." Yet even this criticism revealed deep-seated anti-Catholicism, as the writer compared the actions of the committee with "the very Romanism which they profess so utterly to abhor."[26]

John Bernard Fitzpatrick, the third bishop of Boston, also wrote in protest to the state's House after hearing about the Nunnery Committee's investigations of Roxbury. Fitzpatrick noted that any order of religious women would be willing to explain the nature of their work and life to investigators. Yet when those investigations became offensive or unpleasant, he must object. If such investigations continued, he went on, the Sisters, with his help, would be "compelled legally to assert and defend

the inviolability of their dwellings." Reflecting Hale's critique, Fitzgerald requested
that the legislature remove from its committee those members who lacked "respect,
reserve, and decorum which are due from gentlemen to ladies." Although the legislature ignored Fitzpatrick's protest, they were compelled to respond to the mounting
public criticism of the "Smelling Committee."[27]

Under pressure, the General Court reluctantly established a joint committee to investigate the doings of the nunnery sleuths. Before a standing-room crowd, on the
morning of April 7, 1855, the committee met for an open hearing. Several members of
the Nunnery Committee testified to the "exemplary" nature of their conduct at the
Notre Dame Academy. Charles Hale, who had received permission to participate in
the hearing, asked John Littlefield, the chairman of the Nunnery Committee for the
House, what evidence they cited to justify the search in the first place. Did they have
"good grounds for the belief that there were abuses in these schools demanding legislative interference"? Littlefield replied vaguely that the evidence was sufficient, but
that he "would report to the legislature and not to Mr. Hale." The committee never
subsequently made the evidence public, leading Hale to conclude that "it appeared to
them probable that general rumors and statements were the ground of proceeding."
The subsequent report of the investigation, agreeing with Hale, suggested that
"general rumors" instead of "specific" evidence provided the grounds for the search.
The report stated further that "some of the visitors [to Roxbury] were attracted by
curiosity . . . [and] others were there for no assignable cause."[28]

The only stated justification for the search came from an alleged personal testimony by William B. May, a member of the Nunnery Committee. Before the
Nunnery Committee formed, May told delegates his sister resided at a "similar institution" in Emmitsburg, Maryland. He believed convent authorities held her there
against her will. He also stated that he was not allowed to visit her. May later denied
making any such statement. As Hale reported, May visited his sister in Emmitsburg,
and "no objection whatever was made to his seeing her; she was not detained against
her will; [and] she had no wish to leave the place." This being the only evidence on
which the General Court based its decision to form a Nunnery Committee revealed
the influence of convent narratives and especially that of Josephine Bunkley's, as she
was a resident at the St. Joseph House in Emmitsburg, in shaping public opinion on
nuns. Her story, likely familiar to members of the legislature, provided validation
for May's claims about his sister and reinforced perceptions of convents. May's accusation played on the outrage at the idea of women being beyond traditional male
access and oversight. Bunkley's story of escape, May's testimony, nativist suspicion
of foreign institutions, and mounting public demand for the law to do something
rendered convent investigations an obvious move.[29]

On April 10, Mary Aloysia, the Mother Superior at the Roxbury academy, took the stand. Although the investigators requested the presence of all of the Notre Dame Sisters, only Mary Aloysia appeared. Walking through the courtroom in her full habit, a remnant of a medieval, European custom, the Mother Superior likely resembled all that many of the nativist legislators opposed. She presented a statement from her community, explaining the absence of the other Sisters and why they found fault with the Nunnery Committee's investigation. Instead of appealing to a general invasion of privacy, Aloysia complained that one of the inspectors lingered behind after the rest of the crew departed. He told her that he had drifted from the faith and hoped to return before asking if they could have an "agreeable conversation" on the topic. Believing he had ulterior motives, the Mother Superior suggested "in a very serious way" that he speak with a priest about the matter, at which point he left in a huff. When Hale asked Aloysia to identify the man, she pointed to Joseph Hiss. In a cross-examination, one of the senators asked the Mother Superior if she thought the actions of Hiss improper before she read critical reviews of the committee in the "Jesuit newspapers." The Mother Superior informed him that she did.[30]

Aloysia later wrote that she "tremble[ed] with emotion and indignation, so that I could hardly speak" when the Know Nothings had arrived at the school and announced their intentions to search the building. Although the Mother Superior consented to the search, she described it as a "famous and villainous inquisition" and Hiss as the "biggest rascal" and "wicked fellow" of the search committee for his barging into one of the classrooms and questioning the pupils. After staying on the stand for hours, the committee requested Aloysia's return the next day with Sister Mary Joseph and Caroline Crabb. The following day, Sister Mary Joseph testified to Hiss cornering her in the hall outside the chapel, and Crabb described the men who entered her bedroom where she lay sick.[31]

Aloysia and the other Notre Dame Sisters expressed horror over the public attention they received in light of the Nunnery Committee's investigations. In her daily account, Aloysia wrote of the various papers that took up the story, "some of them being for us and others against us," describing it all as being "mortifying to me." The Sisters, she claimed, "began to fear, and with reason, that we would be cited to appear before the court." For women who had taken vows that wed them to lives of modesty and separation from the world, such attention chafed against their vocational sensibilities. The Nunnery Committee in effect forced these women into the public light, making them a part of the spectacle that had been mounting in popular literature. The women received a notice on Easter Sunday during dinner that their presence was requested the next day in court. "Fatal news for such a holy day!" Aloysia remarked. Reflecting on her entrance into the court, Aloysia wrote, "It seemed to me as if I were being conducted to the gallows." After what turned into three days of questioning, during which time the Sisters had to arrange for substitute teachers to instruct their pupils, the court dismissed the Mother Superior and Sister Mary Joseph.[32]

Shortly after the Easter holiday, the investigative committee issued a report. It upheld "the sacred rights of the domicile, and the right of the press to criticize the action of legislatures," but recommended "no action." The report quoted a spokesperson for the Nunnery Committee stating, "We were appointed to *investigate* only . . . [and] have performed the unwelcomed task fearlessly. Without fear, favor, affection or hope of reward, we have done the work with which we are charged." The report further condoned "the accompaniments of outsiders" in the investigation and "the banquets indulged in by the committee" on the "ground of precedents." As for Hiss, the committee accused him of "improprieties" but not "criminal conduct."[33]

Before being named "Grand Worshipful Instructor" of the Boston Know Nothing Chapter, Hiss, a state representative and leader of the Nunnery Committee, had worked as a tailor. Under pressure from his creditors, he moved from his hometown of Barre, Massachusetts, to Boston, where he rose in the Know Nothing ranks. He presided as secretary of its state convention and judge advocate of the secret order shortly before the state elections. For Hiss, and surely others like him, the fraternal lodge offered a sense of community and purpose. It also afforded those like Hiss, who may have wavered on the verge of economic insecurity and obscurity, greater social mobility and recognition. Nativists became patriots, aligned with the founding fathers, fashioning themselves protectors of their legacy and vision for the nation. This was no short order. In the local fraternity, Hiss could also use personality to his advantage. Known for his "ingratiating personality" and confident smiles, Hiss was well liked by his associates, who mostly overlooked any lack of political acumen.[34]

Not long after the release of the first report, the House voted to scrap the document. The state buzzed with rumors of even greater improprieties taken by members of the committee, including stories of some of them visiting "secular nunneries" or brothels during the romp. Charles Hale pushed hardest for further investigations after uncovering details about the Nunnery Committee's stay in the Washington Hotel following their visit to the Lowell academy. Another special committee was named to investigate these charges. They gathered information on yet another night of carousing, but this time the party went beyond accepted precedent.[35]

During this second investigation, Hale made a startling accusation that Hiss had taken a woman other than his wife to the hotel. At the Washington Hotel, Hiss charged a "woman of the evening" along with dinner, cigars, gin, and lodging to the state. Hale pointed to the name of "Mrs. Patterson" that appeared among the hotel's guest list registered by Joseph Hiss. On the stand, Hiss claimed that he had run into an old friend who had asked him to escort Mrs. Patterson to the hotel. Stumbling through the cross-examination, however, Hiss raised suspicion among the listeners. Did Hiss know Mrs. Patterson? "I don't think so. . . . No. . . . Maybe." The investigative committee further uncovered that Hiss and the so-called "Mrs. Patterson" had adjoining rooms. In further investigations, witness after witness testified to the association between the woman and Hiss, leaving the man known for his smiles uncomfortably unable to defend himself. Days after the hearing, with a pile of accusations stacked against him, Hiss issued his resignation. While not admitting guilt, he claimed this action was necessary to quiet the "hostile press" and save the "American Party."[36]

The House appeared to agree as they dismissed Hiss but exonerated the rest of the Nunnery Committee. In its final report, members claimed that nothing would have come of the committee's actions had it not been for the hostile press and "the Jesuits." The House commended Hiss for his gentlemanly conduct in Roxbury, dismissing all complaints leveled by "the nuns." The report was less forgiving concerning his actions at the Washington House, claiming his conduct was "highly improper and disgraceful both to himself and this body of which he is a member, and we deem it such as to render him unworthy longer to occupy a seat upon the floor of this house." Significantly, however, 150 members of the legislature absented themselves to avoid voting against Hiss. The committee admitted that nothing in the convents searched "warrant[ed] legislation," but that other similar institutions still existed as "prisons of innocent victims."[37]

In contrast to the investigative report, Charles Hale argued that the blame for the Nunnery Committee's misadventures did not "fall on any single member of the committee." He pointed rather to the broader culture of "ignorance and carelessness." Nor did Hale find the Nunnery Committee crew's late-night reveling to be their greatest impropriety. "The cardinal offense," he claimed, "was the entrance, without right or authority, of a party of men into a private house, where their presence was neither desired nor expected." He expressed frustration at the way in which the committee members' partying "tended to attract more of the public attention . . . than the primal offense of the unjustifiable entrance of the house." But Hale was alone in this conclusion. The legislature and the public focused on the Nunnery Committee's nights of carousing, perhaps a more interesting facet, rather than the convent investigations themselves, something that turned out to be uneventful.[38]

Shortly after the Nunnery Committee debacle, Massachusetts Know Nothings fell from public grace. Months after the investigative hearings, Free Soilers—a short-lived political party that opposed the expansion of slavery in favor of free labor—broke their alliance with the Know Nothings, no longer needing their support. They helped form a fusionist group and that would become the Republican Party. In the following fall elections Know Nothings still prevailed, but at a much smaller margin than in 1854. By 1858, the Republican Party triumphed in the state and the Know Nothings disappeared from the political stage. The divisiveness of the slavery issue contributed significantly to this demise, but so did public disapproval of the Know Nothings, furnished in part by their embarrassing investigations of convents.[39]

Massachusetts Know Nothings blamed their demise on a conspiracy. A "corrupt press" had taken advantage of the Nunnery Committee scandal, blowing it out of proportion to wrest political power from the Know Nothings. The defense counselor blamed the "persecution" launched at Hiss on those who aimed to "strike down the party in power." Historian John Mulkern agreed, writing, "Hale's scoop furnished the partisan Boston press with what it had been waiting for—a major Know Nothing scandal—and it pounced on the story with glee." To be sure, criticism from the press, especially Hale's *Daily Advertiser*, ignited disdain for the Nunnery Committee. Yet the lack of incriminating evidence discovered by the investigators in the visited convents also discredited them. Had they found anything to validate the piles of accusations perpetuated for decades against convents, the fate of the Nunnery Committee and perhaps the Massachusetts Know Nothings would have been much different.[40]

At a national level, Know Nothings as a political party disintegrated in the face of the all-encompassing question of slavery. In the North, most Know Nothings vocally opposed the extension of slavery. One of the first acts passed by the Massachusetts Know Nothings prohibited the cooperation of state officials in returning fugitive slaves. Although the law did not condemn slavery morally, rather presenting the issue as a matter of "personal liberty," it placed Massachusetts on a definitive side of the slavery debate. In southern states, Know Nothing legislators cooperated with Democrats. One Know Nothing in Maryland delivered an ambiguous speech in which he upheld "the sovereignty of the States," opposing "any further agitation of the subject of slavery as elevating sectional hostility." Yet sectional hostility infected even the American Party, as Know Nothings formally split in 1855 over the slavery question. Unable to convince the public of the greater evil of "white slavery," or that upholding all things American could keep the country united, the Know Nothings joined the long list of short-lived political parties.[41]

On February 22, 1856, on the anniversary of George Washington's birthday, members of the American Party convened for their first and last national convention. After pledging to "Put none but Americans on guard tonight," the party nominated incumbent candidate Millard Fillmore of New York for the presidency, and Andrew Jackson Donelson of Tennessee as his running mate. Fillmore appeared to be an ideal Know Nothing candidate. He had a record of battling the "foreign vote"; he championed the Compromise of 1850, preserving the Union; and in 1855 he became a member of a Buffalo Know Nothing lodge. Despite recent set-backs, Know Nothings expressed high hopes of securing the presidency. "There can be no room to doubt," augured one Know Nothing author in 1855, as to "the success of the American nominee for the presidency." But his denunciation of the new Republican Party and support of the Kansas-Nebraska Act appeared overly pro-southern, while his conservative pro-Union position displeased the South. The election results signaled Fillmore's defeat and the demise of the American Party. In New England Fillmore received less than thirty thousand votes. He faced similar defeats elsewhere, only carrying electoral votes in the border state of Maryland. At their last national council meeting in June 1857, Know Nothings urged the party faithful to support the local party that best fit the views of the "Americans" and convened without scheduling a future council meeting. By the end of the year the new Republican Party had mostly absorbed the Know Nothings.[42]

The Massachusetts Nunnery Committee may seem like a minor blip on the margins of Know Nothing history. Indeed, many historians have cast it this way. In his book-length discussion of the party, Dale Knobel devoted only half a paragraph to the Massachusetts' Nunnery Committee and the nativist campaign against convents. John Mulkern, who has written the most extensively on the Bay State's Nunnery Committee, described it as a "bitter fruit" of the one-party system that "threw nativist apologists into disarray" as they scrambled to atone for the obvious blunder of their copatriots. Yet the Nunnery Committee as an embarrassing aberration from the party's main goals does not account for the unanimous support the committee received. This argument also ignores the loud and pervasive denigrations of convent life littered throughout popular literature and rhetoric as the movement gained momentum. Although the Nunnery Committee only existed in one state, others, such as Maryland and New York, entertained the idea, and only after the debacle in Massachusetts did demands for such investigations die out elsewhere. That the investigative committee expressed greater horror over the after-hours carousing of the Nunnery Committee than their unconstitutional search of convents further reveals the abiding disdain for convent life and nuns within the Know Nothing movement.

Much more than a "bitter fruit," the Nunnery Committee represented decades of public outcry against convent life and the belief that nuns were either in need of liberation and male protection or complicit in corruption. The anticlimactic results of the Nunnery Committee somewhat sobered the riotous anticonvent movement. People wanted to discover imprisoned nuns; they wanted "inmates" to validate stories of sexual debauchery and torture; they were ready for a new shocking revelation. Yet the "result of the search was a ludicrous disappointment," argued Hale, writing that the committee "would have been glad to find . . . abominations of some sort." The investigations let the air out of public expectations for convent exposures, at least for a time.[43]

The Nunnery Committee marked both the pinnacle and the decline of the Know Nothing Party and the campaign against convents. Although various calls to "invite investigation" into the "cruelty and suffering" of the nun's life appeared throughout the ensuing years, the slavery issue drowned out these cries before enveloping the country in a bloody Civil War. As Sisters of Mercy and nuns from other orders nursed wounded soldiers on both sides of the fight and Catholic men donned the blue and gray, anti-Catholicism abated for a time. Massachusetts, though not always the focal point of the American campaign against convents, neatly bookended the movement, from the burning of Mount Benedict in 1834 to the Nunnery Committee of 1855. Within those two decades, the US witnessed the enormous success of Maria Monk's *Awful Disclosures of the Hotel Dieu*, the ensuing controversy over Monk's "real story," a heightened debate over schooling the nation's youth that focused largely on convent education, the association of convents with slavery, the urban underground, and Mormon plural marriage, and the mounting of a political party whose members made antipopery and convent investigations a major plank of their platform. The Nunnery Committee answered calls dating back to Maria Monk's invocation to "search!" While the public may have scoffed at the Nunnery Committee's "smelling" around convents and their careless late-night carousing, the committee only reflected the demands of large sectors of the American people that had been building for quite some time.[44]

Today, the figure of the nun resides mostly in the realm of kitsch . . . they have become icons without a history.

—Rebecca Sullivan in "A Question of Habit," 2012

More often than not . . . the nun has come to represent something sinister. Many of us only have to see a nun to feel a shiver of fear run down our spine.

—*Scary Nuns*, 2007

Epilogue

SOLVING A PROBLEM LIKE MARIA: IMAGINING SISTERS FROM MARIA MONK TO NUNSENSE

IT HAS BEEN a long time since someone torched a convent. Ambitious politicians do not win elections by promising to ban nunneries. And no escaped nuns capture headlines. Perhaps the ghosts of Maria Monk have finally been exorcised, the flames of the campaign against convents finally snuffed out. And yet unflattering images of nuns still litter American culture, nun kitsch has become a major franchise, and Maria Monk's book has never gone out of print. For well over a decade, the whimsical nun, "caught in the act of cutting loose," has been emblazoned on every month of the year through the popular "Nuns Having Fun" calendar. There is the bitter crone nun ready to slap someone's knuckles with a ruler, nun action figures and nuns of late-night comedy sketches. Television shows, such as *American Horror Story*, have kept alive the scary nun as a modern villain. And Halloween offers a stunning array of sexy, "naughty nun" costumes. Always dressed in a full habit (something few Sisters actually don today), nuns appear on greeting cards, as bowling pins, and in soap. Angelic and childlike nun figurines, boxing nun puppets, "duck nuns," and Sister Mary Margarita cocktail napkins don gift store shelves. Presented as anything other than human, it would seem as though the American campaign against convents continues, albeit in a different tone.

Why are Americans still captivated by nuns? What makes them funny, scary, masculine, or just strange? Does America have a nun problem? Have we still not accepted the idea of a woman living a single, celibate, religious life? Maria Monk's story and other antebellum convent narratives forged the image of the nun that has persisted in American culture. In nineteenth-century convent narratives like *Awful Disclosures*, nuns appeared as vulnerable victims, masculine tyrants, sex slaves, silly idiots, and gothic witchlike figures. While perhaps less sensationalized, this same cast endures. Maria Monk herself continues to haunt American popular culture. Like a jack-in-the-box, she has popped up sporadically at different times. After the Civil War, new "escaped nuns" were likened to Maria Monk. In the early twentieth century, new nativists revived *Awful Disclosures* as part of a reborn anti-Catholic crusade. During the Cold War era, Monk reinforced arguments linking Catholicism to authoritarian regimes. Although most reprints of *Awful Disclosures* since the latter half of the twentieth century introduce the book as a historical example of bigotry and paranoia, the book remains in print by various publishers who promote it as the "shocking truth."[1]

The American Civil War halted the campaign against convents for a time. When war broke out, over six hundred nuns from twenty-one different communities responded by tending to the wounded and the dying. They served at the edges of battles, nursing men regardless of uniform, race, or creed. Sister Mother Angela Gillespie, a Catholic convert and member of the Sisters of Mercy, founded a nursing corps to care for sick and wounded soldiers. She traveled to DC, petitioning Congress for aid, and established a hospital. To commemorate the Sisters' service during the war, Congress erected a monument in the nation's capital, and poets lauded them as "angels of the battlefield." During the war and its immediate aftermath, Sisters faced little hostility in America as they continued to operate schools, tend to the sick, and live lives of prayerful meditation. Historian Margaret Susan Thompson attributed this lull in hostility in part to nuns' unyielding service during the war.[2]

By the 1890s and into the early twentieth century, however, anti-Catholicism and prejudice against nuns resurfaced with a vengeance. A new array of secret, anti-Catholic, nativist groups popped up throughout the country as almost nine million immigrants, many of them Catholic and Jewish, flooded into Ellis Island between the 1880s and 1890s. Unlike earlier groups, these "new immigrants" came from southeastern Europe, the Hapsburg monarchy, Austria-Hungary, and the Russian Empire. Their distinctive culture, language, and religion rendered them unassimilable in the eyes of many Americans. To "protect" American schools from Catholic infiltration and defend their way of life, white, male Protestants formed groups like the National League for the Protection of American Institutions, the United Order of Native Americans, and the American Protective Association (APA).[3]

The APA swelled to half a million members by 1894. Nativist publishing houses reprinted Maria Monk's *Awful Disclosures*, which the APA enthusiastically advertised. Other convent narratives captured public attention, including Edith O'Gorman's *Convent Life Unveiled* (1871). O'Gormon traveled the US and abroad giving anti-Catholic lectures after her book release, which went through thirty-six editions by 1936. Her real presence in a convent, however, was never confirmed. Historian Rene Kollar attributed the success of her book to "the fascination of some non-Catholics with the mysterious inter-workings of sisterhoods." The era also witnessed the rise of a Maria Monk prototype and APA darling, Margaret Shepherd, author of *My Life in a Convent*. Shepherd spoke on a lecture circuit sponsored by the APA throughout the 1890s, telling her story of life as a nun. After fathering a child from a priest, claimed Shepherd, she entered a convent in desperation. While feeling it her "duty to submit," Shepherd suffered at the hands of "licentious and lecherous priests." She related stories of ceremonial orgies and beautiful young women being raped and tortured. Like earlier convent narratives, *My Life in a Convent* offered readers titillating details shrouded in a cautionary tale. No one investigated Shepherd's accusations. A nativist publication at the time, however, offered a dystopian illustration of a future where the "new woman" ruled, suggesting a fear of gender equality at least among some group members. Perhaps this impulse also inspired support for the "escaped nun" legend, as it presented an alternative from marriage and motherhood in a convent as a horror story.[4]

Despite hostility from outsiders, the Sisterhood flourished throughout the US. They built the largest private hospital system in the country, operated the most expansive private school organization in the world, and provided innumerable general welfare services. Sisters were part of the nineteenth-century settlement house movement. Between the Civil War and World War I, women religious established 479 hospitals. They taught English to a flood of immigrants, allowing them to more easily integrate into a society suspicious of non-English-speaking residents. They offered newcomers and other poor members of society services otherwise denied them, such as daycare centers, homes for the aged, and burials for their dead. Sisters established the first form of health insurance, selling $5 tickets to miners, ranchers, and other traveling workers, which when presented at a hospital would allow them access to services. Some scholars claim that these efforts contributed more than anything else in elevating the large number of Catholics in the nation into the upper and middle classes. When their own Catholic institutions would not admit women to universities, Sisters founded their own postsecondary institutions or attended non-Catholic ones. Sister Katherine Drexel founded Xavier University in 1915 to provide

African Americans higher education. The school became accredited in the 1920s and continues to flourish.[5]

From the late nineteenth century to the early twentieth, clerics called on women religious, as a convenient labor source, to run their burgeoning parochial schools. Perceiving public schools in the US to have a decidedly Protestant bias, the Catholic hierarchy mandated the establishment of parochial schools for the ever-growing Catholic population. American nuns almost singlehandedly created the colossus that became the parochial school system in America, educating more than 1.7 million of the nation's Catholic children by 1920. They staffed elementary schools, academies, industrial schools, night schools, and public, private, and parochial schools. By midcentury, however, some women began to feel the toll of trying to keep up with educational standards and school duties while maintaining lives of prayer and their own health. Dropped into classrooms almost as soon as they entered an order, many Sisters received poor and drawn-out training as teachers, which sometimes took twenty years to complete, while deferring their own educational pursuits. Some students taught by overworked, stressed, and underappreciated women, at a time when corporal punishment was encouraged in schools, certainly felt the brunt of "stern nuns." In 1954, a group of Sisters established the Sister Formation Conference (SFC) to promote education among women religious. Unwittingly, they also began discussing how to modernize the Sisterhood, a topic that would be more fully explored in the Second Vatican Council.[6]

The first church council in almost one hundred years, Vatican II (1962–1965) opened a gateway into the twentieth century for the Catholic Church. Notably absent among the thousands of observers and participants, however, were women. A group of women religious accepted an eventual invitation to audit the council by the third session. Mostly notably, Sister Mary Luke Tobin served as a vocal representative for Catholic women. The council ushered in vital reforms, and its resulting documents encouraged a radical rethinking of the church that focused less on the hierarchy and more on the "people of God." The spirit of openness and call to renewal engendered by the council spurred much debate and dialogue, encouraging some Sisters to reconfigure their mission. Other women religious, feeling ignored by the council, awoke to a new sense of feminism. In either case, the council helped to create what the media called "new nuns," women who ditched their habits, earned advanced degrees, and worked in the inner city.

These changes did not suit everyone. Many felt a sense of loss, including Sister Joan D. Chittister, a Benedictine nun who considered leaving the order. "Nothing is the same anymore," she lamented. "They don't want to teach; they don't want to wear the habit; they don't want to live together." Strangely, Vatican II signaled the sharp decline of nuns in the United States. The Sisterhood decreased by 42 percent between 1962 and 1992. Despite lower numbers, Vatican II signaled a shift for Sisters from school rooms to the streets as they took on a plethora of social justice issues. In the second half of the twentieth century Sisters marched alongside civil rights activists, spoke out against anti-Semitism, fought for nuclear disarmament, formed antiwar coalitions, supported the feminist movement, and worked with AIDS patients, among other ventures.[7]

Sisters Mary Joel Read and Mary Austin Doherty served as founding members of the National Organization for Women (NOW). The roots of such feminist impulses among nuns could be traced back to the mid-nineteenth century, with the School Sisters of Notre Dame. These nuns kept files on "women in society," "education of women," and "women and the church." Their focus was on women, elevating them, fostering their skills and talents, and intentionally remaining conscious of their role in society. On August 26, 1970, Sister Margaret Traxler spoke at one of the national "Women Strike" demonstrations in Chicago. "I personally will do anything which will further the cause for women," she said with arm raised and hand clenched in a fist. A few years later the National Coalition of American Nuns (NCAN) demanded "full and equal participation of women in churches." Some Sisters even embraced a prochoice position on abortion and battled the Vatican over the issue. Sisters have continued to have a strong presence regarding social justice in the twenty-first century, dedicating their efforts to such issues as immigration, health care, the death penalty, and civil rights.[8]

Despite the singular role nuns have played in American life, historians for the most part have ignored them. American history textbooks would lead one to believe that nuns never existed in the US. Most histories of religion in America not only marginalize Catholic history but also often neglect information on women's religious orders altogether. Until recently, volumes on Catholicism in the US focused more on the priests, bishops, and laity than on Sisters. Nuns are also conspicuously absent from most women's histories. Although they were on the front lines of much of the women's movement, most feminists write them off as submissively yielding to the patriarchy.[9]

The story of Sisters in America has been largely told through popular culture. Thus, to most people, nuns are caricatures displayed on greeting cards, campy movies, and toys, not real women in real life. The reasons for this historical amnesia are varied. Most historians ignore nuns, but at the same time women religious have traditionally avoided self-promotion, making it difficult for the public to take notice of their lives and actions. A curious public, satiated on a long legacy of anticonvent sentiment, dating back to Maria Monk, has served to create a deep-seated stereotype rather than a history of nuns. At a time when print culture first offered cheap paperbacks and sensationalized stories, the convent narratives impressed on

American minds an image of the nun as a one-dimensional captive, tyrant, fool, or tortured beauty. Nuns became "knowable," amusing, and easy to dismiss.

The Menace, a Missouri-based publishing house, saw to it that Maria Monk's *Awful Disclosures* stayed in print in the 1910s. It advertised the work as "one of the most formidable books ever published," revealing "what takes place when Rome locks out the state and the helpless in her papal prisons." The publisher's newspaper, also titled *The Menace*, sounded much like earlier anti-Catholic papers, such as *The Downfall of Babylon*, which originally promoted Maria Monk. A few years after its printing, a revived and expanded Ku Klux Klan took up the anticonvent campaign. The new Klan proclaimed an objective to "remain until the last son of a Protestant surrenders his manhood, and is content to see America, Catholicized, mongrelized, and circumcised." Members vowed to protect American white women from Jews, African Americans, and Catholic convents. In 1919, Klansmen sponsored a series of lectures delivered by Helen Jackson, an alleged "escaped nun" and author of *Convent Cruelties; or, My Life in a Convent*. Jackson, yet another reincarnation of Maria Monk, regaled listeners with stories of infanticide, illicit relationships among nuns and priests, and gruesome punishments. She was later revealed to be fake. But her story only reinforced the image of vulnerable white womanhood in need of protection, whether from black men or Catholic.[10]

Sounding remarkably like some of the messages distributed by the American Tract Society in the antebellum era were a series of "Tracts" denouncing Catholicism and convents, published by the Protestant Book House, a publisher through the 1910s and 1920s. "Tract No. 8" announced "Catholic Girl Rescued from Roman Convent." With the help of "a lawyer, the Ku Klux Klan, the Editor of the True American, and other loyal Protestants," the girl escaped "papal slavery." Under the title "Know the Truth: Open the Nunneries," the Protestant Book House promoted a series of convent narratives from Margaret Shepherd to Maria Monk in a handy pamphlet. "A convent is far from being what an American institution should be," read the pamphlet, "holding as each and every one does many girls behind iron doors, shut away from parents, friends and homes." From this perspective, convents threatened not only "girls" and family life but also republican ideals. The pamphlet urged readers to carry on the tradition of the pilgrims and the founders, seeking "liberty and escape from papal persecution."[11]

The Protestant Book House prefaced *Awful Disclosures* as a "blood-curdling" narrative of "every crime from seduction to murder." Reinforcing the themes of Monk's book, they published a tract entitled "Convent Horror," featuring a forlorn-looking woman with her hands clutched under her chin and a tear on her cheek. Barbara Ubrick remained locked in a "stone dungeon" for twenty-one years because "she refused to surrender her virtue to a Romish priest." Another tract, whose title harkened back to Rebecca Reed's *Six Months in a Convent*, "My Life in the Convent: Six Years Behind Popish Nunnery Bars," told of a woman who "was the daughter of a priest of Rome—seduced by a priest—married to a priest—abandoned in a convent by a priest—her baby destroyed in a convent." Just as World War I propaganda featuring American women being carted off by a burly, lustful "Hun" in the shape of a gorilla served to dehumanize and discredit the German enemies, anticonvent sentiment continued to present priests and convent life as a danger to female purity, the family, and American ideals.[12]

The following decades saw the entrance of many Catholics into the American religious mainstream due to years of education, their service during World War II, and greater available economic opportunity in the postwar era. Yet anti-Catholicism heated up once more during the Cold War among as some associated Catholicism with authoritarian regimes. In 1949, the Beacon Press published the most famous anti-Catholic work of the twentieth century: Paul Blanshard's *American Freedom and Catholic Power*, which described Soviet Communism and Catholicism as twin evils that threatened the American way of life. Blanshard promoted "candid discussion" about what he called the "Catholic problem." Catholicism "*is* political," he argued, pointing to efforts of bishops to secure tax dollars for parochial schools or to ban the public mailing of birth control literature. Not leaving out nuns, Blanshard described Sisters as being part of "an age when women allegedly enjoyed subjection and reveled in self-abasement." The book remained on the *New York Times* bestseller list for seven months and quickly ran through eleven printings in its first year.[13]

In 1952, the Book and Bible House of Decatur, Georgia, reprinted *Awful Disclosures*. The publisher boasted that "this is the most extensively read book ever printed on the papal curse" and that "Rome fought bitterly but in vain to suppress it." They harkened back to previous editions, including those printed by the Menace, estimating that "10,000,000 copies have been read throughout the world." The Book and Bible House juxtaposed the nun's life with domestic norms, stating, "Rome teaches . . . that the nun is holier in the sight of God than a loving lawful mother with a child in her thrilled and thrilling arms; that a priest is better than a loving father; that celibacy is better than that passion of love that has made everything of beauty in this world." At a time when the suburban nuclear household was perhaps most celebrated, Maria Monk once again gained status as the antithesis to female virtue and family values.[14]

Convent exposés of the mid-twentieth century promised to reveal more shocking details with every publication. "Nothing like this ever published in America!" read a description to "House of Death and Gate of Hell or Convent Brutality," from a 1952 tract by the Book and Bible House. It promised "Horrible and blood-curdling revelations of convent life for the last twenty years—Poison, Murder, Rapine, Torturing and smothering babies." The books and pamphlets freely borrowed from antebellum convent narratives. As in *Awful Disclosures*, "House of Death," told of a nun being made to drink the water from which the Mother Superior washed her feet and another being "bound hand and foot, gagged, lying in a dungeon." Like a carnival line-up of oddities, "House of Death" invited readers to "see" the nun who "dug a hole under wall and made escape from Detroit nunnery"; "see photo of nun shot by a Roman thug"; "see priest and mother superior smothering a baby" in Montreal, Canada; "see nun who struck priest with an ax when he attacked her"; and "see the iron virgin with steel teeth, a murder device." Beauty remained an issue as well. Just as in antebellum narratives, made more dramatic by the entrance of a *beautiful* woman into a convent, later literature lamented the "waste" of attractive women who became nuns. "Almost a Nun!" read the cover of a 1950s tract featuring the mug of a strikingly beautiful woman.[15]

Hollywood picked up on the drama of the beautiful nun but dropped the scathing anti-Catholicism in a series of films that presented the nun as a lovely, angelic figure. The first movie to feature a nun as the lead role, *The Bells of St. Mary's* (1945) displayed a charismatic woman, no stranger to the life of romance and culture, who nevertheless freely chose a nun's life. A story of a good-natured rivalry between Sister Benedict, played by Ingrid Bergman, and Father O'Malley, played by Bing Crosby, unfolded through the film. Despite their differences, the two learned to work together to save their inner-city school from being shut down. *New York Times* reviewer Bosley Crowther wrote that Bergman's performance stereotyped the nun as the "good sister" and Bergman as the "Virgin Mary of films." Audiences enjoyed the film, helping it take in $21,300,000, becoming among the highest grossing of the time. It presented a "feel good" story with affable and attractive lead characters, tensions of chaste romance, and a message of giving and hope. While the film offered a needed antidote to the caricatures of convent propaganda, it was not an entirely realistic portrayal of nuns, presenting a Hollywood ideal rather than a human life.[16]

Other postwar-era films seemed to suggest it was finally okay to be American and Catholic, a citizen and a nun. Released in 1959, the same year as *Ben Hur*, *The Nun's Story*, starring Audrey Hepburn, became an instant success. Based on a true account and best-selling book, *The Nun's Story* traced Gabrielle Van Der Mal, the daughter of a wealthy Belgian surgeon, into a convent where she became Sister Luke. As part of a missionary order, the Mother Superior of the convent sent Sister Luke to assist doctors in the Belgian Congo. Despite having strong convictions to serve, Sister Luke struggled with a sense of pride and independence only to find herself falling in love with Dr. Fortunati, an agnostic and handsome surgeon. While nothing came of their growing mutual affection, Sister Luke continued to chafe against the austerities of convent life. Finally, after her father's death, hastened by the Nazi capture of Belgium, she decided to leave the convent. The camera closed on a woman in civilian clothes walking away into a bustling city, suggesting a hopeful future, likely to include marriage, happiness, and freedom.[17]

A Nun's Story received high reviews by Catholics and the secular press alike. The *Hollywood Reporter* stated that "the picture leaves no doubt that the life of the dedicated nun is courageous and filled with self-sacrificing service." *America*, a Jesuit magazine, praised the film for its portrayal of "devotion to Christ and His work." Some Sisters, however, felt frustrated with the film's picture of convent life as "an imposing asylum," a presentation they felt would harm their efforts to recruit new postulants. A Notre Dame Sister who sat on the panel for the film complained that it reduced religious life to "a series of lectures and processions and exhortations." Indeed, the film presented exaggerated convent austerities for dramatic effect. Despite its shortcomings, the film was one of the first to take seriously the life the nun in a way that was neither dumbed down nor anti-Catholic. Although Sister Luke left the convent, she did not have to run away; she faced no resistance; and her decisions to join and to leave were both her own. Historian Rebecca Sullivan granted that the film was an "ambitious, serious minded, and controversial attempt" to present the story of one nun.[18]

The most famous of all "nun movies," *The Sound of Music*, began as a hit musical by Richard Rogers and Oscar Hammerstein. *The Sound of Music* told the story of a good-hearted novice, Maria, who, after taking an assignment to serve as governess over seven children at the behest of a wealthy Austrian widower, found herself falling in love with him and embroiled in the family's attempts to escape Nazi expansion. Rather than running away from the convent to wed Captain von Trapp, Maria sought refuge back in the convent, where the Mother Superior convinced her to be brave and return, to "climb every mountain." The musical ran from November 1959 to June 1963 before Robert Wise produced the film version in 1965. Rogers and Hammerstein approached the life of the nun with seriousness and respect, consulting with Sister Gregory Duff, OP, a Dominican Sister, to ensure a realistic representation of convent life. Their efforts proved successful. The film version grossed over $60 million in the first year and later received an Oscar for Best Picture.[19]

Although the film avoided vintage anti-Catholicism, it embraced some old caricatures, from stern to silly nuns, and its popularity derived more from its charismatic and uplifting portrayals of female domesticity, romance, and family life. Wise basked in the serendipitous timing of the film. As the US began its war in Vietnam and felt the first waves of a cultural revolution, people longed for "old fashioned ideals" and escape. "Besides an outstanding score and an excellent cast, it has a heartwarming story, good humor, someone to love and someone to hate, and seven adorable children," wrote one reviewer. Maria embodied gender ideals of the age, being chaste, beautiful, and highly deferential, first as a novice and then as a devoted wife. Pauline Kael of *McCalls* criticized Maria's character for being "inhumanly happy . . . [with] a mind as clean and well-brushed as her teeth." Like other postwar-era films about nuns, *The Sound of Music* avoided the cliché of the imprisoned nun, yet relished in an American domestic ideal.[20]

While postwar-era films suggested a final peace among Protestants and Catholics in America, reminiscent of the kind of civil religion described in Will Herberg's *Protestant, Catholic, Jew* (1955), the presidential campaign of 1960 recharged latent anti-Catholic anxieties. On September 8, 1960, the *New York Times'* front page featured an "official statement" regarding John F. Kennedy's religion. Put forward by the National Conference of Citizens for Religious Freedom at the behest of Norman Vincent Peale, the statement compared Kennedy's promises to uphold the separation of church and state with Soviet Premier Khrushchev's alleged commitment to peace, claiming "Rome was little better than Moscow." The article received almost immediate reproof not only from Catholics but also from Protestants and Jews, forcing Peale to backtrack from the statement, but religion haunted Kennedy throughout his campaign. The senator from Massachusetts worked tirelessly to assure voters that he was "not the Catholic candidate for President," but "the Democratic party's candidate for President who happens to be a Catholic." Kennedy's "theologically thin" answer helped ensure the privatization of religion in politics—something many in Peale's camp would later bemoan. His election also represented the integration of Catholics into American society, or at least most Catholics. Nuns would remain foreign, fascinating, or replant for many Americans.[21]

Meanwhile, Maria Monk endured. A string of *Awful Disclosures* reprints and new editions—each more salacious than the next—appeared throughout the 1960s and '70s. Some of the book covers pictured Monk as an attractive veiled woman with red lips and black eyeliner. Another featured a woman clad in a torn habit revealing part of her areola. In 1969, Canova Press, in London, published an edition of *Awful Disclosures* sure to attract interest. The cover pictured a naked nun, bent over in preparation for a priest to whip her. An introduction assured readers the text was "quite authentic," being taken from "a very early edition by T. B. Peterson of Philadelphia [published in 1836]." Reflecting the egalitarian impulses of the late 1960s counterculture, the introduction described *Awful Disclosures* as a work that proved "that all men are equal, that even the good are not always beyond reproach." Like earlier commentary, the Canova edition hailed the enduring popularity of Maria Monk. "Each succeeding generation has read her account of evil practices within the nunnery walls with excitement and absorbed interest, with the result that Maria Monk and her book have passed into the annals of literary legend." This persistence, the editor declared, "proves conclusively and again that truth is stranger and more enduring than fiction."[22]

The 1969 version of *Awful Disclosures* introduced the book as something that shocked its first readers. The introduction praised Monk for her "considerable courage" in publishing the work, presenting her as a Martin Luther–like, lone avenger of truth as opposed to a pawn in the hands of money-grubbing nineteenth-century male publishers. The introduction continued, detailing the "torrent of abuse" Monk faced for her exposures. "Condemnation and refutation . . . raged in the press but the truth contained in this explosive book was unquestionably confirmed." The introduction failed to mention the subsequent investigations of the Hotel Dieu and condemnation of Monk's story issued by a variety of sources, Catholic and otherwise. Instead, the introduction noted that Monk "was able to corroborate her claims by producing reliable witnesses," which "effectively prevented the detractors from taking the matter further" and freed the book "from any suggestion of untruth." Readers of this 1969 edition and a later reissue of it in 1997, featuring a woman wearing nothing other than a nun's short headdress, likely cared little for historical truth.[23]

The late 1960s and '70s witnessed two extreme nun figures, caught between childlike innocence and vixen deviance. Mainstream popular culture stuck to more innocent and benign portrayals, such as *The Flying Nun*, a television show that aired from 1967 to 1970 on ABC. Shortly after her debut as "Gidget," the "ultimate perky teenager," Sally Field played Sister Bertrille, a similarly perky, virginal, and kind-hearted nun. Bertrille's petite frame and large winged coronet enabled her to "fly" in the missionary outpost's windy city of San Juan, Puerto Rico. Like other popular sitcoms from the time, *The Flying Nun* presented small disturbances to everyday life that were neatly resolved within the course of the half-hour time slot. Like its contemporary *Bewitched* and *I Dream of Jeannie*, the show starred a female in possession of some alien force who nevertheless chose a life of containment, be it in the suburban household or the convent. In the midst of the women's movement and radical changes within women's religious orders at the time, *The Flying Nun* represented traditional religious life and controlled female independence. Like nineteenth-century portrayals of nuns, it imagined Sisters as naïve and youthful. The sitcom-ification of convent life initiated by *The Flying Nun* also served as a harbinger for the later emergence of nun kitsch.[24]

The childlike "flying" nun ran counter to the contemporaneous vixen nun. Just as antebellum convent narratives offered readers a thrilling mix of pornographic, gothic, and sadistic imagery, portrayals of nuns in the 1970s combined sex and horror. *The Devils* (1971), directed by Ken Russell, extended an embellished account of a degenerate seventeenth-century priest, Urbain Grandier, and the drama that surrounded his execution for witchcraft in Loudun, France. Vanessa Redgrave starred as a sexually repressed nun obsessed with Grandier, played by Oliver Reed. After being rebuffed by Grandier, who was already preoccupied with an affair of his own, Redgrave's character sought revenge, accusing him of witchcraft and of possessing her and the other nuns of the convent. Clergy members subsequently arrived to perform a mass exorcism, forcing the women to remove all of their clothes. The exorcism devolved into an orgy during which some of the nuns sexually desecrated a statue of Christ. In the end Grandier faced tortures akin to the Inquisition before being burned at the stake. When *The Devils* came out, it received an "X" rating for disturbing violent and sexual content and was banned in several countries.[25]

Flavia the Rebel Nun (1974), an Italian film that became popular in the US, extended a similar story. The film featured a young girl sent to a convent in thirteenth-century Portugal. There she suffered unmentionable horrors of torture, whippings, and rape before finally escaping. As a freed woman, she took a Muslim lover who had devoted his life to castrating rapists. With capture, torture, sex, and liberation, the story uncannily reflected antebellum convent narratives. *The Devils* and *Flavia the Rebel Nun* came out alongside a series of other movies that capitalized on Catholic horror, or what historian Victoria Nelson called "faux Catholicism," including *The Exorcist* (1973) and *The Omen* (1976), each relying on gothic imagery, the supernatural, and a presentation of Catholicism more fantastical than real. Such "faux Catholicism" was nothing new. Convent narratives forged the genre more than a century before.[26]

Nun satire boomed throughout the 1980s, with a parade of ugly, old, funny, goofy, stern, masculine, and "crazy aunt" nuns. Most often these satiric nuns were teachers with ruler in hand, ready to strike at the slightest hint of insubordination. This old crone nun opposed any and all modes of fun, amusement, or frivolity. She appeared famously in the 1980 smash hit *The Blues Brothers*. When Jake and Elwood embarked on their mission from God to save the Catholic home in which they were raised, they stopped to see their old school teacher, a stern nun. The Sister, or "the Penguin"—so called for her black-and-white full habit—insisted that the men sit attentively in small school desks while she bemoaned the school's costly bills. When the brothers offered to give her the funds, she refused their "filthy, stolen money." Jake's retort that she's "up a shit creek" then invoked a barrage of beatings from the nun with a yardstick. As the beatings sent the brothers tumbling down the stairs, still stuck in their desks, the towering Penguin intoned after them that they had "turned into two thieves with filthy mouths and bad attitudes."[27] The *Blues Brothers'* nun embodies the prototype for the quintessential nun figure today. Although most

Sisters are no longer teachers, the image of the angry schoolmarm, though meant to be more comic than offensive, remains ubiquitous.

Five years later, the silly teacher nun (always fully habited) appeared in the famous musical production *Nunsense*. What began as a series of greeting cards developed into a full musical. After its debut, *Nunsense* became the second-longest-running Off-Broadway show in history. In the first act of the show a group of around fifty habited nuns gather around the table for a meal. After a prayer, they silently dip into their bowls, when suddenly one nun after the next drops dead, head-first domino-style into the soup. In the following act or episode, four other nuns, who safely avoided the soup because they were "off playing bingo," host a fundraiser to bury their fellow Sisters. Of the four, one is "Sister Amnesia," who forgot her real name after being hit in the head with a crucifix. The bumbling Sisters run around preparing for their fundraiser to circus music, chant Latin for a few stanzas, and then sing a Broadway-like number about their history, which they get completely wrong. The women argue about the history of their order, suggesting ludicrous ideas as to how they might raise money to pay for the funerals of their poor, dead Sisters. Since its debut, *Nunsense* became so popular that it spawned *Nunsense II, Nuncrackers, Nunsense Jamboree, Nunset Boulevard*, and *Nunsensations*, among other spinoffs that play in New York City and all over the country. Much like *Nunsense, Late Night Catechism*, another spoof on teaching nuns, is a one-woman stand-up act of a stern, somewhat ridiculous nun teacher who lectures her audience on chewing gum and showing cleavage.[28]

Nunsense is not meant to be offensive. Actual nuns often occupy seats in the audience, and the production company regularly donates a percentage of the earnings to various religious houses. These silly nuns harken back to days when the majority of Sisters assumed teaching roles, whether they wanted to or not. They poke fun at outmoded pedagogy and the way some of these women buckled under the pressure of exhaustive teaching and administrative duties. Yet there is something disturbing about the image advanced by these comedies. Over fifty nuns plunging to their deaths in soup makes them appear cartoonlike and ridiculous. The fact that certain nuns avoided this death because they were playing bingo suggests that women religious have nothing important to do. Getting their own history wrong makes it seem as though they actually have none. Likewise, *Late Night Catechism* would have us imagine all nuns as harping, out-of-touch babysitters. Like the benignly silly nuns in *Awful Disclosures*, like "Mad" Jane Ray or the other nuns who did not know how to spell or believed in ghosts, the silly nun of contemporary culture creates an object at which a smug spectator might laugh, maybe feel sorry for, and discard.

Funny nuns burst onto the mainstream scene with the blockbuster hits *Sister Act* and *Sister Act II* (1992, 1993). When a nightclub performer, Deloris Van Cartier, played by Whoopi Goldberg, witnessed a mob murder, the police convinced her to hide out in a convent. Predictably she had a hard time fitting in, especially with the stern Mother Superior, played by the best tight-lipped actor, Maggie Smith. After taking charge of the convent's choir and turning them into an impressive hip-swinging, voice-belting ensemble, Goldberg's character settled into her new role, developing friendships with many of the Sisters. While *Sister Act* did not portray nuns unfavorably—even the stern Mother Superior eventually came around—it capitalized on familiar stock personas. There was the uptight, cold Mother Superior; the old, out-of-touch sexless nun; a sweet, though painfully naïve, Sister; and an overly friendly, zany odd-ball nun who belted random high-pitched soprano notes in glass-shattering vibrato. The film is fun and entertaining. And any one of the scenes, including one where the zany Sister breakdances with kids on the streets, or another where a flock of nuns run throughout a casino in Reno, could make the pages of the "Nuns Having Fun" calendar.[29]

But alongside silly Sisters, scary, veiled nuns still haunt popular culture. A recent book, unambiguously titled *Scary Nuns,* argues that nuns are frightening "because they are different, different in a wholly confusing way." Filled with images of fully habited nuns, *Scary Nuns* lists various nuns throughout history in its "Scary Nuns Hall of Fame." Offering images that often have nothing to do with accompanying quotes, this book merely perpetuates the image of the nun as the other, inviting readers to be amused, if not slightly spooked. One photo features the outline of a faceless veiled nun lurking in the shadows of a dimly lit hallway alongside a quote from Charlotte Brontë's gothic novel *Villette.* "I saw in the middle of that ghostly chamber a figure all black and white; the skirts straight and narrow, black; the head bandaged, veiled, white." Another displays the actual corpse of a Carmelite nun in Spain who was killed during the Spanish Civil War. There's a nun watching children sleep in an orphanage in Havana, Cuba, and even a foldout image of a nun whose tall coronet opens up into a hornlike centerpiece. In being "wholly different," these nuns are scary. They are unknowable. Their lives are to be feared, not imitated, or even understood.[30]

American Horror Story (2011), a miniseries devoted to revamping archetypes in the American horror tradition, presented some of the scariest—if not also formulaic—nuns. Season two, set in an insane asylum in the 1960s, follows the lives of nuns who deliver all sorts of malpractice and abuse on their patients. Sister Jude, played by Jessica Lang, is a severe, cold, judgmental, and intimidating nun who runs the ward. Predictably, Sister Jude doesn't really help her patients. "Mental illness is a fashionable explanation for sin!" she declares before calling her patients "monsters" and using electric shock therapy to "cure" them of homosexuality and other "vices."

Jude's face stares down menacingly with glee as her patients writhe and wriggle under the torture.[31]

Sister Jude also harbors pent-up sexual desire and a secret crush on the monsignor, cofounder of the facility. She dons a red negligee under her habit in the event that he propositions her, about which she frequently fantasizes. Aware of her interest, though not sharing it, the priest plays on the Sister's ambitions, mocking them, to get her approval for various questionable treatments. "When I'm cardinal one day," he tells her, "you will be Mother Superior." Her face shines when he promises, "thousands of nuns . . . will address you as *Reverend Mother*." Like antebellum convent narratives featuring vainly ambitious and tyrannical Mother Superiors, Sister Jude craves power. The show also mimics themes of torture, sex, and sadism found in earlier narratives. In one episode, Sister Eunice, a kind though idiotic nun who lives in deathly fear of Sister Jude, becomes possessed by a demon when an exorcism goes awry in the asylum. In her veiled habit, the unassuming Sister Eunice sadistically carries out a series of murders. Her previously innocent temperament and full habit make her actions all the more frightening. The doctor, played by James Cromwell, experiments with medical treatments that transform his patients into animals and obsesses over the nun-whore figure, demanding a prostitute he hires to dress up as a nun.[32] Tying together the sexual and scary nun in one season, *American Horror Story* does well in keeping alive old traditions.

The fear of nuns has led some on a quest to demystify the veiled Sisterhood. Cheryl L. Reed, a journalist with the *Chicago Sun-Times*, traveled the country interviewing and living among different orders of women religious. What began as a series of articles by Reed turned into a book, *Unveiled: The Hidden Lives of Nuns* (2004). Initially skeptical—Reed wrote that she grew up "afraid of nuns"—she discovered a lasting friendship with many of the women, who opened up to her. Far from being stuffy, subdued, and sulking, Reed wrote that "these women are living the ultimate feminist lives." Rather than seeing women religious as excessively submissive, Reed perceived them as "embracing a radical way of life, a rebellion to societal constraints and demands." Writing of the women of one order, she noted, "I hadn't anticipated that St. Benedict's Sisters would be animated or quizzical or *human*."[33]

Reed spent time interviewing the Visitine Sisters, who run an inner-city ministry in an impoverished town in Minneapolis. The women opened their ministry after years of planning, and described their mission "to be in relationships with these people and to be friends . . . people meet here and get connected." Far from being sheltered or cut off, these women receive constant visitors and phone calls and associate with people on drugs and probation. Yet far from lofty saints, as Reed assured, they "are no different from families; they argue, they fight, and sometimes they let little things get on their nerves." Reed discovered that Suzanne Homeyer joined at the age of forty-five after a long career of peace activism and political involvement as a city council representative. "I had a great sense of how a neighborhood can be a functioning, life-giving place," explained Homeyer. "In a lot of ways, that's why I came here." Other women entered at different ages and for different reasons. No one story was the same. Reed's small snapshot reveals the diversity of nuns and the various ways community can be understood.[34]

Some films and television series have also embarked on presenting a more realistic portrayal of nuns, with *Dead Man Walking* being perhaps the most famous. Based on a true story, Susan Sarandon stars as Sister Helen Prejean, a nun who befriends Matthew Poncelet, a murderer and rapist on death row. Despite an initial revulsion she feels toward Poncelet, played by Sean Penn, and her inexperience as a criminal chaplain, Prejean commits to helping him, even if that only means being a friend. She connects Poncelet with a lawyer and becomes his spiritual counselor. When his appeal is denied, Prejean continues to visit Poncelet, lending a listening ear, meeting his family and the family of his victims, helping him come to terms with his responsibility, and sticking by his side in his final hours. Whereas murderers and nuns usually appear as black-and-white figures, both Poncelet and Prejean are dynamic and complicated, making this a stirring and thought-provoking film.[35]

"Finally a filmic depiction of a nun that is grounded in human emotion," wrote Patricia Kowal in a review of the film for *Magill's Cinema Annual.* Commenting on her role, Sarandon stated she had "never seen a nun on screen who's been a real person." Although *Dead Man Walking* is a type of love story between Sister Helen and Poncelet, it's not a romance. Sister Helen struggles to love the unlovable Poncelet. As she fights a natural aversion to him, she fosters what might be called unconditional love. This surprises and touches Poncelet, who simply says to her in his last hours, "Thank you for loving me." Tim Robbins, the director, said the film "was not a typical love story. . . . The stakes are much higher." Sister Helen risked the disdain of Poncelet's victims' family, while Poncelet risked feeling emotion at a time when callousness would be easier. Perhaps that's what made this film so compelling. While not projecting an angelic nun or a simple plot, *Dead Man Walking* captured something more.[36]

After her experience acting in *Dead Man Walking*, Susan Sarandon narrated an independent, small-budget film, titled *A Question of Habit*. The film opens to the background music from the famed "singing nun," whose short-lived career seemed buoyed more by the novelty of a guitar-strumming, singing nun. As the credits flash on the screen, wind-up nuns march by, bobble-head nuns bounce, and various figurines from bowling nuns to nuns with duck bills flash in and out of view. Interviewing a variety of women religious, including Helen Prejean, the film producers attempt to capture the real lives of women. One Sister, Anna Ida Gannon, BVM (Sister of Charity of the Blessed Virgin Mary), describes the satirical approach to the nun in popular culture as "highly offensive." Cartoon characters paper over a lifetime of work and dedication, she claimed. Scholars of women religious also appear on the film, assessing the current cultural understanding of nuns and the various portrayals of Sisters in popular culture in American history. Although the film has not been released to the general public, it marks a genuine interest in uncovering the life of the nun, of taking women religious seriously and understanding them on their own terms, something due to any and every historical subject.[37]

Some self-identified feminists are also taking a new look at nuns. The highly feminist and visible web-based magazine *Jezebel* ran an article entitled "Nuns Are So Hot Right Now They're Getting Their Own Reality Show." After discussing the potential reality show, *The Sisterhood*, tracing the lives of five women as they consider religious vows, the article went on to analyze interest in nuns. "Are nuns the NEXT BIG THING? Are nuns the new witches? Like how witches are the new zombies and zombies were the new vampires?" On a more serious note, the writers for *Jezebel* asked whether nuns as an institution were feminist. "Obviously Catholicism is markedly *not*, but there's something sisters-doin'-it-for-themselves about nuns." The article referred to nuns' participation in antinuclear peace protests and to nuns as "powerful role models for female friendship."[38]

Even so, one-dimensional portrayals of nuns persist, even in surprising places, such as the 2008 film, *Doubt*. Set in 1964, *Doubt* takes place just one year after the shocking death of John F. Kennedy and untimely death of Pope John Paul XXIII. While the Second Vatican Council (1962–1965) neared its close with a promise of renewal, the convent, parish, and school in the film remain thoroughly entrenched in a malaise of rigid gender roles, repression, and cold regulations. The film offers a sense of foreboding of the coming clerical sex scandals that would become known at the end of the twentieth century, shaking the church's authority, morale, finances, and global reputation to its core. In the film, Sister Aloysius, played by Meryl Streep, comes to doubt the nature of the relationship of Father Flynn, played by Philip Seymour Hoffman, and the school's lone black student, Donald Miller, played by Joseph Foster. Gothic elements run throughout the movie, with the school set in a dark, wintery, gray landscape. Children fear wind storms outside their bedroom windows. Everyone appears lonely and isolated as Streep's character terrifies students and faculty alike and lies in wait to catch Flynn doing something wrong. Under pressure from Streep's character, Sister James (Amy Adams) feels guilty after she implicates Flynn in a scandal about which she is uncertain. In the end Flynn leaves the parish and school, a cloud of suspicion hanging over him, while Sisters and viewers are left in "doubt" as to the veracity of Aloysius's fears.[39]

Reviewers quickly criticized the superficial nature of Streep's and Adams's characters. Maurine Sabine concluded that the "film relies on well-worn gender contrivance of splitting the woman religious in two," with the "admired qualities of youth, beauty, kindness, compassion, and love" to Sister James, and the grotesque and "dangerous properties of authority" to Aloysius. The *Village Voice* wrote of Patrick Shanley's "considerable ambivalence about women" projected by these polar opposite female roles. Although *Doubt* captured a feeling of uncertainty before the revelation of a widespread clerical sex scandal—a serious and tragic moment in the history of Catholicism that continues to be explored—it did little to liberate the nun from the cultural stereotypes in which she has been encapsulated for centuries.[40]

Maria Monk, a mostly unrecognized name today, contributed to a cultural phenomenon much larger than herself or the immediate controversy that surrounded the publication of *Awful Disclosures of the Hotel Dieu.* Her narrative, which became the template for so many other convent narratives in the nineteenth and early twentieth centuries, propelled the American campaign against convents and forged indelible images of nuns as virtuous victims, sex slaves, naïve children, wasted beauties, masculine tyrants, or silly fools. Although some previous anticlerical narratives in Europe had already assigned the nun to such roles, Maria Monk brought the convent legend to America on a grand scale. Her book, along with a growing Catholic and immigrant presence, urbanization, Western expansion, and more fluid female gender roles, served to spark a national obsession with nuns and convents that lasted for decades. As the young US came into its own and became increasingly diverse by the antebellum era, Americans grappled with creating a national identity and character. In the emerging ideals of Protestantism, patriotism, common-man democracy, and the cult of true womanhood, there was no place for the nun. Indeed, convents appeared to many Americans as a threat to womanhood, the family, and national virtue and strength. Although the campaign against convents was short-lived, stymied by a botched nunnery investigation in 1855, the image of the nun forged in the antebellum era has had a lasting legacy, rendering nuns un-American, and as H. L. Mencken put it in 1956, "only half a woman" if indeed wholly human.

_____

INTRODUCTION

1. Samuel Smith, ed., Front page image, *Downfall of Babylon; or, The Truth over Popery* 2, no. 16 (April 16, 1836): 89, courtesy of the American Antiquarian Society; William C. Brownlee, ed., "Maria Monk," *The American Protestant Vindicator and Defender of Civil and Religious Liberty Against the Inroads of Popery* 2, no. 44 (August 3, 1836), courtesy of the New York Public Library.

2. Sales figures cited in Ray Allen Billington, *The Protestant Crusade, 1800–1860: A Study of the Origins of American Nativism* (1938; repr., New York: Quadrangle, 1964), 108.

3. For more on the burning of Mount Benedict, see Nancy Lusignan Schultz, *Fire and Roses: The Burning of the Charlestown Convent, 1834* (Boston: Northeastern University Press, 2000); Rebecca Reed, *Six Months in a Convent; or, The Narrative of Rebecca Theresa Reed, who was under the influence of the Roman Catholics about two years and an inmate of the Ursuline Convent on Mount Benedict* (Boston: Russell, Odiorne, and Metcalf, 1835).

4. Rachel McCrindell, *The Protestant Girl in a French Nunnery*, 4th ed. (Philadelphia: Hooker, 1846); Reed, *Six Months in a Convent*, 7.

5. For more on the domestic ideology of abolitionism, see Kristin Hoganson, "Garrisonian Abolitionists and the Rhetoric of Gender, 1850–1860," *American Quarterly* 45, no. 4 (December 1993): 558–95; and Ronald G. Walters, "The Erotic South: Civilization and Sexuality in American Abolitionism," *American Quarterly* 25, no. 2 (May 1973): 177–201; George Bourne, *Lorette. The History of Louise, Daughter of a Canadian Nun, Exhibiting the Interior of Female Convents* (New York: C. Small, 1834).

6. George G. Foster, *New York by Gas-Light and Other Urban Sketches*, ed. with an introd. by Stuart M. Blumin (Berkeley: University of California Press, 1990), 83; for more on city mysteries, see David M. Henkin, "City Streets and the Urban World of Print," in *The Industrial*

Book, 1840–1880, vol. 3 of *A History of the Book in America*, ed. Scott E. Casper et al. (Chapel Hill: University of North Carolina Press, 2007), 344–45; my analysis here builds on Tracy Fessenden, "The Convent, the Brothel, and the Protestant Woman's Sphere," *Signs* 25, no. 2 (Winter 2000): 451–78.

7. My analysis builds on David Brion Davis, "Some Themes of Counter-Subversion: An Analysis of Anti-Masonic, Anti-Catholic, and Anti-Mormon Literature," *Mississippi Valley Historical Review* 47, no. 2 (September 1960): 205–24; N.A., *Awful Disclosures of Mormonism and Its Mysteries* (n.p.: Printed for the Booksellers, 1866), NYPL; Frederick Rinehart Anspach, *The Sons of the Sires: A History of the Rise, Progress, and Destiny of the American Party* (Philadelphia: Lippincott, Grambo, & Co., 1855); for more on the Nunnery Committee, see John R. Mulkern, "Scandal Behind Convent Walls: The Know-Nothing Nunnery Committee of 1855," *Historical Journal of Massachusetts* 11, no. 1 (1983): 22–34.

8. Amy Leonard, *Nails in the Wall: Catholic Nuns in Reformation Germany* (Chicago: University of Chicago Press, 2005), 1–2; see also Beth Kreitzer, *Reforming Mary: Changing Images of the Virgin Mary in Lutheran Sermons of the Sixteenth Century* (New York: Oxford University Press, 2004); and Merry E. Wiesner, "Luther and Women: The Death of Two Marys," in *Disciplines of Faith: Studies in Religion, Politics, and Patriarchy*, ed. Jim Obelkevich, Lyndal Roper, and Raphael Samuel (New York: Routledge & Kegan Paul, 1987).

9. For more on the dissolution of the monasteries under Henry VIII, see Geoffrey Moorhouse, *The Last Divine Office: Henry VIII and the Dissolution of the Monasteries* (New York: BlueBridge, 2009); and Richard Rex, *Henry VIII and the English Reformation* (New York: St. Martin's Press, 1993); for more on women religious migrating from England to the continent, see Kathleen Cooke, "The English Nuns and the Dissolution," in *The Cloister and the World: Essays in Medieval History in Honor of Barbara Harvey*, ed. John Blair and Brian Golding (Oxford: Clarendon Press, 1996).

10. Matthew G. Lewis, *The Monk* (1796; repr., New York: Grove Press, 1952); for an analysis of *The Monk*, see Victoria Nelson, "Faux Catholic: A Gothic Subgenre from Monk Lewis to Dan Brown," *Boundary 2* 34, no. 3 (2007): 87–107; for more on the role of Protestant anticlericalism in gothic literature, see Robert F. Geary, *The Supernatural in Gothic Fiction: Horror, Belief, and Literary Change* (Newiston, NY: Edwin Mellen Press, 1992); and Victor Sage, *Horror Fiction and the Protestant Tradition* (London: Macmillan, 1988); for an overview of medieval convent literature, see Graciela S. Daichman, *Wayward Nuns in Medieval Literature* (Syracuse, NY: Syracuse University Press, 1986).

11. Antonio Gavin, *The Master-Key to Popery* (Dublin, 1724; repr., London: J. Walthoe, 1725); Gavin, *The Great Red Dragon; or, The Master-Key to Popery* (New York: H. Dayton, 1860); Joan R. Gundersen, "Anthony Gavin's 'A Master-Key to Popery': A Virginia Parson's Best Seller," *Virginia Magazine of History and Biography* 82 (January 1974): 39–46; Jenny Franchot, *Roads to Rome: The Antebellum Protestant Encounter with Catholicism* (Berkeley: University of California Press, 1994), 106.

12. Ray Allen Billington, "Tentative Bibliography of Anti-Catholic Propaganda in the United States (1800–1860)," *Catholic Historical Review* 18, no. 4 (January 1933): 492–513; Billington, *The Protestant Crusade*; for more on the literature published by American Protestant Reformation societies, see David Paul Nord, *Faith in Reading: Religious Publishing and the Birth of Mass Media in America* (New York: Oxford University Press, 2004).

13. *The Statistical History of the United States* (Stamford, CT: Fairfield Publishers, 1865), ser. C88–114, p. 57; see also Arnold Schrier, *Ireland and the American Emigration, 1850–1900*

(Minneapolis: University of Minnesota Press, 1958), 151; D. B. Debow, *Statistical View of the United States: Compendium of the Seventh Census* (Washington, DC: Senate Printer, 1854), 119; and Edwin Scott Gaustad, *Historical Atlas of Religion in America* (New York: Harper & Row, 1962), 101–10.

14. Emily Clark, *Masterless Mistresses: The New Orleans Ursulines and the Development of a New World Society, 1727–1834* (Chapel Hill: University of North Carolina Press, 2007), 4–5; for more on republican motherhood, see Linda K. Kerber, *Women of the Republic: Intellect and Ideology in Revolutionary America* (Chapel Hill: University of North Carolina Press, 1980); Samuel Smith, "On Nunneries," *Downfall of Babylon* 1, no. 4 (December 6, 1834).

15. George C. Stewart Jr., "Women Religious in America, Demographic Overview," in *The Encyclopedia of American Catholic History*, ed. Michael Glazier and Thomas J. Shelley (Collegeville, MN: Liturgical Press, 1997), 1496–97; Clark, *Masterless Mistresses*, 261–62; Mary Ewens, *The Role of the Nun in Nineteenth Century America: Variations on an International Theme* (Thiensville, WI: Caritas, 2014), 32, 45, 61, 64; see also Barbara Misner, *Highly Respectable and Accomplished Ladies: Catholic Women Religious in America, 1790–1850* (New York: Garland, 1988), 203–4; and "Women in the Convent," in Karen Kennelly, ed., *American Catholic Women: A Historical Exploration* (New York: Macmillan, 1989), 17–47.

16. Barbara Welter, "The Cult of True Womanhood: 1820–1860," *American Quarterly* 18, no. 2 (Summer 1966): 152. While dated, Welter's landmark article is still cited and expanded on by historians of gender in America. Michael D. Pierson, *Free Hearts and Free Homes: Gender and American Antislavery Politics* (Chapel Hill: University of North Carolina Press, 2003), 4–12. Pierson shows how antislavery women used domestic feminism to push for more equitable gender relationships. See also Mary Kelley, "Beyond the Boundaries," *Journal of the Early Republic* 21, no. 1 (Spring 2001): 73–78.

17. Pierson, *Free Hearts and Free Homes*, 11–12; Karen Halttunen, *Confidence Men and Painted Women: A Study of Middle-Class Culture in America, 1830–1870* (New Haven, CT: Yale University Press, 1982), 29, 191–97; see also Stuart M. Blumin, *The Emergence of the Middle Class: Social Experience in the American City, 1760–1900* (Cambridge: Cambridge University Press, 1989); Sandra Frink, "Women, the Family, and the Fate of the Nation in American Anti-Catholic Narratives, 1830–1860," *Journal of the History of Sexuality* 18, no. 2 (May 2009): 242–43.

18. Franchot, *Roads to Rome*; Marie Anne Pagliarini, "The Pure American Woman and the Wicked Catholic Priest: An Analysis of Anti-Catholic Literature in Antebellum America," *Religion and American Culture: A Journal of Interpretation* 9, no. 1 (Winter 1999): 98, 116, 100; Fessenden, "The Convent, the Brothel, and the Protestant Woman's Sphere," 452–53.

CHAPTER 1

1. W. Robertson, "Affidavit of Dr. Robertson," in appendix to the new edition of *Awful Disclosures by Maria Monk, of the Hotel Dieu Nunnery of Montreal, Revised with an Appendix*, by Maria Monk (1836; repr., New York: Arno Press, 1977), 212.

2. Robertson, "Affidavit," 212–13.

3. Robertson, "Affidavit," 212–13.

4. Maria Monk, *Awful Disclosures by Maria Monk of the Hotel Dieu Nunnery of Montreal, Revised with an Appendix* (New York, 1836), preface, 181, 12, 47, 140, 128.

5. Monk, *Awful Disclosures*, 148, 69, 49, 103.

6. Monk, *Awful Disclosures*, 178–79, 186, 183, 30, 84.

7. Monk, *Awful Disclosures*, 16, 186, 140, 128–29.

8. Monk, *Awful Disclosures*, 110–11, 122–23, 115–16.

9. "Appendix," in Monk, *Awful Disclosures*, 265–66, 256. All regular editions of *Awful Disclosures* are bound with the sequel.

10. "Appendix," in Monk, *Awful Disclosures*, 274, 287–88, 291–94. For more on the advent of the almshouses, see David J. Rothman, *The Discovery of the Asylum: Social Order and Disorder in the New Republic* (Boston: Little, Brown, and Company, 1971); for more information on the Tappans' finances, see Robert H. Abzug, *Cosmos Crumbling: American Reform and the Religious Imagination* (New York: Oxford University Press, 1994), 220.

11. Figures in Ray Allen Billington, *The Protestant Crusade, 1800–1860: A Study of the Origins of American Nativism* (1938; repr., New York: Quadrangle, 1964), 108; "Harper and Brothers, 1833–1962," in *American Literary Publishing Houses, 1638–1899*, part 1, ed. Peter Dzwonkoski (Detroit: A Bruccoli Clark Book, 1986), 192; Eugene Exman, *The Brothers Harper: A Unique Publishing Partnership and Its Impact upon the Cultural Life of America, from 1817 to 1853* (New York: Harper and Row, 1865), 61.

12. *Downfall of Babylon* 1, no. 1 (August 14, 1834), AAS; *Downfall* 1, no. 34 (July 4, 1835), AAS; "Credibility of the Awful Disclosures," *Downfall* 2, no. 2 (February 6, 1836), AAS; "Dreadful Scenes in the Awful Disclosures of Maria Monk," *Downfall* 2, no. 15 (April 2, 1836), AAS.

13. William Brownlee, *America Protestant Vindicator* (August 20, 1834), NYPL; "Maria Monk," *Protestant Vindicator* 2, no. 41 (July 13, 1836), NYPL; George Bourne, "Nunneries Are Unconstitutional," *Protestant Vindicator* 2, no. 40 (July 6, 1836), NYPL; for more on these periodicals, see Billington, *The Protestant Crusade*, 92–93.

14. For more information on the Tappan brothers, see Abzug, *Cosmos Crumbling*, 107–111, 150–61, 220–27; Ronald G. Walters, *American Reformers, 1815–1860* (New York: Hill and Wang, 1978), 33–34; and Lewis Tappan, *The Life of Arthur Tappan* (New York: Hurd and Houghton, 1870).

15. "Maria Monk: Villainy Exposed!," *L'Ami du Peuple* quoted in "Appendix," Monk, *Awful Disclosures*, 208; John W. Christie and Dwight L. Dumond, *George Bourne and* The Book and Slavery Irreconcilable (Wilmington: Historical Society of Delaware, 1969), 17–19; for information on George Bourne, see Abzug, *Cosmos Crumbling*, 134–35, 151; see also Billington, *Protestant Crusade*, 53; George Bourne, *Picture of Quebec in Its Vicinity* (New York, 1830); Bourne, *The Book and Slavery, Irreconcilable* (Philadelphia: J. M. Sanderson, 1816); Bourne, *Picture of Slavery in the United States of America* (Middletown, CT: Edwin Hunt, 1834); Bourne, *Slavery Illustrated in Its Effects upon Woman and Domestic Society* (1837; repr., Freeport, NY: Books for Libraries Press, 1972); Bourne, ed., *The Protestant* (New York, 1830–1832); Bourne, *Lorette: The History of Louise, Daughter of a Canadian Nun, Exhibiting the Interior of Female Convents* (New York: William A. Mercein, 1833).

16. For information on Theodore Dwight, see Rothman, *Discovery of the Asylum*, 240. Theodore Dwight, *Open Convents; or, Nunneries and Popish Seminaries, Dangerous to the Morals and Degrading to the Character of a Republican Community* (New York: Van Nostrand and Dwight, 1836), 5, 6. Information on Morse's support to Monk and his courtship with her cited in a letter by James Fenimore Cooper to his wife postmarked New York, October 27, 1835, *The Letters and Journals of James Fenimore Cooper*, ed. James Franklin Beard (Cambridge: Harvard University Press, 1960), 3:220.

17. "Maria Monk and Her Impostures: Awful Disclosures," *Quarterly Christian Spectator* 9, no. 2 (June 1, 1837): 263, 270; Samuel B. Smith, *Rosamond; or, A Narrative of the Captivity and Sufferings of an American Female Under the Popish Priests, in the Island of Cuba* (New York: Leavitt, Lord & Co., 1836), 11; Harry Hazel, *The Nun of St. Ursula; or, The Burning of the Convent: A Romance of Mount Benedict* (Boston: Gleason, 1845); Charles W. Frothingham, *The Convent's Doom: A Story of Charlestown in 1834* (Boston: Graves & Weston, 1854); Josephine Bunkley, *The Escaped Nun; or, The Disclosures of Convent Life; and The Confessions of a Sister of Charity* (New York: DeWitt & Davenport, 1855), 153.

18. Statistics quoted in Thomas T. McAvoy, CSC, *A History of the Catholic Church in the United States* (Notre Dame, IN: University of Notre Dame Press, 1969), 133; for more on American conversions to Catholicism, see Eleanor Simpson, "The Conservative Heresy: Yankees and the 'Reaction in Favor of Roman Catholics'" (PhD diss., University of Minnesota, 1974); "Our Country," *American Protestant Vindicator* 2, no. 52 (September 28, 1836), NYPL.

19. For more information on these organizations, see Billington, *The Protestant Crusade*, 95–97. These Protestant societies were modeled on well-established organizations in England, such as the British Society for Promoting the Principles of the Protestant Reformation, which formed in 1827.

20. Billington, "Maria Monk and Her Influence," *Catholic Historical Review* 22, no. 3 (October 1936): 283; Barbara Welter, "The Cult of True Womanhood: 1820–1860," *American Quarterly* 18, no. 2 (Summer 1966): 151–74. While Welter's article is dated, her description of the ideals of "true womanhood" are still recognized among American women's and gender historians. While not all women conformed to these ideals, the model appeared most prominently in prescriptive literature and hence had significant influence on the cultural understanding of proper female gender roles. For more on sentimentality and women in antebellum America, see Mary G. De Jong, ed., *Sentimentalism in Nineteenth-Century America: Literary and Cultural Practices* (Madison, NJ: Fairleigh Dickinson University Press, 2013).

21. Monk, *Awful Disclosures*, 183.

22. Nancy Woloch, *Women and the American Experience* (New York: Alfred A. Knopf, 1984), 136; Terrance Murphy, ed., *A Concise History of Christianity in Canada* (Toronto: Oxford University Press, 1996), 12, 94–95.

23. Monk, *Awful Disclosures*, 14.

24. By the 1820s Lower Canada had five Catholic hospitals that cared for the elderly and the sick. In Montreal was the Hotel Dieu and the Hospital General. They cared for citizens during the frequent epidemics, like the cholera epidemic that struck in 1832 and 1834. See Terrence Murphy and Roberto Perin, eds., *A Concise History of Christianity in Canada* (New York: Oxford, 1996), 94; *The Montreal Courier* (November 16, 1835) in "Appendix," in Monk, *Awful Disclosures* (1836; repr., New York: Arno Press, 1977), 211.

25. George Bourne described his missionary efforts in Canada in *The Picture of Quebec and Its Vicinity* (1831); reference from a prospectus and promotion of *The Protestant* in the New York *Observer*, November 14, 1829, quoted in Billington, *Protestant Crusade*, 54; "Appendix," in Monk, *Awful Disclosures*, 270–71; for an overview of anti-Canadian sentiment and its relation to anti-Catholic literature, see Rebecca Sullivan, "A Wayward in the Wilderness: Maria Monk's *Awful Disclosures* and the Feminization of Lower Canada in the Nineteenth Century," *Essays on Canadian Writing* 62 (Fall 1997): 201–22.

26. *Albany Argus* quoted in the *Vermont State Paper* 1, no. 34 (February 9, 1836); *New Hampshire Sentinel* 38, no. 6 (February 11, 1836); New York *Sunday Morning News* and *New Yorker* quoted in *New Hampshire Sentinel*, 38, no. 6, (February 11, 1836).

27. New York *Journal of Commerce* quoted in *New Hampshire Sentinel*, 38, no. 6, (February 11, 1836); "Living Death: New Carmelite Nuns," *Baltimore Literary and Religious Magazine* 2, no. 3 (March 1836); "Interview with Maria Monk," *Zion's Herald* 7, no. 36 (September 7, 1836); "Maria Monk," *Baltimore Literary and Religious Magazine* 2, no. 9 (September 1836).

28. "Hotel Dieu Nunnery at Montreal," *American Protestant Vindicator* 2, no. 39 (June 29, 1836), NYPL.

29. "Affidavit of My Mother," in "Appendix," in Monk, *Awful Disclosures*, 215–17.

30. In the Jacksonian era, in the beginning stages of the development of the insane asylum, most general practitioners believed insanity was a disease of the brain that could be caused by "blows on the head." See Rothman, *Discovery of the Asylum*, 110–11; "Affidavit of My Mother," in Monk, *Awful Disclosures*, 217. There was a general ecumenical spirit among Protestants and Catholics in Canada before the 1840s when tens of thousands of Irish famine migrants moved into the British North American colonies after 1845. See Murphy and Perin, eds., *A Concise History of Christianity in Canada*, especially chapters 2 and 3.

31. Mrs. L. St. John Eckel, *Maria Monk's Daughter: An Autobiography* (New York: United States Publishing Company, 1875), 171; "Affidavit of My Mother," in Monk, *Awful Disclosures*, 217–19.

32. "Maria Monk," *Barre Gazette* 2, no. 40 (February 19, 1836); *New Bedford Mercury* 29, no. 34 (February 26, 1836); "Appendix," in Monk, *Awful Disclosures*, 213–14, 220–21.

33. One Who Knows, "Maria Monk and Her Awful Disclosures," *New York Evangelist* 7, no. 15 (April 9, 1836); "Resolutions Regarding Maria Monk," *Downfall of Babylon* 2, no. 28 (October 1, 1836); "The Testimony of Maria Monk Considered," *Protestant Vindicator* 2, no. 45 (August 11, 1836); Rev. J. J. Slocum, *Confirmation of Maria Monk's Disclosures Concerning the Hotel Dieu Nunnery of Montreal; Preceded by a Reply to the Priests' Book*, 2nd ed. (London: James S. Hodson, 1837), 3.

34. "Sequel," in Monk, *Awful Disclosures*, 257–69, 321, 323; "Maria Monk and Her Awful Disclosures: From One Who Knows," *New York Evangelist* 7, no. 15 (April 9, 1836).

35. "Dreadful Scenes in the Awful Disclosures of Maria Monk," *Downfall of Babylon* 2, no. 15 (April 2, 1836), AAS.

36. Description of the investigation and statements by the investigators were subsequently published in J. Jones, *Awful Exposure Awful Exposure of the Atrocious Plot Formed by Certain Individuals Against the Clergy and Nuns of Lower Canada, Through the Intervention of Maria Monk. With an Authentic Narrative of Her Life, from Her Birth to the Present Moment and an Account of Her Impositions, etc.* (New York: Jones & Co. of Montreal, 1836). They were also reprinted in "Maria Monk and Her Impostures," *Quarterly Christian Spectator*, (June 1, 1837); *L'Ami du Peuple* was a "moderate" paper of Montreal that did not support Lower Canada's revolutionary movement; "Maria Monk, the Nun-Such," *Atkinson's Saturday Evening Post*, (August 13, 1836); *Portsmouth Journal of Literature and Politics*, (August 20, 1836).

37. Both stories printed in "Interview with Maria Monk," *Zion's Herald*, (September 7, 1836); Samuel B. Smith, a late popish priest, *The Escape of Sainte Frances Patrick, Another Nun from the Hotel Dieu Nunnery of Montreal, to Which Is Appended a Decisive Confirmation of the Awful Disclosures of Maria Monk* (New York: Office of the Downfall of Babylon, 1836), 5–8; George Bourne, "Romanism in Canada," *American Protestant Vindicator* 2, no. 50 (September 14, 1836).

38. Description of Patridge's retreat in "Maria Monk and Her Impostures," *Quarterly Christian Spectator*; *Atkinson's Saturday Evening Post* 15, no. 794 (October 15, 1836); see also Billington, "Maria Monk and Her Influence," 295; statement of Brownlee quoted in New York *Observer*, (October 6, 1838).

39. Jones, *Awful Exposure*, 15, 6, 13, 47, 36.

40. Jones, *Awful Exposure*, 41, 78, 98; Mary Anne Poutanen, *Brutal Passions: Prostitution in Early Nineteenth-Century Montreal* (Montreal: McGill-Queens University Press, 2015), 153–54. For more information on Magdalen asylums, see Steven Ruggles, "Fallen Women: The Inmates of the Magdalen Society Asylum of Philadelphia, 1836–1908," *Journal of Social History* 14, no. 4 (Summer 1983): 65–82.

41. Jones, *Awful Exposure*, 32, 124, 40, 88, 32, 66; Poutanen, *Brutal Passions: Prostitution in Nineteenth-Century Montreal*, 154.

42. Jones, *Awful Exposure*, 32, 124, 40.

43. Ruggles, "Fallen Women," 66, 67; Poutanen, *Brutal Passions*, 153–55.

44. Slocum, *Confirmation of Maria Monk's Disclosures Concerning the Hotel Dieu Nunnery of Montreal*, 142–43; "Maria Monk," *Zion's Herald* 7, no. 35 (August 31, 1836); *Protestant Vindicator* 2, no. 45 (August 11, 1836), NYPL; *Downfall of Babylon*, no. 28 (October 1, 1836), AAS.

45. "Maria Monk and Her Impostures," *Quarterly Christian Spectator*; "Was Maria Monk a Nun at the Hotel Dieu Convent at Montreal?," *American Protestant Vindicator*, (August 11, 1836); "Appendix," in Monk, *Awful Disclosures*, 205; "Maria Monk," *Baltimore Literary and Religious Magazine* (September 1836); American Tract Society resolution published in Slocum, "Resolutions Respecting Maria Monk," *Confirmation of Maria Monk's Disclosures*, 85.

46. *Catholic Diary, Boston Pilot*, and "From Father McMahon's Letter to the Editor of the N. Y. *Catholic Diary* of March, 1836," in "Appendix," in Monk, *Awful Disclosures*, 206, 210, 226–28; *Catholic Telegraph*, November 24, 1836; "Maria Monkism," *Catholic Telegraph* 9, no. 10 (March 7, 1840).

47. Stone was the editor of the New York *Commercial Advertiser*, where he also published his incriminating evidence against Monk; William L. Stone, *A Complete Refutation of Maria Monk's Atrocious Plot Concerning the Hotel Dieu Convent, in Montreal, Lower Canada* (1837), 7, 6, 20, 22, 25, 26, 33.

48. Stone, *A Complete Refutation*, 32, 44, 35.

49. Stone, *A Complete Refutation*, 37, 46, 43.

50. "Colonel Stone," *Downfall of Babylon*, March 18, 1837, AAS; *Protestant Vindicator*, October 26, 1836, NYPL; Stone, *A Complete Refutation*, 58, 51, 48, 47.

51. "Resolutions Respecting Maria Monk," in Slocum, *Confirmation of Maria Monk's Disclosures*, 85–88; N.A., *Evidence Demonstrating the Falsehoods of William L. Stone, Concerning the Hotel Dieu Nunnery of Montreal* (New York, c. 1837), American Antiquarian Society; Samuel F. B. Morse, *Imminent Dangers to the Free Institutions of the United States and Foreign Conspiracy Against the Liberties of the United States* (New York: E. B. Clayton, 1835); *Downfall of Babylon*, (October 29, 1836); "Maria Monk vs. Col. Stone," *Haverville Gazette*, (November 19, 1836); "The Hotel Dieu Nunnery in Labor Hath Brought Forth a Jesuitical Hoax," *Protestant Vindicator*, (July 27, 1837).

52. *Protestant Vindicator*, (November 16, 1836), and (November 23, 1836), NYPL; Laughton Osborn, *Vision of Rubeta: An Epic Story of the Island of Manhattan, with Illustrations Done on Stone* (Boston: Weeks, Jordan, and Company, 1838), AAS; Autodicus, *A Critique of the Vision of*

Rubeta: A Dramatic Sketch in One Act (Philadelphia: Printed for the Trade, 1838), AAS; response from the American Tract Society printed in Slocum, *Confirmation of Maria Monk's Disclosures*, 85.

53. "Maria Monk and Her Impostures," *Quarterly Christian Spectator*.

54. W. W. Sleigh, *An Exposure of Maria Monk's Pretended Abduction and Conveyance to the Catholic Asylum, Philadelphia, by Six Priests, on the Night of August 15, 1837, with Numerous Extraordinary Incidents During Her Residence in This City* (Philadelphia: T. K. and P. G. Collins' Printers, 1837), 3–13.

55. Sleigh, *An Exposure of Maria Monk's Pretended Abduction and Conveyance*, 14–18.

56. Sleigh, *An Exposure of Maria Monk's Pretended Abduction*, 23–29.

57. Sleigh, *An Exposure of Maria Monk's Pretended Abduction*, 34–36.

58. Maria Monk, *Further Disclosures by Maria Monk Concerning the Hotel Dieu Nunnery of Montreal, also Her Visit to Nuns' Island, and Discourses Concerning That Secret Retreat, Preceded by a Reply to the Priest's Book, by Rev. J. J Slocum* (New York: Leavitt, Lord, 1837).

59. "Maria Monk," *New Hampshire Patriot*, (August 1, 1836); information on the court proceeding in New York *Observer*, (November 26, 1836), as cited in Billington, "Maria Monk and Her Influence," 287; Bourne, *Lorette*, 208, 173. I am indebted for this interpretation of *Lorette* to Marie Anne Pagliarini, "The Pure American Woman and the Wicked Catholic Priest: An Analysis of Anti-Catholic Literature in Antebellum America," *Religion and American Culture: A Journal of Interpretation* 9, no. 1 (Winter 1999): 112.

60. New York *Observer*, October 6, 1838; *American Protestant Vindicator*, (April 28, 1841), quoted in Billington, "Maria Monk and Her Influence," 295; *Morning News* (Connecticut), (September 2, 1847). Sing-Sing was the New York State prison at Auburn, its nickname derived from its location in Ossining. For more on Sing-Sing, see Rothman, *Discovery of the Asylum*, 79–108; *Barre Patriot* (Massachusetts), (August 18, 1848); *Weekly Eagle* (Vermont), (July 9, 1849).

CHAPTER 2

1. Louisa Goddard Whitney, *The Burning of the Convent. A Narrative of the Destruction by a Mob, of the Ursuline School on Mount Benedict, Charlestown, as Remembered by One of the Pupils* (Cambridge: Welch, Bigelow, and Company, 1877), 75–81.

2. Whitney, *The Burning of the Convent*, 33, 81–84; "Letter from Mother St. Augustine O'Keefe to Rev. F. Flynn, June 17, 1887," *Historical Records and Studies* 4 (1906): 227; for more on the burning of the convent, see Nancy Lusignan Schultz, *Fire and Roses: The Burning of the Charlestown Convent, 1834* (Boston: Northeastern University Press, 2000); George Hill Evans, *The Burning of the Mount Benedict Ursuline Community House*, Somerville Historical Monographs (Somerville, MA: Somerville Public Library, 1934); Robert H. Lord, John E. Sexton, and Edward T. Harrington, *History of the Archdiocese of Boston*, 3 vols. (New York: Pilot Publishing Co., 1944), 205–39; Jeanne Hamilton, "The Nunnery as Menace: The Burning of the Charlestown Convent, 1834," *U.S. Catholic Historian* 14, no. 1 (Winter 1996): 35–65; and Daniel A. Cohen, "Passing the Torch: Boston Firemen, 'Tea Party' Patriots, and the Burning of the Charlestown Convent Riot," *Journal of the Early Republic* 24 (2004): 528–86.

3. "Statement by the Leader of the Know Nothing Mob, Destruction of the Charlestown Convent," *U.S. Catholic Historical Records and Studies* 12 (1918): 66, in Lusignan Schultz, *Fire and Roses*, 5; "Report," in *Documents Relating to the Ursuline Convent in Charlestown* (Boston: Reprinted by Samuel N. Dickinson, 1842), 13; Whitney, *The Burning of the Convent*, 86.

4. Whitney, *The Burning of the Convent*, 10, 46; Schultz, *Fire and Roses*, 21–30; see Schultz, *Fire and Roses* for a thorough account of Moffatt's early life.

5. Schultz, *Fire and Roses*, 97; for remarks on Moffatt, see "The Black Nuns," *Boston Monthly Magazine* 1, no. 4 (September 1825): 184; Moffatt, "To the Editor," *Recorder* (September 18, 1834), as cited in Hamilton, "The Nunnery as Menace," 50; for comments on Moffatt's sometimes abrupt temperament, see "Letter from Mother St. Augustine O'Keefe to Rev. F. Flynn, June 17, 1887," *Historical Records and Studies* 4 (1906): 228; for a description of early nineteenth-century American female gender norms, see Barbara Welter, "The Cult of True Womanhood: 1820–1860," *American Quarterly* 18 (Summer 1966): 151–74; and Jeanne Boydston, *Home and Work: Housework, Wages, and the Ideology of Labor in the Early Republic* (New York: Oxford University Press, 1990).

6. Schultz, *Fire and Roses*, 81; "Report," *Documents*, 10.

7. "Prospectus," original in Archives of Catholic University of America, cited in Hamilton, "The Nunnery as Menace," 41; for a description of the education received at Mount Benedict, see Daniel A. Cohen, "The Respectability of Rebecca Reed," *Society for Historians of the Early Republic* 16, no. 3 (Autumn 1996): 427; Mary J. Oates, "Catholic Female Academies on the Frontier," *U.S. Catholic Historian* 12 (Fall 1994): 124–30; and Margaret M. McGuinness, *Called to Serve: A History of Nuns in America* (New York: New York University Press, 2013), 71–72.

8. Whitney, *The Burning of the Convent*, 96–103; "Letter from Mother St. Augustine O'Keefe to Rev. F. Flynn, June 17, 1887," *Historical Records and Studies* 4 (1906): 225; O'Keefe was a resident at Mount Benedict when the attack occurred and wrote to Rev. F. Flynn after Louisa Goddard's account of the attack was published to confirm or counter certain details therein.

9. Daniel A. Cohen, "Miss Reed and the Superiors: The Contradictions of Convent Life in Antebellum America," *Journal of Social History* 30, no.1 (Fall 1996): 162; Evans, *The Burning of the Mount Benedict Community*, 7. For more on the economic decline in Boston and neighboring cities in the 1830s, see Peter R. Knights, *The Plain People of Boston, 1830–1860: A Study in City Growth* (New York: Oxford University Press, 1971). Knights calculated that Boston's skilled workers were twice as likely to experience economic decline than advancement through the 1830s, and that percentages were worse for unskilled workers.

10. "Report," 13; Schultz, *Fire and Roses*, 3–5. At the time, Charlestown contained about ten thousand people and Boston close to seventy-two thousand, according to Evans, *The Burning of the Mount Benedict Community*, 3, 13; this meeting is described in Mary Ewens, *The Role of the Nun in Nineteenth Century America*, (Thiensville, WI: Caritas, 2014), 150.

11. Whitney, *The Burning of the Convent*, 93; Hamilton, "The Nunnery as Menace," 43; Evans, *The Burning of the Mount Benedict Community*, 9; Daniel A. Cohen challenges the class-conflict analysis of the burning of Mount Benedict by pointing to the involvement and socioeconomic status of the firefighters in the event in his "Passing the Torch: Boston Firemen, 'Tea Party' Patriots, and the Burning of the Charlestown Convent," 527–86; for studies on mob violence and rioting in early America, see David Grimsted, *American Mobbing, 1826–1861: Toward Civil War* (New York: Oxford University Press, 1998); Theodore Hammett, "Two Mobs of Jacksonian Boston: Ideology and Interest," *Journal of American History* 62 (March 1976): 845–68; Jack Tager, *Boston Riots: Three Centuries of Social Violence* (Boston: Northeastern University Press, 2001), 108–20; and Paul A. Gilje, *Rioting in America* (Bloomington: Indiana University Press, 1996).

12. John England, "Documents Relating to the Burning of the Charlestown Convent, The Imposture of Rebecca Reed, The Boston Riots, Etc.," *Works of the Right Rev. John England, First Bishop of Charleston*, vol. 5, ed. Sabastian G. Messmer (Baltimore: John Murphy & Co., 1849),

252; Whitney, *The Burning of the Convent*, 105; Schultz, *Fire and Roses*, 5–6; Hamilton, "The Nunnery as Menace," 43.

13. "Letter from Mother St. Augustine O'Keefe to Rev. F. Flynn, June 17, 1887," *Historical Records and Studies*, 226; Schultz, 6–7; Hamilton, "The Nunnery as Menace," 48; "Report," 16.

14. "Report," 12; *Supplement* to *Six Months in a Convent* in Reed, *Six Months in a Convent*, (Boston: Russell, Odiorne & Metcalf, 1835), 73–89; Edward Cutter, "Letter to the Editor," *Independent Inquirer* (Vermont) 1, no. 49 (August 16, 1834): 2.

15. Whitney, *The Burning of the Convent*, 18; "Report," 8; England, "Documents," vol. 5, 243; "Mysterious," *Mercantile Journal* (August 1834); England, vol. 5, 243, 260.

16. See, for instance, "Convent at Charlestown," *Boston Recorder* 19, no. 33 (August 15, 1834); and "Mysterious," *Mercantile Journal* (August 1834); England, vol. 5, 243, 245; "Report," 8.

17. Whitney, *The Burning of the Convent*, 55–57.

18. Cutter, "Letter to the Editor," *Independent Inquirer*, 2; "Report," 10; England, "Documents," 243; Whitney, *The Burning of the Convent*, 55–57, 62–65.

19. Analysis of criticism of male celibacy from Maria Anne Pagliarini, "The Pure American Woman and the Wicked Catholic Priest: An Analysis of Anti-Catholic Literature in Antebellum America," *Religion and American Culture: A Journal of Interpretation* 9, no. 1 (Winter 1999): 97–128.

20. Sales figures for *Six Months in a Convent* found in Ray Allen Billington, *The Protestant Crusade, 1800–1860: A Study of the Origins of American Nativism* (1938; repr., New York: Quadrangle, 1964), 90; Moffatt, *An Answer to Six Months in a Convent*, iii, vii.

21. For social background on Reed and vocational prospects available to her and women of her social conditions, see Cohen, "Miss Reed and the Superiors," 156.

22. Information about Reed's life before entering the Ursuline convent found in Cohen, "The Respectability of Rebecca Reed," 419; and Cohen, "Miss Reed and the Superiors," 156–57; details also taken from Reed, *Six Months*, 52–68; Moffatt, *An Answer to Six Months*, xv–xix, 2, 3, 8, 12, 57–61.

23. Cohen, "The Respectability of Rebecca Reed," 442–43; Schultz, *Fire and Roses*, 120–21; *Supplement to Six Months in a Convent*, 154–55, 160, 219–21.

24. Reed, *Six Months in a Convent*, 7, 11, 16, 23–24.

25. Moffatt, *An Answer to Six Months*, 16.

26. Reed, *Six Months in a Convent*, 6.

27. Reed, *Six Months*, 2; *Literary and Catholic Sentinel*, September 12, 1835; *American Traveler* April 14, 1835, cited in Cohen, "The Respectability," 451.

28. *Report of the Committee*; Boston *Daily Advocate*, August 14, September 30, 1834; Boston *Daily Advocate*, October 10, 1834; Fay's letter and Reed's response printed in Boston *Courier*, January 5 and 7, 1835.

29. George Bourne, *The Protestant* (New York) 1 (May 22, 1830): 165; Bourne, *The Protestant* 1, no. 34 (August 31, 1830); Bourne, *The Protestant* 1, no. 45 (November 6, 1830).

30. Thomas Roscoe, "Introduction," in Scipione de Ricci, *Female Convents* (New York: D. Appleton & Co., 1834), xiv, viii.

31. "Mothers' Lyceums," *Ladies' Magazine and Literary Gazette* 5, no. 9 (September 1832): 424; "The Convent of St. Clare," *Ladies' Magazine and Literary Gazette* 5, no. 6 (June 1832): 244; see Linda K. Kerber, *Women of the Republic: Intellect and Ideology in Revolutionary America* (Chapel Hill: Published for the Institute of Early American History and Culture by the University of North Caronia Press, 1980).

32. England, "Documents," 232; Lyman Beecher's three sermons were reprinted in Lyman Beecher, DD, *Plea for the West* (New York: Leavitt, Lord, & Co., 1835), 54–56.

33. Beecher, *Plea for the West*, 127; England, "Documents," 232; Beecher, *Autobiography of Lyman Beecher*, ed. Barbara Cross (Cambridge, MA: Harvard University Press, 1961), 2:167–68.

34. "Report," 1–20, 10–11, 14–20; Hamilton, "The Nunnery as Menace," 46.

35. Evans, *The Burning of the Mount Benedict Ursuline Community House*, 15; England, "Documents," 234, 257; Ephraim Tucker, "The Burning of the Ursuline Convent," *Collections of the Worcester Society of Antiquities* IX (1890), 40–41; Richard S. Fay, *An Argument Before the Committee of the House of Representatives upon the Petition of Benedict Fenwick and Others, with a Portion of the Documentary History* (Boston: J. H. Eastburn, 1835), 36.

36. England, "Documents," 248.

37. England, "Documents," 253–54.

38. Evans, *The Burning of the Mount Benedict Ursuline Community House*, 7, 18; Lord, Sexton, and Harrington, *History of the Archdiocese of Boston*, vol. II, 234–35; "Report," 8; England, "Documents," 255, 257, 248; Fay, *An Argument Before the House of Representatives*, 50.

39. Evans, *The Burning of the Mount Benedict Ursuline Community House*, 18; Sr. Mary St. George to Dr. Hooker, February 25, 1834 (Mass. State Archives, Pardons, 1835, M. Marcy), Lord Papers, archives of the Archdiocese of Boston, cited in Schultz, *Fire and Roses*, 227–28. The American Ursulines and the bishop held the Mount Benedict property in trust; see Hamilton, "The Nunnery as Menace," 40.

40. Fay, *An Argument*, 36, 14, 17, 21, 19, 22, 33, 37, 41; for more background information on Judge Fay, see William T. Davis, *Bench and Bar of the Commonwealth of Massachusetts,* 2 vols. (Boston, 1895), 1:447.

41. Fay, *An Argument*, 33; Letter from Peter O. Hatch, Boston, September 1, 1834, as cited in Fay, *An Argument*, 52; *Evening Transcript* (1834), cited in Evans, *The Burning of the Mount Benedict Ursuline Community House*, 14.

42. Mathew Carey, "Circular," Philadelphia, 1834; for more on Carey, see William Clarkin, *Mathew Carey: A Biography of His Publications, 1785–1824* (New York, 1984); and James N. Green, *Mathew Carey: Publisher and Patriot* (Philadelphia: Library Company of Philadelphia, 1985).

43. Boston *Daily Advocate,* October 10, 1835.

44. "Carmelite Convent in Baltimore: An Outrage Which Was Probably Committed Therein," *Baltimore Literary and Religious Magazine* 1, no. 5 (May 1835).

45. For more on the riot, see Joseph G. Mannard, "The 1839 Baltimore Nunnery Riot: An Episode in Jacksonian Nativism and Social Violence," in *Urban American Catholicism: The Culture and Identity of the American Catholic People,* ed. Timothy J. Meagher (New York: Garland Publishing, 1988), 192–206; details on Neal's diagnosis in *National Intelligencer*, August 22, 1839; for news coverage, see "Escape of a Nun from the Carmelite Prison in Aisquith Street," *Baltimore Literary and Religious Magazine* 5, no. 9 (September 1839).

46. Thomas W. Spalding, *The Premier See: A History of the Archdiocese of Baltimore, 1789–1989* (Baltimore: Johns Hopkins University Press, 1989), 55–56, 108, 112–15.

47. Mannard, "The 1839 Baltimore Nunnery Riot," 193–94.

48. "Escape of a Nun from a Carmelite Prison in Aisquith Street," *Baltimore Literary and Religious Magazine* 5, no. 9 (September 1839).

49. "Carmelite Convent in Baltimore," *Baltimore Literary and Religious Magazine* 1, no. 5 (May 1835); *Downfall of Babylon* 2, no. 2 (February 6, 1836), AAS.

50. Damon Norwood, *The Chronicles of Mount Benedict: A Tale of the Ursuline Convent* (Boston: Printed for the Publisher, 1837), 153, 147.

51. Norwood, *The Chronicles of Mount Benedict*, xiii, 149, 178, 180–81.

52. Norwood, *The Chronicles of Mount Benedict*, 187, xi, xiii.

53. Hamilton, "The Nunnery as Menace," 49; Evans, *The Burning of the Mount Benedict Ursuline Community House*, 18.

CHAPTER 3

1. Sales figures cited in Ray Allen Billington, *The Protestant Crusade, 1800–1860: A Study of the Origins of American Nativism* (1938; repr., New York: Quadrangle, 1964), 108.

2. See "Harper and Brothers, 1833–1962," in *American Literary Publishing Houses, 1638–1899*, part 1, ed. Peter Dzwonkoski (Detroit: A Bruccoli Clark Book, 1986), 192; William L. Stone, *The True History of Maria Monk: A Reprint of the Famous Report on her Charges*, Original Title: *A Refutation of the Fabulous History of the Arch-Impostor Maria Monk Being the Result of a Minute and Searching Inquiry by William L. Stone, Esq. of New York* (1836; repr., New York: Paulist Press, c. 1920), Anti-Catholic Printed Material Collection, UNDA; Comments on *Awful Disclosures* in *Albany Argus* quoted in the *Vermont State Paper* 1, no. 34 (February 9, 1836).

3. William Lloyd Garrison, "To the Public," *The Liberator* 1, no. 1 (January 1, 1831); Joyce Birt, *Catalogue of a Collection of Anti-Slavery Tracts and Pamphlets in the Possession of the Anti-Slavery Society for the Protection of Human Rights* (PhD diss., University of London, May 1958), ii; See also Kristin Hoganson, "Garrisonian Abolitionists and the Rhetoric of Gender, 1850–1860," *American Quarterly* 45, no. 4 (December 1993): 558–95.

4. Ronald G. Walters, "Anti-Slavery," in Walters, *American Reformers: 1815–1860* (New York: Hill and Wang, 1978), 77; Samuel B. Smith, ed., *Downfall of Babylon; or, The Truth Over Popery* (Philadelphia, New York, 1834–37), AAS; William C. Brownlee, "Nunneries Are Unconstitutional," *American Protestant Vindicator* (New York) 2, no. 40 (July 6, 1836), NYPL; for anti-Catholic literature published in the 1830s, see Ray Allen Billington, "Tentative Bibliography of Anti-Catholic Propaganda in the United States (1800–1860)," *Catholic Historical Review* 18, no. 4 (January 1933): 492–513.

5. Stephen S. Foster, *The Brotherhood of Thieves; or, A True Picture of the American Church and Clergy: A Letter to Nathaniel Barney, of Nantucket* (Boston: Anti-Slavery Office, 1844), 9; George Bourne, *Slavery Illustrated in Its Effects upon Woman and Domestic Society* (1837; repr., Freeport, NY: Books for Libraries Press, 1972), 11; Harriet Martineau, "Morals of Slavery," in *Society in America*, vol. II (1837; repr., New York: AMS Press, 1966), 320–28.

6. Nathaniel Southard, David Lee Child, and Lydia Marie Child, *The American Anti-Slavery Almanac for 1840* 1, no. 5 (Boston: Webster & Southard, 1840); Harriet Beecher Stowe, *The Annotated Uncle Tom's Cabin*, ed. with an introd. notes by Henry Louis Gates Jr. and Hollis Robbins (New York: W. W. Norton & Company, 2007), 138–40; for more examples, see "The Mother and Babe," *Slave's Friend* 2, no. 4 (n.d.): 14–16, and "The Nine Mothers," *Slave's Friend*, no. 10 (1836), 2.

7. George Bourne, Comments on Thome's Address, *Liberator*, May 10, 1834; see Ronald G. Walters, "The Erotic South: Civilization and Sexuality in American Abolitionism," *American Quarterly* 25, no. 2 (May 1973): 177–201; Martineau, "Morals of Slavery," in *Society in America*, 329–30; Theodore Bourne, "George Bourne: The Pioneer of American Anti-Slavery," *Methodist*

Quarterly Review 64 (1882): 68–91; George Bourne, Letter to Rhode Island Anti-Slavery Society, *Liberator*, February 6, 1836.

8. Theodore Dwight Weld, *American Slavery as It Is: Testimony of a Thousand Witnesses* (New York, 1839), 11, 15; "A Puritan," [George Bourne], in *The Abrogation of the Seventh Commandment in the American Churches* (New York, 1835), 3–4; Lydia Maria Child, *An Appeal in Favor of That Class of Americans Called Africans* (Boston, 1836), 22–24; "Preamble & Constitution of the Canton [OH] Ladies Anti-Slavery Society," Canton Ladies Anti-Slavery Society, Records, Ms. 26, Western Reserve Historical Society, quoted in Carol Lasser, "Voyeuristic Abolitionism: Sex, Gender, and the Transformation of Anti-Slavery Rhetoric," *Journal of the Early Republic* 28, no. 1 (Spring 2008): 91.

9. Lasser, "Voyeuristic Abolitionism," 92–95; for more on female antislavery efforts, see Jean Fagan Yellin and John C. Van Horne, eds., *The Abolitionist Sisterhood: Women's Political Culture in Antebellum America* (Ithaca, NY: Cornell University Press, 1994); and Debra Gold Hansen, *Strained Sisterhood: Gender and Class in the Boston Female Anti-Slavery Society* (Amherst: University of Massachusetts Press, 1993); David Brion Davis, "Some Themes of Counter-Subversion: An Analysis of Anti-Masonic, Anti-Catholic and Anti-Mormon Literature," *Mississippi Valley Historical Review* 47 (September 1960): 205–24; see statistics in Lasser, "Voyeuristic Abolitionism," 101–3.

10. David Brion Davis, "The Emergence of Immediatism in British and American Antislavery Thought," in *History of the American Abolitionist Movement: A Bibliography of Scholarly Articles,* ed. John R. McKirvigan (New York: Garland Publishing, 1999), 15; George Bourne, *The Book and Slavery Irreconcilable: With Animadversions upon Dr. Smith's Philosophy* (Philadelphia: J. M. Sanderson & Co., 1816); John W. Christie and Dwight L. Dumond, *George Bourne and The Book and Slavery Irreconcilable* (Wilmington: Historical Society of Delaware, 1969), 17–19; Bourne, *Man-Stealing and Slavery Denounced* (Boston: Garrison & Knapp, 1834); Bourne, *Picture of Slavery in the United States of America* (Middletown, CT: Edwin Hunt, 1834); Bourne, *Slavery Illustrated in Its Effects upon Woman and Domestic Society* (Boston: Isaac Knapp, 1837); Christie and Dumond, *George Bourne*, 77, 86; William Lloyd Garrison, "The Protestant," *Liberator* 2, no. 11 (March 17, 1832): 43; Bourne, *Protestant* (New York, 1830–1831).

11. Davis, "Immediatism in Antislavery Thought," in McKivigan, ed., *Abolitionism and American Reform*, 4–6.

12. Bourne, *Slavery Illustrated in Its Effects upon Woman and Domestic Society*, 33, 45, 74, 39.

13. Bourne, *Slavery Illustrated*, 34, 39, 44

14. William Hogan, *Popery! As It Was and as It Is; Also, Auricular Confession; and Popish Nunneries* (1845; repr., Hartford, CT: Andrus & Son, 1854), 246–84; Maria Monk, *Awful Disclosures of the Hotel Dieu Nunnery of Montreal, Revised with an Appendix* (New York: Howe & Bates, 1836), 24, 40, 15, 54.

15. Smith, ed., *Downfall of Babylon* (New York) 2, no. 22 (July 9, 1836), AAS; Ned Buntline, *The Beautiful Nun* (Philadelphia: T. B. Peterson & Brothers, 1866); "Flogging American Women," "Selling Females by the Pound," and "Ladies Whipping Girls" from Bourne, *Picture of Slavery in the United States of America*; for more analysis of the images in Bourne's book, see Lasser, "Voyeuristic Abolitionism," 84–89.

16. Walters, "The Erotic South," 187; Bourne, *Lorette. The History of Louise, Daughter of a Canadian Nun, Exhibiting the Interior of Female Convents* (New York: C. Small, 1834); Christie and Dumond, *George Bourne*, 10.

17. Bourne, *Lorette*, 1, 12, 57, x.

18. Colleen McDannell, *The Christian Home in Victorian America, 1840–1900* (Bloomington: Indiana University Press, 1986), xv; Barbara Welter, "The Cult of True Womanhood, 1820–1860," *American Quarterly* 18, no. 2, pt. 1 (Summer 1966): 151–74; Marie Anne Pagliarini, "The Pure American Woman and the Wicked Catholic Priest: An Analysis of Anti-Catholic Literature in Antebellum America," *Religion and American Culture: A Journal of Interpretation* 9, no. 1 (Winter 1999): 98.

19. Daniel R. Vollaro, "Lincoln, Stowe, and the 'Little Woman/Great War' Story: The Making, and Breaking, of a Great American Anecdote," *Journal of the Abraham Lincoln Association* 30 (Winter 2009): 18–34; Nancy Koester, *Harriet Beecher Stowe: A Spiritual Life* (Grand Rapids, MI: William B. Eerdmans, 2014), x; *National Era* (April 15, 1852), on Railton website, accessed March 18, 2016, http://utc.iath.virginia.edu/notices/noar01ft.html; Amy Dru Stanley, "Home Life and the Morality of the Market," in *The Market Revolution in America*, ed. M. Stokes and S. Conway (Charlottesville: University of Virginia Press, 1996), 88; Lasser, "Voyeuristic Abolitionism," 109.

20. "Harriet Beecher Stowe and 'The Man That Was a Thing,'" in *The Annotated Uncle Tom's Cabin*, , xxxv; Harriet Beecher Stowe, [Letter to the Abolitionist Eliza Cabot Follen], in Harriet Beecher Stowe, *Uncle Tom's Cabin*, Norton Critical Edition, ed. E. Ammons (New York: W. W. Norton, 1994), 413; "Harriet Beecher Stowe and 'The Man That Was a Thing,'" in *Annotated Uncle Tom's Cabin*, xxxvii; *National Era,* October 2, 1851; Paula Garrett, "*Legacy* Profile: Grace Greenwood (Sarah Jane Lippincott), 1823–1904," *Legacy* 14, no. 2 (1997): 137–53; see also David S. Reynolds, *Mightier Than the Sword: Uncle Tom's Cabin and the Battle for America* (New York: W. W. Norton & Company, 2011).

21. Charles Dudley Warner, "The Story of *Uncle Tom's Cabin*," in *Critical Essays on Harriet Beecher Stowe*, ed. E. Ammons (Boston: G. K. Hall, 1980), 64–65; William Lloyd Garrison, *The Liberator* 22, no. 13 (March 26, 1852): 50; "Literary," *Independent* 4, no. 180 (May 13, 1852): 79; "Harriet Beecher Stowe and 'The Man That Was a Thing," in *The Annotated Uncle Tom's Cabin*, xl; Maria Monk, *Awful Disclosures of the Hotel Dieu* (New York, 1836); Monk, *Further Disclosures by Maria Monk Concerning the Hotel Dieu Nunnery of Montreal; and Also Her Visit to Nuns Island and Disclosures Concerning That Retreat* (New York, 1836).

22. *The Annotated Uncle Tom's Cabin*, chapters 1–5.

23. *The Annotated Uncle Tom's Cabin*, 9, 57, 67, 90–91; Elizabeth Ammons describes the stereotypical Victorian heroine as "pious, domestic, self-sacrificing, emotionally uninhibited in response to people and ethical questions" in "The Heroines of *Uncle Tom's Cabin*," in Ammons, ed., *Critical Essays on Harriet Beecher Stowe* (Boston: G. K. Hall & Co., 1980), 159; *The Annotated Uncle Tom's Cabin*, 384–85.

24. Ammons, "Stowe's Dream of the Mother-Savior: *Uncle Tom's Cabin* and American Women Writers Before 1920," in *New Essays on* Uncle Tom's Cabin, ed. Eric J. Sundquist (New York: Cambridge University Press, 1986), 158–59; for more on the development of moral motherhood, see Ruth H. Bloch, "American Feminine Ideals in Transition: The Rise of the Moral Mother, 1785–1815," *Feminist Studies* 4 (June 1978): 105; *The Annotated Uncle Tom's Cabin*, 144, 144, 150, 151.

25. Ammons, 164–65; *The Annotated Uncle Tom's Cabin*, 155–56; for a description of Eva's grandmother, see *The Annotated Uncle Tom's Cabin*, 234–37; Charles Edward Stowe, *Life of Harriet Beecher Stowe Compiled from Her Letters and Journals* (Boston: Houghton Mifflin, 1890), 154; Martineau, "Morals of Slavery," in *Society in America* vol. 2, 342; for more on the

high status afforded to motherhood as articulated by Stowe's sister, see Katheryn Kish Sklar, *Catherine Beecher: A Study in American Domesticity* (New Haven, CT: Yale University Press, 1973); Elizabeth Ammons, "Heroines in *Uncle Tom's Cabin*," in Ammons, ed., *Critical Essays on Harriet Beecher Stowe* (Boston: G. K. Hall & Co., 1980), 152–65.

26. Gates and Robbins, "Introduction," in *The Annotated Uncle Tom's Cabin*, xiii; *Annotated Uncle Tom's Cabin*, 18, 121, 23, 148–49.

27. *The Annotated Uncle Tom's Cabin*, 148–50; Ammons, "Heroines in *Uncle Tom's Cabin*," 157–58; see also Stephanie Coontz, *Marriage, a History: From Obedience to Intimacy, or How Love Conquered Marriage* (New York: Viking Press, 2005), chapters 10 and 11.

28. *The Annotated Uncle Tom's Cabin*, 166–67, 174, 180, 190; Ammons, "Stowe's Dream of the Mother-Savior," 164–65.

29. Monk, *Awful Disclosures*, 8, 12, 5, 14, 24, 40, 119.

30. Joan D. Hedrick, *Harriet Beecher Stowe: A Life* (New York: Oxford University Press, 1994), 353ff; Ammons, "Stowe's Dream of the Mother-Savior," 160; Nina Baym, *Women's Fiction: A Guide to Novels by and about Women in America, 1820–1860* (Ithaca, NY: Cornell University Press, 1978), 27; Hogan describes nuns as "poor, helpless females" in *A Synopsis of Popery*, 133; *Awful Disclosures* refers to nuns as "helpless females," preface; Bourne describes nuns as "slaves to his [a priest's] will" in *Lorette*, 61.

31. *The Annotated Uncle Tom's Cabin*, 365; Monk, *Awful Disclosures*, 118; *Annotated*, 360; Samuel S. Smith, "On Nunneries," *Downfall of Babylon* 1, no. 2 (October 30, 1834), AAS; Monk, *Awful Disclosures*, 117.

32. For a discussion of sexuality and power in the context of antislavery rhetoric, see Walters, "The Erotic South," 180, 186; Lydia Marie Child, *An Appeal in Favor of Americans Called Africans* (1836; repr., New York: Arno Press, 1968), 101; *The Annotated Uncle Tom's Cabin*, 17, 236, 374, 376, 351, 362, 390, 356, 391, 360, 363.

33. Monk, *Awful Disclosures*, 26; Pagliarini, "The Pure American Woman and the Wicked Catholic Priest," 98; Monk, 94, 95.

34. James Baldwin, "Everybody's Protest Novel," in Ammons, ed., *Critical Essays on Harriet Beecher Stowe*, 92; Alfred Kazin, *God and the American Writer* (New York: Alfred A. Knopf, 1997), 83; George Orwell, "Good Bad Books," in *The Collected Essays, Journalism, and Letters of George Orwell*, vol. 4, ed. S. Orwell and I. Angus (New York: Harcourt, Brace & World, 1968), 21; Ethan J. Kytle, *Romantic Reformers and the Antislavery Struggle in the Civil War Era* (New York: Cambridge University Press, 2014), 116–17.

35. Ammons, "Harriet Beecher Stowe and 'The Man That Was a Thing,'" in *The Annotated Uncle Tom's Cabin*, xlvii, xliii.

36. Reynolds, *Mightier Than The Sword*, xi–xii; Walters, "The Erotic South," 191–92, 187.

CHAPTER 4

1. T. S. Arthur, "The Young Music Teacher," *Ladies' Magazine, of Literature, Fashion, and the Fine Arts* 1 (January–July 1844): 191–96.

2. Jo Anne Preston, "Domestic Ideology, School Reformers, and Female Teachers: Schoolteaching Becomes Women's Work in Nineteenth-Century New England," *New England Quarterly* 66, no. 4 (December 1993): 531–51; Thomas Woody, *A History of Women's Education in the United States*, vol. 1 (New York: Octagon Books, 1966), 499.

3. Thomas Roscoe, "Introduction," in Scipione de Ricci, *Female Convents* (New York: D. Appleton & Co., 1834), xxi; Rachel McCrindell, *The Protestant Girl in a French Nunnery*, 4th American ed. (Philadelphia: Hooker, 1846), preface, 104, 161.

4. McCrindell, *The Protestant Girl in a French Nunnery*, 217–19, 196, 138, 82.

5. Press coverage printed in Rachel McCrindell, *The Protestant Girl in a French Nunnery; or, The Snares of Popery: A Warning to Protestants Against Education in Catholic Seminaries*, 10th ed. (New York: Wellman, 1846); "New Publications," *New York Evangelist* 23, no. 21 (May 20, 1852); "Literary," *New York Observer and Chronicle*, May 13, 1852, 158.

6. *The Presbyterian* quoted in *The Catholic Advocate* (Louisville), August 26, 1837; "Nunneries and the Confessional," *Boston Recorder* 30, no. 41 (October 9, 1845).

7. Harry Hazel, *The Nun of St. Ursula; or, The Burning of the Convent: A Romance of Mount Benedict* (Boston: Gleason, 1845); "The Grey Nuns of Montreal," *Christian Parlor Magazine* (New York), September 1844; Maria D. Weston, *Luzette: Good Brought Out of Evil* (Boston: Massachusetts Sabbath School Society, 1847), AAS; Ray Allen Billington, *The Protestant Crusade, 1800–1860: A Study of the Origins of Nativism* (1938; repr., Chicago: Quadrangle Paperbacks, 1952), 142; William Hogan, *Popery! As It Was and as It Is; Also, Auricular Confession; and Popish Nunneries* (1845; repr., Hartford, CT: Silas Andrus and Son, 1854), 247–48; Weston, *Luzette*, 12.

8. McCrindell, *The Protestant Girl in a French Nunnery*, preface; Hazel, *The Nun of St. Ursula*, 10, 12; Hogan, *Popery! As It Was and as It Is*, 238; Roscoe, "Introduction," *Female Convents*, xxii.

9. Letter reprinted in *Catholic Telegraph* (Cincinnati) 11, no. 35 (August 27, 1842): 278; "The Grey Nuns of Montreal," *Christian Parlor Magazine*; William Brownlee, "Nunneries Are Unconstitutional," *American Protestant Vindicator* 2, no. 4 (July 4, 1836), NYPL; McCrindell, *The Protestant Girl in a French Nunnery*.

10. Henry Barnard, *Second Annual Report of the Board of Commissioners of Common Schools in Connecticut* (1840), 6–7; Redding S. Sugg Jr., *Motherteacher: The Feminization of American Education* (Charlottesville: University Press of Virginia, 1978), 86; Horace Mann, *Fourth Annual Report of the Massachusetts Board of Education* (Washington, DC: National Education Association, 1947), 24; Preston, "Domestic Ideology, School Reformers, and Female Teachers," 533; Catherine Beecher, *Essay on the Education of Female Teachers* (New York: Van Nostrand & Dwight, 1835), 16.

11. Heather Julien, "School Novels, Women's Work, and Maternal Vocationalism," *NWSA Journal* 19, no. 2 (Summer 2007): 118; Sugg, *Motherteacher*, 18; Horace Mann, *A Few Thoughts on the Powers and Duties of Woman. Two Lectures* (Syracuse, NY: Hall, Mills & Co., 1853), 10, 23.

12. Henry Barnard quoted in Anne L. Kuhn, *The Mother's Role in Childhood Education: New England Concepts, 1830–1860* (1861; repr., New Haven, CT: Yale University Press, 1947), 55; Horace Bushnell, *Christian Nurture*, with an introd. by Luther A. Weigle (New Haven, CT: Yale University Press, 1947), 12–14; 202; Sugg, *Motherteacher*, 28; see also Colleen McDannell, *The Christian Home in Victorian America, 1840–1900* (Bloomington: Indiana University Press, 1994).

13. Mary Peabody Mann, *Life of Horace Mann* (Boston: Walker, Fuller & Co., 1865), 424; Catherine Beecher to Horace Mann, in *Common School Journal* (Boston) 5 (1843): 353; Mann, *Fourth Annual Report*, 24.

14. Catherine Beecher, *An Address to the Protestant Clergy of the United States* (New York, 1846), 29; Kathryn Kish Sklar, *Catherine Beecher: A Study in American Domesticity* (New York: W. W. Norton, 1976), 172; Mann, *A Few Thoughts on the Powers and Duties of Woman*, 35, 47.

15. Catherine Beecher, *The Evils Suffered by American Women and American Children: The Causes and the Remedy* (New York: Harper & Bros., 1846), 9–10; Sklar, *Catherine Beecher*, 174; Lyman Beecher, *Plea for the West* (New York: Leavitt, Lord, & Co., 1835), 11–12, 110, 113; *Annual Reports of the General Agent of the Board of National Popular Education* (Hartford, CT, 1848–57), cited in Sklar, *Catherine Beecher*, 184.

16. Mary Ewens, *The Role of the Nun in Nineteenth Century America: Variations on the International Theme* (1970; repr., Thiensville, WI: Caritas Communications, 2014), 37–41; St. Charles, Missouri: Bicentennial: Historical Program Book: 1769–969, R70: 10.4.5.2: St. Charles, SSND, St. Louis, Missouri; Barbara Brumleve, ed., *The Letters of Caroline Friess: School Sisters of Notre Dame* (Winona, MN: Saint Mary's Press, 1991), 45.

17. "The Educational Mission of the Society of the Sacred Heart, 1800–1979," RSCJ, St. Louis, Missouri; Louise Callan, RSCJ, *The Society of the Sacred Heart of North America* (New York: Longmans, Green and Co., 1937), 38, 45, 59; Ruth Cunningham, RSCJ, *First American Daughter: Mary Aloysia Hardey, 1809–1886* (Accra: Kenwood, 1981), 1.

18. Callan, *The Society of the Sacred Heart of North America*, 205–9; "The Educational Mission of the Society of the Sacred Heart, 1800–1979," RSCJ; "Education and Educators Described by Saint Madeleine Sophie Barat," Work undertaken by Clare Dykmans, RSCJ, using some of the letters, 1987, translated by Barbara Hogg, RSCJ.

19. Mann, *First Annual Report*, 58, 66; Mann, *Reply to the Remarks of Thirty-One Boston School-Masters on the Seventh Annual Report of the Secretary for the Massachusetts Board of Education* (Boston: W. B. Fowle and N. Capen, 1844), 130–31; Horace Mann, *Tenth Annual Report of the Secretary of the Board of Education* (1846), in *Antebellum American Culture*, ed. David Brion Davis (University Park: Pennsylvania State University Press, 1979), 40–42.

20. James Pyle Wickersham, *A History of Education in Pennsylvania, Private and Public, Elementary and Higher* (Lancaster, PA: Inquirer Publishing Co., 1886), 293.

21. For more on the "Bible Wars," see Katie Oxx, *The Nativist Movement in America: Religious Conflict in the Nineteenth Century* (New York: Routledge, 2013), 59–60; Diane Ravitch, *The Great School Wars* (New York: Basic Books, 1974); and Joseph J. McCadden, "Bishop Hughes Versus the Public School Society of New York," *Catholic Historical Review* 50, no. 2 (July 1964): 188–207; James W. Fraser, ed., *The School in the United States: A Documentary History* (Boston: McGraw-Hill, 2001), 77.

22. Oxx, *The Nativist Movement in America*, 53–82; Michael Feldberg, *The Philadelphia Riots of 1844: A Study in Ethnic Conflict* (Westport, CT: Greenwood Press, 1975), 49–77.

23. "The Philadelphia Riots," *Barre Gazette* 11, no. 2 (May 24, 1844); "Great Riot in Philadelphia," *Farmer's Cabinet* 42, no. 39 (May 16, 1844); Feldberg, *The Philadelphia Riots of 1844*, 99–106, 111–15; Oxx, 72.

24. For a description of the parade, see Feldberg, 136–38.

25. "Nunneries and the Confessional," *Boston Recorder* 30, no. 41, (October 9, 1845); William Hogan, *Popery! As It Was and as It Is*, 264, 246.

26. Hogan, *Popery!*, 253–54; for more on the anti-Catholic views of confessionals, see Marie Anne Pagliarini, "The Pure American Woman and the Wicked Catholic Priest: An Analysis of Anti-Catholic Literature in Antebellum America," *Religion and Culture: A Journal of Interpretation* 9, no. 1 (Winter 1999): 105–10.

27. Hogan, *Popery!*, 255, 285, 554.

28. Letter from Philippine Duchesne to Madame de Rollin, May 1836, "Duchesne to Her Family and Lay People," Box 5, RSCJ, translation from the French provided by Antoine Matondo;

Letter from Mary Hardy, March 15, 1884, cited in Cunningham, *First American Daughter: Mary Aloysia Hardy*, 12, 13.

29. Benilda Dix, SSND, *Love Cannot Wait: Life of Mary Theresa of Jesus Gerhardinger, Foundress of the School Sisters of Notre Dame* (Milwaukee: School Sisters of Notre Dame, 1987), 173.

30. "The Family," *Parent's Monitor and Young People's Friend* (Gilmanton, NH) 4, no. 4 (December 1840): 90; "On the Domestic Constitution, and Its Obvious Advantages in the Promotion of Piety and Happiness," *Parent's Magazine* 1, no. 1 (September 1840): 1–9.

31. Callan, *The Society of the Sacred Heart of North America*, 201; Cunningham, *First American Daughter*, 2, 7; Callan, 209.

32. Letters from Sophia Barat to Mary Hardy, 1847 and 1851, printed in "Education and Educators Described by Saint Madeleine Sophie Barat," RSCJ; Callan, *The Society of the Sacred Heart of North America*, 228.

33. Preston, "Domestic Ideology, School Reformers, and Female Teachers," 542–47; Hannah More, "Female Virtues and Pursuits," *Parent's Magazine* 1, no. 1 (September 1840): 68.

CHAPTER 5

1. George G. Foster, *New York by Gas-Light and Other Urban Sketches*, ed. with an introd. by Stuart M. Blumin (Berkeley: University of California Press, 1990), 69; Ned Buntline, *The Mysteries and Miseries of New York: A Story of Real Life* (New York: W. F. Burgess, 1849), preface; Buntline, *The Beautiful Nun* (Philadelphia: T. B. Peterson, 1866).

2. James Rees, *Mysteries of City Life* (Philadelphia: J. W. Moore, 1849); Buntline, *Mysteries and Miseries of New York*; George Foster, *New York Naked* (New York: De Witt & Davenport, 1850); George Lippard, *The Quaker City; or, The Monks of Monk Hall, a Romance of Philadelphia Life* (Philadelphia: T. B. Peterson, 1845); Foster, *New York by Gas-Light*, 69; Buntline, *Mysteries and Miseries of New York*, title page; Jacob Riis, *How the Other Half Lives: Studies Among the Tenements of New York* (New York: Charles Scribner's Sons, 1890).

3. For further analysis of the city mystery genre in the early nineteenth century, see David M. Henkin, "City Streets and the Urban World of Print," in *The Industrial Book, 1840–1880*, vol. 3 of *A History of the Book in America,* ed. Scott E. Casper et al. (Chapel Hill: University of North Carolina Press, 2007), 344–45; David Reynolds, *Beneath the American Renaissance: The Subversive Imagination in the Age of Emerson and Melville* (New York: Oxford University Press, 1988), 206.

4. Stuart M. Blumin, "George G. Foster and the Emerging Metropolis," introduction in *New York by Gas-Light and Other Urban Sketches*, 13–16; John Tebbel, *A History of Book Publishing in the United States*, vol. 1: *The Creation of an Industry, 1630–1865* (New York: R. R. Bowker, 1972), 240–51; Lippard, *The Quaker City*, opening page; Reynolds, *Beneath the American Renaissance*, 207; Henkin, "City Streets and the Urban World of Print," 345; Blumin, "George G. Foster," 38; *New York Tribune*, January 13, 1849, January 25, 1850, and January 28, 1850.

5. David Reynolds, *George Lippard* (Chapel Hill: University of North Carolina, 1982), 30.

6. J. Wayne Laurens, *The Crisis; or, The Enemies of America Unmasked* (Philadelphia: G. D. Miller, 1855), preface; George Lippard, *Washington and His Men* (Philadelphia: Jos. Severns and Company, 1849); Lippard, *The Blanche of Brandywine; or, September the Eleventh, 1777. A Romance, Combining the Poetry, Legend, and History of the Battle of Brandywine* (Philadelphia: G. B. Zieber & Co., 1846); Reynolds, *Beneath the American Renaissance*, 205; *Democratic*

Standard quoted in Lippard, *The Nazarene; or, The Last of the Washingtons* (Philadelphia: G. Lippard and Co., 1846); William M. Bobo, *Glimpses of New York* (Charleston: J. J. McCarter, 1852), 103; Reynolds, *George Lippard*, 30, 51.

7. Alfred B. Ely, *American Liberty: Its Sources, Its Dangers, and the Means of Its Preservation: An Oration, Delivered at the Broadway Tabernacle, in New York, Before the Order of United Americans, on the 22nd of February* (New York: Seaman & Dunham, 1850), 20.

8. Thomas R. Whitney, *A Defense of the American Policy, as Opposed to the Encroachments of Foreign Influence, and Especially to the Interference of the Papacy in the Political Interests and Affairs of the United States* (New York: De Witt & Davenport, 1856), 257–66, 371–72, 116; John Dowling, *The History of Romanism, From Its Earliest Corruptions of Christianity to the Present Time* (New York: Edward Walker, 1853), 812.

9. Josephine Bunkley, *The Escaped Nun; or, Disclosures of Convent Life* (New York: De Witt & Davenport, 1855), 24–25; A Clergyman's Widow, *Sister Agnes; or, The Captive Nun* (New York: Riker, Thorne & Co., 1854), 342; Benjamin Barker, *Cecilia; or, The White Nun of the Wilderness, a Romance of Love and Intrigue* (Boston: United States Publishing Co., 1845), introduction.

10. Jemima Luke, *The Female Jesuit; or, The Spy in the Family* (New York: M. W. Dodd, 1851), 18–19; 47, 352; Whitney, *A Defense of the American Policy*, 116.

11. Karen Halttunen, *Confidence Men and Painted Women: A Study of Middle-Class Culture in America, 1830–1870* (New Haven, CT: Yale University Press, 1982), xiv, xv; Foster, *New York by Gas-Light*, 72.

12. Ned Buntline, *The G'hals of New York: A Novel* (New York: De Witt & Davenport, 1850); Lippard, *Quaker City*, 20; Buntline, *The Mysteries and Miseries*, 92; see also Halttunen, *Confidence Men and Painted Women*, 1–33.

13. Whitney, *A Defense*, 112; Whitney, *An Address Delivered by Thomas R. Whitney, Esq., December 22, 1851, at Hope Chapel, New-York City, On the Occasion of the Seventh Anniversary of the Alpha Chapter, Order of United Americans* (New York: John A. Gray, 1852), Order of the United Americans Records, NYPL; Whitney, *Defense*, 269.

14. Lippard, 10; Bobo, *Glimpses of New York City*, 31, 128–29.

15. Reynolds, *George Lippard*, 10; *The Magdalen Report: First Annual Report of the Executive Committee of the New-York Magdalen Society* (New York: Printed for the Publishers, 1831); for more analysis on this report, see Larry Whiteaker, *Seduction, Prostitution, and Moral Reform in New York, 1830–1860* (New York: Garland Publishing, 1997), 32–35; Buntline, *The Mysteries and Miseries of New York*, 41; Foster, *New York by Gas-Light*, 93; see also Karen J. Renner, "Seduction, Prostitution, and the Control of Female Desire in Popular Antebellum Fiction," *Nineteenth-Century Literature* 65, no. 2 (September 2010): 166–91.

16. William C. Brownlee, "Female Convents," *American Protestant Vindicator* 2, no. 41 (July 13, 1836), courtesy of the New York Public Library; Lewis Tonna, *Nuns and Nunneries: Sketches Compiled Entirely from Romish Authorities* (London: Seeley's, 1852), 17; One of 'Em, *The Wide-Awake Gift: A Know-Nothing Token for 1855* (New York: J. C. Derby, 1855), 98.

17. Monk, *Awful Disclosures*, 99–103; Buntline, *The Beautiful Nun*, 178.

18. Buntline, *The Mysteries and Miseries of New York*, 118; Foster, *New York Naked*, 158; Karen Halttunen, "Humanitarianism and the Pornography of Pain in Anglo-American Culture," *American Historical Review* 100, no. 2 (April 1995): 303–34; Daniel A. Cohen, "The Beautiful Female Murder Victim: Literary Genres and Courtship Practices in the Origins of a Cultural Motif, 1590–1850," *Journal of Social History* 31, no. 2 (Winter 1997): 277–306.

19. Foster, *New York by Gas-Light*, 83; Thomas Roscoe, "Introduction," in Scippio di Ricci, *Female Convents: Secrets of Nunneries Disclosed* (New York: D. Appleton & Co., 1834), xiv.

20. *Wide-Awake Gift*, 198–201; "Mothers' Lyceums," *Ladies' Magazine and Literary Gazette* (Boston) 5, no. 9 (September 1832): 424.

21. Foster, *Quaker City*, 43; Andrew B. Cross, *Priests' Prisons for Women; or, A Consideration of the Question Whether Unmarried Foreign Priests Ought to be Permitted to Erect Prisons, into Which, Under Pretense of Religion, to Seduce or Entrap, or by Force Compel Young Women to Enter, and After They Have Secured Their Property Keep Them in Confinement, and Compel Them as Slaves to Submit Themselves to Their Will* (Baltimore: Sherwood & Co., 1854), 12–16, 23, 40–41, 11; *Sister Agnes*, 364.

22. Bunkley, *The Escaped Nun*, 182, 277.

23. Foster, *New York by Gas-Light*, 10.

24. Lippard, *Quaker City*, 20, 40, 46–48.

25. Lippard, *Quaker City*, 48, 88–91; Reynolds, *George Lippard*, 77.

26. Ely, *American Liberty*, 21, 28; Laurens, *The Crisis; or, The Enemies of America Unmasked*, 44; Whitney, *A Defense*, 84.

27. Bobo, *Glimpses of New York*, 11; Foster, *New York in Slices*, 94; Buntline, *The Mysteries and Miseries*, 92; Lippard, *New York: Its Upper Ten and Lower Million* (Cincinnati: H. M. Rulison, 1853), 156, 148; see Elizabeth Kelley Gray, "The World by Gaslight: Urban-Gothic Literature and Moral Reform in New York City, 1845–1860," *American Nineteenth Century History* 10, no. 2 (June 2009): 137–61.

28. Foster, *New York by Slices*, 16, 18, 93–95; Lippard, *New York: Its Upper Ten and Lower Million*, 155.

29. Samuel B. Smith, *Rosamond; or, A Narrative of the Captivity and Suffering of an American Female Under the Popish Priests, in the Island of Cuba* (New York: Leavitt, Lord, 1836), 188–89; Maria Monk, *Further Disclosures by Maria Monk, Concerning the Hotel Dieu Nunnery of Montreal, Also Her Visit to Nun's Island* (New York: Leavitt, Lord, 1837); "The Convent in the Desert," *Wesleyan Magazine* (February 1857).

30. Harry Hazel, *The Nun of St. Ursula; or, The Burning of the Convent, a Romance of Mount Benedict* (Boston: Gleason, 1845), AAS.

31. Hazel, *The Nun of St. Ursula*.

32. For information on American Party electoral victories, see David H. Bennett, *The Party of Fear: The American Far Right from Nativism to the Militia Movement*, revised and Updated (New York: Vintage Books, 1988), 153, 142–43; John R. Mulkern, *The Know-Nothing Party in Massachusetts: The Rise and Fall of a People's Movement* (Boston: Northeastern University Press, 1990); W. Darrell Overdyke, *The Know-Nothing Party in the South* (Baton Rouge: Louisiana State University Press, 1950); and Dale T. Knobel, *"America for Americans": The Nativist Movement in the United States* (New York: Twayne Publishers, 1996), 95–97. Charles Frothingham, *The Convent's Doom, a Tale of Charlestown in 1834; also, The Haunted Convent*, 5th ed. (Boston: Graves & Weston, 1854), title page, 9, 15, 12; see also description of Frothingham's conspiracy theory–driven fiction in Terryl Givens, *Viper on the Hearth: Mormons, Myths, and the Construction of Heresy* (New York: Oxford University Press, 1997), 132.

33. W. L. Garrison, "Triumph of 'Know-Nothingism,'" *Liberator* 24, no. 46 (November 17, 1854): 182; Bennett, *The Party of Fear*, 153, 142–43; *Brownlow's Knoxville Whig* 6, no. 2 (October 7, 1854).

CHAPTER 6

1. N.A., *Awful Disclosures of Mormonism and Its Mysteries* (n.p.: Printed for the Booksellers, 1866), NYPL.

2. Terryl L. Givens, *The Viper on the Hearth: Mormons, Myths, and the Construction of Heresy* (New York: Oxford University Press, 1997), 4–6, 109, 124–25; John Russell, *The Mormoness; or, The Trials of Mary Maverick* (Alton, IL: Courier Steam Press, 1853); Maria Ward, *Female Life Among the Mormons* (London: Routledge, 1855); Orvilla S. Bellisle, *The Prophets; or, Mormonism Unveiled* (Philadelphia: W. W. Smith, 1855); Alfreda Eva Bell, *Boadicea: The Mormon Wife, Life Scenes in Utah* (Baltimore: A. R. Orton, 1855); Metta Victoria Fuller Victor, *Mormon Wives: A Narrative of Facts Stranger Than Fiction* (New York: Derby and Jackson, 1856); Givens, *The Viper on the Hearth*, 106, 113.

3. Givens, *The Viper on the Hearth*, 4–6, 107.

4. Joseph Smith, *Joseph Smith Tells His Own Story* (Desert City, UT: Salt Lake News Press, 1920), 1; I Nephi 14:10, The Book of Mormon; John G. Turner, *The Mormon Jesus: A Biography* (Cambridge, MA: Belknap Press of Harvard University Press, 2016), 15; for more on the background of Joseph Smith, see Richard Lyman Bushman, *Joseph Smith: Rough Stone Rolling* (New York: Alfred A. Knopf, 2006).

5. Smith, *Joseph Smith Tells His Own Story*, 8; *Desert News 1995–96 Church Almanac* (Salt Lake City: Desert News, 1994), 418; Turner, *The Mormon Jesus*, 37; *Doctrine and Covenants of the Church of Jesus Christ of Latter Day Saints; Carefully Selected from the Revelations of God*, compiled by Joseph Smith, 2nd ed. (Nauvoo, IL: John Taylor, 1844); for more on the Book of Mormon, see Turner, *The Mormon Jesus*, 19–22, 28–48.

6. Lucy Smith, *Biographical Sketches of Joseph Smith the Prophet*, Religion in America (New York: Arno Press & The New York Times, 1969), 1–2; Turner, *The Mormon Jesus*, 128–39.

7. Givens, *The Viper on the Hearth*, 138; Chris Beneke, "What Kind of Prejudice Was Anti-Mormonism?: Review Essay," *Mormon Studies Review* 2 (2015): 76; *Warsaw Signal*, June 19, 1844, quoted in Dallin H. Oaks and Marvin S. Hill, *Carthage Conspiracy: The Trial of the Accused Assassins of Joseph Smith* (Urbana: University of Illinois Press, 1975).

8. Sarah Barringer Gordon, "'The Liberty of Self-Degradation': Polygamy, Woman Suffrage, and Consent in Nineteenth-Century America," *Journal of American History* 83, no. 3 (December 1996): 819; J. Spencer Fluhman, *"A Peculiar People": Anti-Mormonism and the Making of Religion in Nineteenth-Century America* (Chapel Hill: University of North Carolina Press, 2012), 107–8; *Official Proceedings of the National Republican Conventions* (Minneapolis: Charles W. Johnson, 1903), 358; Fluhman, *"A Peculiar People,"* 5.

9. David Brion Davis, "Some Themes of Counter-Subversion: An Analysis of Anti-Masonic, Anti-Catholic, and Anti-Mormon Literature," *Mississippi Valley Historical Review* 47, no. 2 (September 1960): 205; Beneke, "What Kind of Prejudice Was Anti-Mormonism," 77; for more on the Mormon War, see Ronald W. Walker, Richard E. Turley, and Glen M. Leonard, *Massacre at Mountain Meadows* (New York: Oxford University Press, 2011).

10. William Hogan, *Popery!: As It Was and as It Is* (Hartford, CT: Silas, Andrus & Son, 1854), 320; Thomas R. Whitney, *A Defense of the American Policy, as Opposed to the Encroachments of Foreign Influence, and Especially to the Interference of the Papacy into the Political Affairs of the United States* (New York: DeWitt & Davenport, 1856), 103; Harriet Beecher Stowe, *The Minister's Wooing* (Boston: Houghton, Mifflin & Co., 1881); see also Neil Meyer, "'One Language in

Prayer': Evangelicalism, Anti-Catholicism, and Harriet Beecher Stowe's *The Minister's Wooing*," *New England Quarterly* 85, no. 3 (September 2012): 468–90; Mrs. T. B. H. Stenhouse, *Tell It All: The Story of a Life's Experience in Mormonism,* with introductory preface by Harriet Beecher Stowe (Hartford, CT: A. D. Worthington, 1874); Orvilla S. Belisle, *The Archbishop; or, Romanism in the United States* (Philadelphia: William White Smith, 1854); Belisle, *The Prophets; or, Mormonism Unveiled* (Philadelphia: W. W. Smith, 1855), 204.

11. Beneke, "What Kind of Prejudice Was Anti-Mormonism," 77; Fluhman, *"A Peculiar People,"* 118; see Linda K. Kerber, *Women of the Republic: Intellect and Ideology in Revolutionary America* (Chapel Hill: University of North Carolina Press, 1980).

12. Ann Eliza Young, *Wife No. 19; or, The Story of a Life in Bondage: Being a Complete Exposé of Mormonism* (Hartford, CT: Dustin, Gilman & Co., 1876), 32, 290–93, 307, 305.

13. Young, *Wife No. 19,* 444, 536, 530, 545–46, 572; Gary L. Bunker and Davis Bitton, *The Mormon Graphic Image, 1834–1914: Cartoons, Caricatures, and Illustrations* (Salt Lake City: University of Utah Press, 1983), 41.

14. Young, *Wife No. 19,* 294, 313, 321.

15. John Russell, *The Mormoness; or, The Trials of Mary Maverick* (Alton, IL: Courier Steam Press, 1853); Givens, *The Viper on the Hearth,* 126.

16. Russell, *The Mormoness*; Givens, *The Viper on the Hearth,* 126–27.

17. Fluhman, 105 paraphrase; Horace Bushnell, *Barbarism the First Danger. A Discourse for Home Missions* (New York: Printed for the American Home Missionary Society, 1847); D. H. Riddle, *Our Country for the Sake of the World: A Sermon Delivered on Behalf of the Home Missionary Society* (New York: American Home Missionary Society, 1851), 23–24; Fluhman, *"A Peculiar People,"* 117.

18. Davis, "Some Themes of Counter-Subversion: An Analysis of Anti-Masonic, Anti-Catholic, and Anti-Mormon Literature," 216.

19. Reference to Smith's magnetism in Maria Ward, *Female Life Among the Mormons. A Narrative of Many Years' Experience Among the Mormons* (London: Routledge, 1855), 38; *Awful Disclosures of Mormonism,* viii, 40–41, 53, 33.

20. Ward, *Female Life Among the Mormons,* 38, 9, 230; Givens, 139–40; *New York Herald* article reprinted in *Times and Seasons* 3 (May 1842); *New York Herald* (April 2, 1842), in Givens, *The Viper and the Hearth,* 140; William C. Brownlee, "Female Convents," *American Protestant Vindicator* 2, no. 41 (July 13, 1836), courtesy of the New York Public Library.

21. Gordon, "The Liberty of Self-Degradation," 833–34.

22. Charles Frothingham, *The Convent's Doom, a Tale of Charlestown in 1834; also, The Haunted Convent,* 5th ed. (Boston: Graves & Weston, 1854), 21; Givens, *The Viper and the Hearth,* 121–22; Bellisle, *The Prophets; or, Mormonism Unveiled,* 409; Fluhman, *"A Peculiar People,"* 122; *Awful Disclosures of Mormonism,* viii.

23. *Awful Disclosures of Mormonism,* 13, 17; Ward, *Qvinnan Bland Mormonerna* (Stockholm, Sweden: Schuck and Josephson, 1857).

24. *Awful Disclosures of Mormonism,* 10; Young, 295, 305; Josephine M. Bunkley, *The Escaped Nun; or, Disclosures of Convent Life* (New York: DeWitt & Davenport, 1855), 277; "Female Convents," *American Protestant Vindicator* 2, no. 31 (July 13, 1836); *Awful Disclosures,* 16.

25. Fluhman, *"A Peculiar People,"* 117; Eliza R. Snow and Others, "Great Indignation Meeting of the Ladies of Salt Lake City, to Protest Against the Passage of Cullom's Bill," *Desert Evening News,* (January 19, 1870); Givens, *The Viper and the Hearth,* 149; *Proceedings in Mass Meeting of*

the Ladies of Salt Lake City to Protest Against the Passage of Cullom's Bill (Salt Lake City) 4, no. 6 (1870): 7, cited in Laurel Thatcher Ulrich, A House Full of Females: Plural Marriage and Women's Rights in Early Mormonism, 1835–1870 (New York: Alfred A. Knopf, 2017), xii; "Polygamy: Mass Meeting of Mormon Women in Salt Lake City," Daily Evening Bulletin, January 18, 1870, in Ulrich, A House Full of Females, xii; Gordon, "The Liberty of Self-Degradation," 817.

26. "Another Startling Tragedy," New York Herald, May 28, 1857, 8; Ulrich, A House Full of Females, 352; Eleanor J. McComb, Account of the Death of Parley P. Pratt, ca. 1857, Church of Jesus Christ of Latter-day Saints, Church History Library, Salt Lake City, Utah, quoted in Ulrich, A House Full of Females, 352.

27. Turner, The Mormon Jesus, 104–5; Doctrine and Covenants, 132:52, 54; see also Linda King Newell and Valeen Tippets Avery, Mormon Enigma: Emma Hale Smith, 2nd ed. (Champaign: University of Illinois Press, 1994), 132–39; and Ulrich, A House Full of Females, 89–92.

28. Gordon, "The Liberty of Self-Degradation," 825; Givens, The Viper on the Hearth, 149; William H. Hooper, "The Utah Delegate and Female Suffrage Advocate," Phrenological Journal and Science of Health (Philadelphia) 51, no. 5 (November 1870): 328; Gordon, "The Liberty of Self-Degradation," 826–27.

29. Ulrich, A House Full of Females, xix, 349–51; Gordon, "The Liberty of Self-Degradation," 821; Givens, The Viper on the Hearth, 144; story of Agnes Hoagland in Scott G. Kenney, ed., Wilford woodruff's Journal: 1833–1898, 9 vols. (Midvale, UT: Signature Books, 1983–85), cited in Ulrich, A House Full of Females, 350.

30. Ulrich, A House Full of Females, xiii, xvii; Jill Mulvay Derr and Karen Lynn Davidson, eds., Eliza R. Snow Smith: The Complete Poetry (Provo, UT: Brigham Young University Press, 2009), 376, 377; Ulrich, A House Full of Females, xix, 241.

31. Givens, The Viper on the Hearth, 130–31; E. D. Howe, History of Mormonism (Painesville, NY: E. D. Howe, 1834), 12; Benjamin G. Ferris, Utah and the Mormons (New York: Harper, 1854), 247; Justin S. Morrill, Speech of Hon. Justin S. Morrill, of Vermont, on Utah Territory and Its Law—Polygamy and Its License; Delivered in the House of Representatives, February 23, 1857 (Washington, 1857), 10; Givens, The Viper on the Hearth, 136; Surgeon General's Office, Statistical Report on the Sickness and Mortality in the Army of the United States . . . From January, 1855 to January 1860 (Washington, DC: George W. Bowman, 1860), 301–2, cited in Givens, The Viper on the Hearth, 136–37; Jennie Anderson Froiseth, The Women of Mormonism; or, The Story of Polygamy as Told by the Victims Themselves (Detroit: C. G. G. Paine, 1884), 163.

32. Gordon, "The Liberty of Self-Degradation," 822, 832; Official Proceedings of the National Republican Conventions, 358.

33. Gordon, "The Liberty of Self-Degradation," 820, 822; Morrill, Speech of Hon. Justin S. Morrill, of Vermont, on Utah Territory and Its Law—Polygamy and Its License; Delivered in the House of Representatives, February 23, 1857, 10; Givens, The Viper on the Hearth, 38–39; for more on the Mormon War, see Walker, Turley, and Leonard, Massacre at Mountain Meadows, and Will Bagley, Blood of the Prophets: Brigham Young and the Massacre at Mountain Meadows (Norman: University of Oklahoma Press, 2002).

34. Givens, The Viper on the Hearth, 37; Fluhman, "A Peculiar People," 103; see also Kathleen Flake, The Politics of American Religious Identity: The Seating of Senator Reed Smoot, Mormon Apostle (Chapel Hill: University of North Carolina Press, 2004).

35. Givens, The Viper on the Hearth, 120.

36. Awful Disclosures of Mormonism, viii.

CHAPTER 7

1. "Convent Annals, Roxbury, 1854–1868," March 1855, SSNDEN (Boston/Ipswich Archives), 14; for a description of the Massachusetts Nunnery Committee, see John R. Mulkern, "Scandal Behind the Convent Walls: The Know-Nothing Nunnery Committee of 1855," *Historical Journal of Massachusetts* 11, no. 1 (1983): 22–34.

2. Mulkern, "Scandal Behind the Convent Walls," 25; "Investigation into the Conduct of the Nunnery Committee at Roxbury," *Barre Patriot,* April 13, 1855; "Statement of the Lady Superior and Sisters to the Honorable the 'Committee to Investigate Charges Against the Committee on Nunneries," Roxbury, April 9, 1855, printed in "Appendix" to Charles Hale, *"Our Houses Are Our Castles": A Review of the Proceedings of the Nunnery Committee, of the Massachusetts Legislature; and Especially Their Conduct and That of Their Associates on the Occasion of the Visit to the Catholic School in Roxbury, March 26, 1855* (Boston: Published at the Office of the Boston *Daily Advertiser,* 1855), 48–50; "Convent Annals, Roxbury," March 1855, SSNDEN, 16.

3. Hale, *"Our Houses Are Our Castles,"* 46–47.

4. Hale, *"Our Houses Are Our Castles,",* 17–18, 48–49; Robert H. Lord, John E. Sexton, and Edward T. Harrington, *History of the Archdiocese of Boston: In the Various Stages of Its Development, 1604–1943,* vol. 1 (Boston: Pilot Publishing Company, 1945), 616–18; for more on the Sisters of Notre Dame de Namur, see A Member of the Congregation, *The Educational Ideals of Blessed Julie Billiart, Founder of the Congregations of the Sisters of Notre Dame de Namur* (London: Longmans, Green & Co., 1922).

5. "Convent Annals, Roxbury," May–January 1854, SSNDEN, 3–6, 9.

6. "Convent Annals, Roxbury," January–March 1855, SSNDEN, 14; "Convent Annals, Lowell, 1855," SSND; for more on the Lowell factory girls, see William Moran, *The Belles of New England: The Women of the Textile Mills and the Families Whose Wealth They Wove* (New York: St. Martin's Press, 2002).

7. "Convent Annals, Roxbury," January–March 1855, SSNDEN, 10–11; 13–14; "Convent Annals, Lowell," 1854, SSNDEN.

8. Thomas R. Whitney, *A Defense of the American Policy, as Opposed to the Encroachments of Foreign Influence, and Especially to the Interference of the Papacy in the Political Interests and Affairs of the United States* (New York: De Witt & Davenport, 1856), 257–66, 371–72, 116; Andrew B. Cross, *Priests' Prisons for Women* (Baltimore: Sherwood & Co., 1854), 12–16, 23, 40–41, 11.

9. Frederick Rinehart Anspach, *The Sons of the Sires; A History of the Rise, Progress, and Destiny of the American Party, and Its Probable Influence on the Next Election* (Philadelphia: Lippincott, Grambo, & Co., 1855), 200; "Nunneries," *Christian Watchman and Reflector* (Boston), September 14, 1854; "A Nunnery Law Wanted," *New York Observer and Chronicle,* November 30, 1854, 382.

10. John Dowling, *The History of Romanism, from Its Earliest Corruptions of Christianity to the Present Time* (New York: Edward Walker, 1853), 812; Cross, *Priests' Prisons for Women*; Sarah Richardson, *Life in the Grey Nunnery at Montreal: An Authentic Narrative of the Horrors, Mysteries and Cruelties of Convent Life* (Boston: Damrell & Moore Printers, 1858), 25–27.

11. "Massachusetts Legislature," *Sun* (Pittsfield), January 25, 1855; Mass., *Supplement to the Revised Statutes of Massachusetts, 1855* (Boston, 1855), chapter 28, 108, cited in Mulkern, "Scandal Behind the Convent Walls," 23; the petitions can be found in the *Massachusetts State Archives, Sen. Doc. 4015* (1855), cited in Lord et al., *History of the Archdiocese of Boston,* 686.

12. "A Nunnery Law Wanted," *New York Observer*; "Escape of a Nun," *German Reformed Messenger*, December 13, 1854, 4210.

13. Josephine M. Bunkley, *The Escaped Nun; or, Disclosures of Convent Life and the Confessions of a Sister of Charity: Giving a More Minute Detail of Their Inner Life and a Bolder Revelation of the Mysteries and Secrets of Nunneries Than Have Ever Before Been Submitted to the American Public* (New York: De Witt & Davenport, 1855), 208–209, 250, 232.

14. Seminary Sisters, 1853–1964, November 9, 1954, courtesy of Daughters of Charity Archives, Emmitsburg, MD; "Confessions of a Sister of Charity" and "Horrors of a Nunnery," in Bunkley, *The Escaped Nun*, 199–242; "Review of Current Literature," *The Metropolitan: A Monthly Magazine Devoted to Religion, Education, Literature and General Information* 4 (Baltimore: John Murphy & Co., 1856), 246–47.

15. "Miss Bunkley," *New York Herald*, September 3, 1855; "List of New Works: American," *American Publishers' Circular and Literary Gazette*, December 22, 1855, 253; John Harper was a member of the Order of United Americans; for more on his nativist affiliations, see David H. Bennett, *Party of Fear: The American Far Right from Nativism to the Militia Movement*, revised and updated (New York: Vintage Books, 1988), 107; and *Directory, Alpha Chapter No. 1, OUA, August 1848* (New York: R. C. Root & Anthony, 1848), NYPL.

16. "Literary Notices," *Zion's Herald and Wesleyan Journal*, January 16, 1856; "The Escaped Nun," *Western Reserve Chronicle* (Warren, Ohio), August 1, 1855; "Short Reviews and Notices of Books," *Methodist Quarterly Review* (April 1856); "To the Editor of the New York Herald," *New York Herald*, August 20, 1855.

17. Jean H. Baker, *Ambivalent Americans: The Know-Nothing Party in Maryland* (Baltimore: Johns Hopkins Press, 1977), 4–5, 81, 88–80; see also Benjamin Tuska, *Know-Nothingism in Baltimore, 1854–1860* (New York, 1930); Sister Mary McConville, *Political Nativism in the State of Maryland* (Washington, DC: Catholic University of America, 1930); and Laurence Frederick Schmeckebier, *History of the Know-Nothing Party in Maryland* (Baltimore: Johns Hopkins University Press, 1899).

18. "Literary Notices," *Zion's Herald and Wesleyan Journal* (Boston), January 16, 1856; "Report of the Committee of Inquiry," Appendix D, in Hale, *"Our Houses Are Our Castles,"* 55; Hale, *Our Houses Are Our Castles,"* 12–13.

19. Karen M. Kennelly, "Women Religious in America," in *The Encyclopedia of American Catholic History*, ed. Michael Glazier and Thomas J. Shelley (Collegeville, MN: Liturgical Press, 1997), 1496, 1491; "Closing Statement of the Editors of the Boston Daily Advertiser," Appendix C, in Hale, *"Our Houses Are Our Castles,"*, 50; "Two Articles from the Boston Daily Advertiser," Appendix A, in Hale, *"Our Houses Are Our Castles,"*, 44.

20. "Report to the Joint Committee on the Inspection of Nunneries and Convents," April 24, 1855, *House Doc. 4015* (Mass. State Archives), cited in Lord, *History of the Archdiocese*, 687; Hale, *"Our Houses Are Our Castles,"*, 18, 15, 39.

21. "Convent Annals, Lowell," 1854, SSNDEN, 5.

22. Hale, *"Our Houses Are Our Castles,"* 26, 20; Hale's criticism in the *Boston Daily Advertiser* appeared first on March 31, 1855.

23. Hale, *"Our Houses Are Our Castles,"* 30, 32, 37.

24. Charles and Nathan Hale, *Journal of Debates and Proceedings in the Convention of Delegates, Chosen to Revise the Constitution of Massachusetts* (Boston: Office of the Daily Advertiser, 1853); Charles Hale, *Debates and Proceedings in the Convention of the Commonwealth of Massachusetts,*

Held in the Year 1788, and Which Finally Ratified the Constitution of the United States (Boston: W. White, 1856); "Honorable Charles Hale, Speaker of the Massachusetts House of Representatives," *Ballou's Pictorial Drawing-Room Companion (1855–1859)* 16, no. 4 (January 22, 1859); "Hale, Charles," in *Dictionary of American Biography* (New York: Charles Scribner's Sons, 1932), 96–97.

25. "The Nunnery or 'Smelling Committee,'" *Sun* (Pittsfield, MA), April 12, 1855, 2; Lord, *Archdiocese*, 689.

26. "The Nunnery Visitation," *Barre Patriot*, April 13, 1855, quoting from the New York *Commercial Advertiser*.

27. Bishop Fitzpatrick to the Massachusetts General Court, undated (Boston Dioceses Archives), cited in Lord, *Archdiocese*, 690–91.

28. Mulkern, "Scandal Behind Convent Walls," 24; *Boston Daily Advertiser,* April 11, 1855; Hale, *"Our Houses Are Our Castles,"* 14; "Report of the Committee of Inquiry," cited in Hale, *"Our Houses Are Our Castles,"* Appendix D, 57–58.

29. Hale, *"Our Houses Are Our Castles,"* 15.

30. Mulkern, "Scandal Behind Convent Walls," 24–25; *Boston Daily Advertiser*, April 2 and 13, 1855; Investigating Committee to the Sisters of Notre Dame and Caroline Crabb, April 9, 1855, *Senate Doc. 4295* (Mass. State Archives), cited in Lord, *Archdiocese*, 692; "Convent Annals, Roxbury" (March 1855), 17–18.

31. "Convent Annals, Roxbury," March 1855, SSNDEN, 16–17; Investigating Committee to the Sisters of Notre Dame and Caroline Crabb, April 9, 1855, *Senate Doc. 4295* (Mass. State Archives), cited in Lord, *Archdiocese*, 692.

32. "Convent Annals, Roxbury," April 1855, SSNDEN, 18–21.

33. "Another Farce Closed," *Farmers' Cabinet*, April 26, 1855.

34. Mulkern, "Scandal Behind Convent Walls," 25; Lord, 689; *Boston Daily Advertiser,* April 18, 1855.

35. Mulkern, "Scandal Behind Convent Walls," 26; *Boston Daily Advertiser,* April 23, 1855.

36. Lord, *Archdiocese*, 694–98; Mulkern, 27; *Boston Daily Advertiser,* April 23, 1855; "Mr. Hiss and the Nunnery Committee," *National Era,* April 26, 1855, 67; Mulkern, "Scandal Behind Convent Walls," 29.

37. *Report of the Joint Committee to Investigate the Nunnery Committee, April 17, 1855, Sen. Doc. 4295* (Mass. State Archives), cited in Lord, 695–96; Mulkern, "Scandal Behind Convent Walls," 29; Ray Allen Billington, *The Protestant Crusade, 1800–1860: A Study of the Origins of American Nativism* (1938; repr., Chicago: Quadrangle Books, 1952), 415; Hale, *"Our Houses Are Our Castles,"* 53–59.

38. Hale, *"Our Houses Are Our Castles,"* 31, 22.

39. Mulkern, "Scandal Behind Convent Walls," 31; see also William E. Gienapp, "Nativism and the Creation of a Republican Majority in the North Before the Civil War," *Journal of American History* 72, no. 3 (December 1985): 529–59.

40. *Boston Daily Bee,* April 3, 1855; *Boston Daily Courier,* April 24, 1855; Mulkern, "Scandal Behind Convent Walls," 31, 30, 24.

41. Massachusetts, *Senate Documents* 1855 (Boston, 1855), no. 162, cited in Mulkern, "Scandal Behind Convent Walls," 23; *Journal of Proceedings of the House of Delegates of the State of Maryland* (Annapolis, MD: Requa and Wilson, Printers, 1856), 53; see also Tyler Anbinder, *Nativism and Slavery: The Northern Know Nothings and the Politics of the 1850s* (New York: Oxford University Press, 1992); William E. Gienapp, *The Origins of the Republican Party, 1852–1856* (New York: Oxford University Press, 1987), 260–72.

42. Tuska, *Know-Nothingism in Baltimore*, 12; Anspach, *Sons of the Sires*, 178; Dale Knobel, *"America for the Americans": The Nativist Movement in the United States* (New York: Twayne Publishers, 1996), 142–44; Gienapp, *The Origins of the Republican Party*, 189–90.

43. Knobel, *"America for the Americans,"* 122; Mulkern, *The Know-Nothing Party in Massachusetts*, 180; "Report of the Committee of Inquiry," Appendix D, in Hale, *"Our Houses Are Our Castles,"* 57; Hale, *"Our Houses Are Our Castles,"* 31. Pointing to the importance of convent literature, Allan Billington in *The Protestant Crusade, 1800–1860* argues that the Nunnery Committee searched "to find the dread evidences of Popery which propaganda writers had convinced them should be there," 414; Hale, *"Our Houses Are Our Castles,"* 30.

44. Richardson, *Life in the Grey Nunnery of Montreal*, n.p.

EPILOGUE

1. Ray Allen Billington, "Maria Monk and Her Influence," *Catholic Historical Review*, October 1936, 283–96; Allen Churchill, "Awful Disclosures of Maria Monk," *American Mercury* 37 (January 1936): 94; see, for instance, Edward Hendrie, *Murder, Rape, and Torture in a Catholic Nunnery: Maria Monk's Awful Disclosures Proven True* (n.p.: Great Mountain Publishing, 2015).

2. See George Barton, *Angels of the Battlefield: A History of the Labors of the Catholic Sisterhoods in the Late Civil War* (Philadelphia: Catholic Art Publishing Company, 1898); Mary Denis Maher, *To Bind Up the Wounds: Catholic Sister Nurses in the U.S. Civil War* (Westport, CT: Greenwood Press, 1989); Margaret Susan Thompson as quoted in the film *A Question of Habit*, directed by Mike Whalen (Whalen Films, a Bren Ortega Murphy Film, 2012).

3. David H. Bennett, *The Party of Fear: The American Far Right from Nativism to the Militia Movement*, revised and updated (New York: Vintage Books, 1995), 160–70; see also John Higham, *Strangers in the Land: Patterns of American Nativism, 1860–1925*, with a new epilogue (1955; repr., New Brunswick: Rutgers University Press, 2004), chapter 4; and Mark S. Massa, *Anti-Catholicism in America: The Last Acceptable Prejudice* (New York: A Crossroad Book, 2003), 29–30; for more on the APA, see Donald L. Kinzer, *An Episode in Anti-Catholicism: The American Protective Association* (Seattle: University of Washington Press, 1964).

4. Bennett, *Party of Fear*, 171; see Maria Monk, *Awful Disclosures of Maria Monk: Illustrated with 40 Engravings and the Startling Mysteries of a Convent Exposed!* (Philadelphia: T. B. Peterson, 1870); Monk, *Awful Disclosures of Maria Monk as Exhibited in a Narrative of Her Suffering During Her Residence of Five Years as a Novice and Two Years as a Black Nun in the Hotel Dieu Nunnery at Montreal* (New York: D. M. Bennett, Liberal and Scientific Publishing House, 1878); and Monk, *Awful Disclosures of the Hotel Dieu Convent of Montreal; or, The Secrets of the Black Nunnery Revealed* (Philadelphia: Jordon Bros., 1892); *A.P.A. Magazine* 2 (March 1896): 943–44; Edith O'Gorman, *Trials and Persecutions of Miss Edith O'Gorman, Otherwise Sister Teresa de Chantal, of St. Joseph's Convent, Hudson City, N.J.* (Hartford, CT: Connecticut Publishing Company, 1871); O'Gormon's book subsequently took the title *Convent Life Unveiled*; for more on O'Gormon, see Augustine J. Curley, "The Identity of Edith O'Gormon, the 'Escaped Nun'"; Rene Kollar, *A Foreign and Wicked Institution?: The Campaign Against Convents in Victorian England* (Cambridge: James Clare & Co., 2011), 103; Margaret Shepherd, *My Life in the Convent* (Philadelphia: Jordan Bros., 1893); for more on Shepherd, see Bennett, *Party of Fear*, 175–76.

5. Mary Ewens, "The Leadership of Nuns in Immigrant Catholicism," in *Women and Religion in America*, vol. 1: *The Nineteenth Century*, ed. Rosemary Radford Ruether and Rosemary Skinner

Keller (New York: Harper & Row, 1981), 101–12; *A Question of Habit*, 2012; statistics on hospitals found in George C. Stewart Jr., "Women Religious in America," in *The Encyclopedia of American Catholic History*, ed. Michael Glazier and Thomas J. Shelley (Collegeville, MN: Liturgical Press, 1997), 1492; for more on the role of Sisters in providing welfare services, see Maureen Fitzgerald, "Irish Catholic Nuns and the Development of New York City's Welfare System, 1840–1900" (PhD diss., University of Wisconsin, 1992); Margaret McGuinness, "Body and Soul: Catholic Social Settlements and Immigration," *U.S. Catholic Historian* 13 (Summer 1995): 63–75; for sources on nuns' involvement in health care, see Sioban Nelson, *Say Little, Do Much: Nurses, Nuns, and Hospitals in the Nineteenth Century* (Philadelphia: University of Pennsylvania Press, 2001); and Dorothy M. Brown and Elizabeth McKeown, *The Poor Belong to Us: Catholic Charities and American Welfare* (Cambridge, MA: Harvard University Press, 1997).

6. Stewart, "Women Religious in America," *Encyclopedia of American Catholic History*, 1493–95; Ewens, "The Leadership of Nuns in Immigrant Catholicism," in *Women and Religion in America*, 101; Mary J. Henold, *Catholic and Feminist: The Surprising History of the American Catholic Feminist Movement* (Chapel Hill: University of North Carolina Press, 2008), 20; see also Annabelle Raiche and Ann Marie Biermaier, *They Came to Teach: The Story of Sisters Who Taught in Parochial Schools and Their Contribution to Elementary Education in Minnesota* (St. Cloud, MN: North Star Press, 1994).

7. John J. Fialka, *Sisters: Catholic Nuns and the Making of America* (New York: St. Martin's Press, 2003), 200–206, 17; Henold, *Catholic and Feminist*, 20–23; see also Carmel Elizabeth McEnroy, *Guests in Their Own House: The Women of Vatican II* (New York: A Crossroad Book, 1996); Sister Rose Thering's efforts to combat anti-Semitism within the Catholic Church led to Vatican II's publication of "Nostra Aetate," declaring the Jews not guilty for the death of Jesus and condemning any displays of anti-Semitism. See film *Sister Rose's Passion*, directed by Oren Jacoby (Storyville Films, 2004).

8. Carole Garibaldi Rogers, *Habits of Change: An Oral History of American Nuns* (New York: Oxford University Press, 1996), 148, 297, 69; Rebecca Sullivan, *Visual Habits: Nuns, Feminism, and American Postwar Popular Culture* (Toronto: University of Toronto Press, 2005), 48; Henold, *Catholic and Feminist*, 1; for more on Sisters' involvement in the civil rights movement, see Suellen Hoy, "No Color Line at the Loretto Academy: Catholic Sisters and African Americans on Chicago's South Side," *Journal of Women's History* 4, no. 1 (Fall 2002): 4–23; and Amy Koehlinger, "From Selma to Sisterhood: Race and Transformation in Catholic Sisterhoods in the 1960s" (PhD diss., Yale University, 2002); for an account of nuns' battles with the Vatican over abortion, see Barbara Ferraro and Patricia Hussey with Jane O'Reilly, *No Turning Back: Two Nuns' Battle with the Vatican over Women's Right to Choose* (New York: Poseido Press, 1990).

9. There is no mention of nuns in major US history textbooks, such as Eric Foner's *Give Me Liberty!: An American History*, 3rd ed., vols. 1–2 (New York: W. W. Norton, 2012); James Oakes et al., *Of the People: A History of the United States*, 2nd ed., vols. 1–2 (New York: Oxford University Press, 2013); and Alan Brinkley, *The Unfinished Nation: A Concise History of the American People*, 3rd ed., vol. 1 (Boston: McGraw-Hill, 2000). In Jon Butler, Grant Wacker, and Randall Balmer's summary of American religious history, *Religion in American Life: A Short Summary* (New York: Oxford University Press, 2000), only two pages reference only two orders of women religious (pp. 47, 269); Mark A. Noll's *America's God: From Jonathan Edwards to Abraham Lincoln* (New York: Oxford University Press, 2002) includes no reference to

Sisters. There is only one brief reference in a note to nuns in Linda K. Kerber and Jane De Hart-Mathews, eds., *Women's America: Refocusing the Past*, 2nd ed. (New York: Oxford University Press, 1987). There is no mention of nuns in Sara Delamont's and Lorna Duffin, eds., *The Nineteenth-Century Woman: Her Cultural and Physical World* (New York: Barnes and Nobel Books, 1978). Some notable recent works on women religious in America include Kathleen Sprows Cummings, *New Women of the Old Faith: Gender and American Catholicism in the Progressive Era* (Chapel Hill: University of North Carolina Press, 2009); Emily Clark, *Masterless Mistresses: The New Orleans Ursulines and the Development of A New World Society, 1727–1834* (Williamsburg: Published for the Omohundro Institute of Early American History and Culture, 2007); Nancy Lusignan Schultz, *Fire and Roses: The Burning of the Charlestown Convent, 1834* (Boston: Northeastern University Press, 2000); and Maureen McGuinness, *Called to Serve: A History of Nuns in America* (New York: New York University Press, 2013).

10. "Three Books for the Price of One" (advertisement), *The Menace* (Aurora, MO), December 28, 1918, 2; Kelly J. Baker, *Gospel According to the Klan: The KKK's Appeal to Protestant America, 1915–1930* (Lawrence: University Press of Kansas, 2011), 44; Exalted Cyclops of the Order, "Principles and Purposes of the Knights of the Ku Klux Klan," *Papers Read at the Meeting of the Grand Dragons, Knights of the Ku Klux Klan, at Their First Meeting Held in Asheville, North Carolina, July 1923,* in *Anti-Movements in America,* ed. Gerald N. Grob (New York: Arno Press, 1977), 125; Baker, *Gospel According to the Klan,* 148–52; Helen Jackson, *Convent Cruelties; or, My Life in a Convent* (Detroit: n.p., 1919), UNDA.

11. "Nunneries Must Be Abolished from American Soil," Tract No. 40, Protestant Book House (Toledo, OH, n.y.), located in the Anti-Catholic Printed Material Collection, box 5, folder 1, UNDA; "Catalogue of Anti-Papal Books" (Toledo: Protestant Book House, 1925).

12. "Convent Horror," Tract No. 40, Protestant Book House (Toledo, OH), UNDA; "My Life in The Convent," Tract No. 40, Protestant Book House; "Black Convent Slave," excerpt in "Catalogue of Anti-Papal Books."

13. Paul Blanshard, *American Freedom and Catholic Power* (Boston: Beacon Press, 1949), 3, 43–44, 67; Massa, *Anti-Catholicism in America,* 59; Blanshard, *Personal and Controversial: An Autobiography by Paul Blanshard* (Boston: Beacon Press, 1973), 195.

14. "Maria Monk," Tract and Book Ad Combined, Tract No. 27, 1952 Series (Decatur, GA: Book and Bible House, 1952), UNDA.

15. "House of Death and Gate of Hell; or, Convent Brutality," Tract No. 31, 1952 Series (Decatur, GA: Book and Bible House, 1952), UNDA; "Almost a Nun!" (Havertown, PA: Conversion Center, c. 1950), UNDA.

16. *The Bells of St. Mary's,* directed by Leo McCarey (Rainbow Productions, 1945); Maurine Sabine, *Veiled Desires: Intimate Portraits of Nuns in Postwar Anglo-American Film* (New York: Fordham University Press, 2013), 29–31; Bosley Crowther, "The Screen," *New York Times,* December 7, 1945, 26; Mary Gordon, "Father Chuck: A Reading of *Going My Way* and *The Bells of St. Mary's;* or, Why Priests Make Us Crazy," *Southern Atlantic Quarterly* 93, no. 3 (1994): 592; see also Anthony Burke Smith, *The Look of Catholics: Portrayals in Popular Culture from the Great Depression to the Cold War* (Lawrence: University of Kansas Press, 2010).

17. *The Nun's Story,* directed by Fred Zimmermann (Warner Brothers, 1959); Sullivan, *Visual Habits,* 101–2.

18. Sullivan, *Visual Habits,* 119; Harold C. Gardiner, "Story on *The Nun's Story,*" *America,* December 8, 1956, 300–301; for the Notre Dame Sister's response and the response of other

Sisters to the film, see Gardiner, ' "The Nun's Story'—A Symposium," *America,* June 27, 1959, 468–71; Sullivan, *Visual Habits,* 103, 98, 105, 115, 4.

19. *The Sound of Music,* directed by Robert Wise (Twentieth Century Fox, 1965); Sullivan, *Visual Habits,* 163–64, 85.

20. Sabine, *Veiled Desires,* 164; Pamela Grace, *The Religious Film* (Chichester: Wiley-Blackwell, 2009), 3–5; Pauline Kael, "The Sound of . . . *The Sound of Music* and *The Singing Nun,*" in *Kiss Bang* (London: Calder and Boyars, 1970), 176–78; Sullivan, *Visual Habits,* 80–85.

21. Massa, *Anti-Catholicism in America,* 77–83; John F. Kennedy, "On Church and State," in *The Kennedy Reader,* ed. Jay David (Indianapolis: Bobbs-Merrill, 1967), 363–64; Kennedy, "The Responsibility of the Press: Address to the American Society of Newspaper Editors, Washington D.C., April 12, 1960," in *"Let the Word Go Forth": The Speeches, Statements, and Writings of John F. Kennedy,* ed. Theodore Sorensen (New York: Delacorte Press, 1988), 126–28; Will Herberg, *Protestant, Catholic, Jew: An Essay in American Religious Sociology* (1955; repr., Chicago: University of Chicago Press, 1983); Peter Braestrup, "Protestant Group Wary on Kennedy: Statement by Peale Group Sees Vatican 'Pressure' on Democratic Nominee," *New York Times,* September 8, 1960.

22. Maria Monk, *Awful Disclosures of Maria Monk* (London: Canova Press, 1969).

23. "Introduction," in Monk, *Awful Disclosures* (1969), xii; Maria Monk, *Awful Disclosures of Maria Monk: The Hidden Secrets of Convent Life, Together with the Cardiere Case* (1969; repr., London: Random House, 1997).

24. *The Flying Nun* (1967–70), ABC Television; Sullivan, "Gidget Joins a Convent: Television Confronts the New Nuns," in Sullivan, *Visual Habits,* 190–213.

25. *The Devils,* directed by Ken Russell (Warner Bros., 1971); *The Devils* was based on Aldous Huxley's *The Devils* (1952; repr., New York: Harper Perennial, 2009).

26. *Flavia the Rebel Nun,* directed by Gianfranco Mingozzi (1974); Victoria Nelson, "Faux Catholic: A Gothic Subgenre from Monk Lewis to Dan Brown," *Boundary 2* 34, no. 3 (2007): 87–107.

27. Mary Ann Janosik, "Madonnas in Our Midst: Representations of Women Religious in Hollywood Film," *U.S. Catholic Historian* 15, no. 3 (Summer 1997): 75–98; *The Blues Brothers,* directed by John Landis (Universal Pictures, 1980).

28. *Nunsense,* book, music, and lyrics by Dan Goggin, Off-Broadway, New York, 1985–present; *Late Night Catechism,* written by Vicki Quade and Maripat Donovan, premiered at Life Bait Theater, Chicago, 1993.

29. *Sister Act,* directed by Emile Ardolino (Touchstone Pictures, 1992).

30. N.A., *Scary Nuns: Sisters at Work and Play* (New York: Harper Entertainment, 2007).

31. *American Horror Story: Asylum,* Season 2 (American FX, 2012–2013).

32. *American Horror Story,* Season 2, episodes 1–3.

33. Cheryl L. Reed, *Unveiled: The Hidden Lives of Nuns* (New York: Berkeley Books, 2004), xvi, 23–24.

34. Reed, *Unveiled,* 35, 39, 42.

35. *Dead Man Walking*, directed by Tim Robbins (Polygram Film Entertainment, 1995). The film is based on Helen Prejean's memoir, *Dead Man Walking: An Eye Witness Account of the Death Penalty in the United States* (New York: Vintage Books, 1996).

36. Patricia Kowal, Review of *Dead Man Walking, Magill's Cinema Annual 1996: A Survey of Films of 1995*, ed. Beth A. Fhaner and Christopher B. Scanlon (Detroit: Gale, 1996), 125–27; Rachel Abramowitz, "Mother Superior: Interview with Susan Sarandon," *Premier* 9, no. 5 (1996): 56; Sabin, *Veiled Desires*, 254–55.

37. *A Question of Habit*, directed by Michael Whalen (2012).

38. Lindy West, "Nuns Are So Hot Right Now They're Getting Their Own Reality Show," *Jezebel,* April 4, 2014, accessed July 12, 2014, http://jezebel.com/nuns-are-so-hot-right-now-theyre-getting-their-own-real-1567201174.

39. Sabine, *Veiled Desires*, 276–79; *Doubt*, directed and written by John Patrick Shanley (Miramax, 2009).

40. Sabine, *Veiled Desires*, 282; Ella Taylor, "*Doubt* Wags the Finger of Moral Relativism," *Village Voice,* December 9, 2008, accessed August 26, 2014, http://www.villagevoice.com/2008-12-10/film/doubt-wags-the-finger-of-moral-relativism/full/.

INDEX

background, 7, 52
missionary to Canada, 7
views on marriage, 38, 52–53
Bowery, The, 97
Breckinridge, Robert J., 44, 131
Brontë, Charlotte, 156
brothel. *See also* prostitute and prostitution
and antislavery literature, 50
and city mysteries, 85, 90, 92–93, 97–98, 100
comparison to convent, xvi, xxi, 6, 133, 138
and nativism, 88, 99
Brownlee, William C., xiii, 7, 9, 17, 49, 92
Buchanan, James, 121
Buck, Henry, 41
Bunkley, Josephine M., 111, 129–32, 136
Buntline, Ned, 54, 85, 86, 88, 90–94, 99
Bushnell, Horace, 71, 113
Buzzell, John R., 27, 29, 41–42
Byrne, Father Patrick, 35

Canada. *See also* anti-Canadian sentiment
and *Awful Disclosures of the Hotel Dieu Nunnery*, xiv, 11, 17, 24, 150
in convent narratives, 36, 54–55, 100
and Maria Monk, 1, 18
missionary work in, 7, 11
Society of the Sisters of the Sacred Heart in, 74
Canova Press, 152
captivity narrative
convent, 105 (*see also* convent narrative)
Mormon, xvi, 105–7, 111, 113–14, 116–17, 119, 122–23
Carey, Mathew, 43
Carmelite
convent in Maryland, xix, 44–45, 127, 131
nuns, 156
Carroll, Edward Zane. *See* Buntline, Ned
Catholic Diary, 12, 19
Catholic Telegraph, The, 20
Catholicism. *See also* anti-Catholicism
in Canada, 11, 27, 54
conversions to, 27, 35, 74, 113, 129
growth of in the US, xix–xx, 9
Celia (Barker, Benjamin), 89
Child, Lydia Marie, 51
Chittister, Sister Joan D., 146
Christian Home in Victorian America, The (McDannell, Colleen), 56

Chronicles of Mount Benedict, The (Norwood, Damon), 46
Church of Jesus Christ of Latter-day Saints. *See also* Mormonism
and doctrine of plural marriage, 118
founding and growth of, 108–9
and Utah War, xvi, 110, 120–21
city mysteries
compared to convent narratives, 87–89, 95, 99–103
compared to Mormon captivity narratives, 107, 116
disguised villains in, 87, 89
the foreign or exotic, 99–100
and nativism, 88–89, 95, 102–3
popularity of, 86
and prostitution, 92, 94
and underground vice, xvi, 86, 90
Civil War
and anti-Mormonism, xvi, 120
nuns' aid during, 142, 144
political divisions before, 103
popular literature before, xiv, 8, 9, 48, 123
and slavery, 142
Clark, Emily, xix
Cohen, Daniel, 28, 94
Cold War, The, 144, 149
Commercial Advertiser (New York), 20, 135
common school movement
and anti-Catholicism, 75–76
and the Bible, 75
in competition with convent schools, 84
and the feminization of teaching, 66
reformers' vision of, 71–72, 75
Compromise of 1850, 141
confession
and convent schools, 69
and female sexual purity, xxi, 78, 116
practice of, 41
confidence man, 90, 91
confraternity, 82
Convent Cruelties (Jackson, Helen), 148
Convent Life Unveiled (O'Gorman, Edith), 145
convent narrative. See also *Awful Disclosures of the Hotel Dieu Nunnery*
and anti-Mormon literature, xvi, 105–7, 109, 111–12, 114–16, 120
and antislavery literature, xv, 54, 61–62, 64